Language: From Meaning to Text

Igor MEL'ČUK

LANGUAGE:

From Meaning to Text

Edited by David Beck

Moscow & Boston
2016

Library of Congress Cataloging-in-Publication Data:
A catalog record for this book as available from the Library of Congress.

Copyright © 2016 LRC Publishing House
Copyright © 2016 I. A. Mel'čuk

All rights reserved

ISBN 978-1-61811-769-4

ISBN 978-1-61811-457-0 (electronic)

Typeset by LRC Publishing House
Russia, Moscow, Bolshaya Lubyanka, 13/16
http://www.lrc-press.ru/?lang=en

Published by Academic Studies Press in 2016
28 Montfern Avenue
Brighton, MA 02135, USA
press@academicstudiespress.com
www.academicstudiespress.com

Contents

Acknowledgments ix
The Author's Foreword x

Chapter 1. The Problem Stated 1
1.1 What is natural language and how to describe it? 1
1.2 Illustrations of some basic notions 6
1.3 The structure of this book 14
1.4 Limitations accepted 15

Chapter 2. Functional Modeling in Linguistics 17
2.1 A model as a means of study and description 17
2.2 Functional models 19
2.3 The Meaning-Text model: a global functional linguistic model ... 23
    2.3.1 Introductory remarks 23
    2.3.2 Three postulates of the Meaning-Text theory 23
    2.3.3 Main formal properties of a Meaning-Text model 31
    2.3.4 Two central notions of the Meaning-Text approach:
           linguistic meaning and paraphrasing 34
    2.3.5 General characterization of the Meaning-Text approach 37

Chapter 3. An Outline of a Particular Meaning-Text Model 41
3.1 Deep and surface sublevels of linguistic representations 41
3.2 Linguistic representations in a Meaning-Text model 43

    3.2.1 Introductory remarks 43
    3.2.2 The semantic structure of a sentence 46
    3.2.3 The deep-syntactic structure of a sentence 52
    3.2.4 The surface-syntactic structure of a sentence 59
    3.2.5 The deep-morphological structure of a sentence 64
    3.2.6 The surface-morphological structure of a sentence 65
    3.2.7 Prelinguistic representation of the world:
          conceptual representation 66
3.3 The modules of the Meaning-Text model 69
    3.3.1 Introductory remarks 69
    3.3.2 Semantic module 71
        3.3.2.1 Semantic paraphrasing: rules
              of the form "$\text{SemR}_i \equiv \text{SemR}_j$" 71
        3.3.2.2 Semantic transition: rules
              of the form "$\text{SemR}_i \Leftrightarrow \text{DSyntR}_k$" 72
        3.3.2.3 Deep-syntactic paraphrasing: rules
              of the form "$\text{DSyntR}_{k_1} \equiv \text{DSyntR}_{k_2}$" 76
    3.3.3 Deep-syntactic module 77
    3.3.4 Surface-syntactic module 80
    3.3.5 Deep-morphological module 84
    3.3.6 Surface-morphological module 84

**Chapter 4. Modeling Two Central Linguistic Phenomena:
Lexical Selection and Lexical Cooccurrence** 86
4.1 Modeling lexical selection (paradigmatics):
    semantic decompositions 87
4.2 Modeling lexical cooccurrence (syntagmatics):
    lexical functions 90
4.3 Correlations between paradigmatic and syntagmatic
    aspects of lexeme behavior 103

CONTENTS

Chapter 5. Meaning-Text Linguistics 109

5.1 Meaning-Text linguistics and the direction
    of linguistic description: from meaning to text 109

   5.1.1 Example 1: Spanish "semivowels" 110

   5.1.2 Example 2: Russian binominative sentences 112

5.2 Meaning-Text linguistics and a linguistic
    conceptual apparatus 116

   5.2.1 Introductory remarks 116

   5.2.2 Linguistic sign 118

   5.2.3 Word 130

   5.2.4 Cases, ergative construction, voices 136

5.3 Meaning-Text linguistics and the description
    of linguistic meaning 142

5.4 Meaning-Text linguistics and the lexicon:
    the Explanatory Combinatorial Dictionary [= ECD] 151

   5.4.1 Introductory remarks 151

   5.4.2 The three main properties of an ECD 153

   5.4.3 A lexical entry in an ECD: three major zones 155

      5.4.3.1 The semantic zone in an ECD lexical entry 155

      5.4.3.2 The syntactic cooccurrence zone
              in an ECD lexical entry 158

      5.4.3.3 The semantic derivation and lexical
              cooccurrence zone in an ECD lexical entry 160

   5.4.4 Two sample lexical entries of a Russian ECD 164

5.5 Meaning-Text linguistics and dependencies
    in natural language 170

   5.5.1 Three types of linguistic dependency 171

   5.5.2 Criteria for syntactic dependency 173

Summing Up 180

Appendices 182
Appendix I : Phonetic Table 182
Appendix II: Surface-Syntactic Relations of English 184
Appendix III: Possible Combinations of the Three Types of Linguistic Dependency between Two Lexemes in a Clause 195

Notes 199
References 217
Abbreviations and Notations 226
Subject and Name Index with a Glossary 229
Index of Languages 255

Acknowledgments

This book was written at the suggestion of, and under gentle pressure from, A. Koshelev, who also helped me with advice and commentary. In the initial stages, the multiple discussions with D. Beck, L. Iomdin, L. Iordanskaja, S. Kahane, J. Milićević and A. Polguère were of crucial importance. The first version of the text was read and criticized—as always—by Lidija Iordanskaja; the subsequent version underwent the scrutiny of Ian Mackenzie, whose numerous remarks and suggestions led to significant changes, which no doubt constitute a serious improvement. Then *Language: From Meaning to Text* was reread once more —by Haitao Liu, Máirtín Mac Aodha, Jasmina Milićević and Alain Polguère. Finally, David Beck fully edited the manuscript; without his friendly and highly professional help, the book would have never achieved its present quality.

Of course, the usual disclaimers apply: none of the persons mentioned above is responsible for any mistakes and blunders that survived their scrutiny.

The Author's Foreword

My dear reader! This small book, which is now in your hands, represents a desperate attempt to introduce you to a science that is of crucial importance for understanding the world and Mankind, but—in spite of this—is little known to the public. I am referring to linguistics (from *Lat. lingua* 'language'), the science of human language.

As I write this paragraph, I realize that it raises (at least) three questions that require immediate answers.

- Why do I declare my attempt "desperate" before I have even begun? The reason is that one book cannot present, even partially, the contents of an entire science. First, from a theoretical perspective, linguistics, as I see it, uses a complicated notional apparatus, which would require several volumes to fully explain (since many formalisms are involved). Second, from a practical point of view, linguistics deals with a staggering number of facts: there are about seven thousand languages spoken in the world today, ranging from Aasax to Zulu, plus many well-known dead ones—including Latin, Ancient Greek, Old Church Slavonic, Hittite, Assyro-Babylonian, Biblical Hebrew, Ancient Chinese, Hurrian, Sumerian, etc.[1] Each language is a vast and complex system. Therefore, obviously, this book cannot entirely fulfill its mission.

- Why is linguistics of crucial importance for understanding the world and us, who live in it? Because to understand and describe anything—**anything** at all—we need language, the main tool of thought. But this tool is as yet itself very poorly understood. It would be no gross exaggeration to suggest that human language, human thinking and human psychology are the least-studied and the least-explained parts of the universe; they represent the last frontier of our scientific explorations. Linguistics is important because it tackles the phenomenon without which all sciences and humanity itself could not exist—human language.

- Why is linguistics so little known to the public? Simply because it is a science never taught in primary or high school. (Spelling and grammar rules, those instruments used to torture students of all ages, are based on linguistics, but are by no means linguistics.) Two reasons underlie this neglect. On one hand, everybody speaks his native language as naturally as he walks, eats, sleeps, etc. We thus acquire a subconscious conviction that there is nothing to study. On the other hand, because of this fact, linguistics is one of the youngest sciences, if not simply the youngest (it has existed for fewer than 100 years). Since it deals with human language, linguistics is still considered one of the humanities—along with history, philosophy, theology, and literary studies—or a social science. But in fact, linguistics is no less a hard science than physiology or medicine. Being a hard science implies that linguistics operates with complex intertwined notions and elaborated formalisms applied to a huge range of highly variegated phenomena. A modest volume like the present cannot touch on them all; I am forced at the outset to maximally narrow my task. In particular, the following three topics and the corresponding branches of linguistics have to be completely left out, despite the interest they present.

"**Language in time.**" By this I mean, first, diachronic linguistics, which studies the development of individual languages and their historical links (language relatedness), as well as the history of human language; and second, the acquisition of language by children, language attrition in old age, adult learning of foreign languages, etc.

"**Language in society.**" This is sociolinguistics, which deals with relations between languages and their speakers (language use in different social and age groups; language contacts; language politics and language planning; language and verbal art).

"**Language in the brain.**" First, neurolinguistics, which carries out a direct study of the chemical-physiological coding of language in the brain, and, second, **psycholinguistics**, which targets the perception of linguistic behavior by speakers.

However, the present book is by no means a popular introduction to "pure" synchronic linguistics that has simply cut off the problems of language in time, in society and in the brain. I limit myself to just one linguistic methodology, known as **Meaning-Text approach**. More specifically, I will focus on linguistic models of the Meaning-Text type. At this point, my reader might well raise a very legitimate question: "What is meaning and what is text? And what does a language do, sandwiched between them?" Please, be patient: this book, *Language: From Meaning to Text* [= LMT], aims at providing a detailed answer exactly to this question.

I have tried to make my exposition available to any educated reader (not just to linguists and their ilk) while remaining precise and professional. In other words, I am trying both to run with the hare and to hunt with the hounds; the result may well be unsatisfactory for both audiences. However, I have no choice—the only option is a reasonable compromise.

Chapter 1
The Problem Stated

I want to begin by giving a rough idea of two things: the nature of human language and the means we have to describe it (*1.1*). Short remarks on these subjects serve to underpin what follows. Then I present the general organization of the book, in order to help the reader navigate it (*1.2*). Finally, I mention some unavoidable limitations of my exposition (*1.3*).

1.1 What is natural language and how to describe it?

This question has been asked innumerable times and has received innumerable answers. Nevertheless, I have to answer it once more, since the answer I intend to give is not—as far as I can judge—universally accepted, at least not in a clear and precise form.

Intuitively, everybody knows what language is. But it is difficult to formulate this knowledge in words: language is an abstract entity unavailable for direct observation. Only the results of its functioning—speaking and understanding of speech—are observable. Therefore, our discussion of language can only be based on the observation of how a language functions.

Suppose I want to use language to communicate something to somebody, or simply to express something. What happens?

- The first thing I, the Speaker,* need is this "something," which is— let me emphasize this point—quite different from the language

---

* To simplify, I ignore writing, which is, by all means, secondary with respect to speaking.

I will use, yet intimately related to it. This "something" is what I want to express or communicate, and it can be called linguistic meaning. (The construction of this meaning by the Speaker is a prelinguistic operation.) Meaning is primary in speech acts: I cannot say anything if I do not know what to say.

> ☞ The term *Speaker*—with a capital "S"—refers to the author of the given speech act, that is, to the person who actually produces the utterance we are considering; *speaker* stands for anyone who speaks the language.

- The second—and the last—step for me as the Speaker is to construct an utterance (or a series of utterances) corresponding to my initial meaning; this utterance can be called (linguistic) text. Producing utterances is speaking. Speaking is also primary in speech acts: you cannot start to understand speech before it has been produced.

Here my role as the Speaker ends. If there is an Addressee—for instance, you, my reader—you perform an inverse operation: first, you receive my text and, second, you extract its meaning. (Then you have to process this meaning in order to incorporate the information into your knowledge database; but this is a postlinguistic operation.) However, the functioning of language is fully characterized by the behavior of the Speaker: speech can take place even in the absence of an Addressee.

Let me start with two basic assumptions, which underlie the whole subsequent exposition.

Assumption 1

> A natural language can be described as a logical device—that is, a system of rules stored in the brain of a speaker that allows him to **speak** and to **understand speech**.

- Speaking is then modeled as implying two operations: 1) associating with an intended meaning 'σ' all the texts that can carry 'σ', and 2) choosing from these texts one that corresponds best to the specific situation of the given speech act. In linguistic lingo, the combination of these operations is called (linguistic) **synthesis**.

1.1 WHAT IS NATURAL LANGUAGE AND HOW TO DESCRIBE IT? 3

- Understanding speech implies two inverse operations: 1′) associating with the received text T all the meanings this text can carry, and 2′) selecting the meaning which best corresponds to the situation of the given speech act. This operation complex is called (linguistic) analysis.

 Remember, real speakers of a language do not, of course, behave as stated above. The notions of linguistic synthesis and linguistic analysis just introduced are simply one of many possible formalizations of speaker's activities.

Now I can formulate a definition of natural language.

Definition 1: Natural language

> A natural language **L** is a specific correspondence² between meanings and texts, encoded in the brains of **L**'s speakers and inaccessible for direct observation by linguists.

This definition, while being absolutely crucial, is often misunderstood, in spite of its seeming simplicity. Hopefully, a metaphor will help.

To begin with, language is like a meat grinder, which receives as its input a piece of meat (≈ meaning) and produces ground meat (≈ text) as its output. If a meat grinder is a meat-to-ground-meat transformer, language can be viewed as a meaning-to-text transformer. This simile is, however, too rough: a meat grinder does not allow for an inverse operation—you cannot return ground meat to its prior state, since it is impossible to turn a hamburger back into a piece of "solid" meat. But the meaning, even transformed into a corresponding text, does not disappear: it can be re-extracted from the text at any given moment.

A better approximation would be to compare language to a human translator, who is translating from language $\mathbf{L_1}$ to language $\mathbf{L_2}$. A translator reads a sufficient—more or less self-contained—fragment of the input text (in $\mathbf{L_1}$) and understands it; doing this he is functioning as $\mathbf{L_1}$, performing linguistic analysis of the input text. As a result, he gets a chunk of meaning that he is supposed to render in $\mathbf{L_2}$. This meaning is then expressed in the output language $\mathbf{L_2}$; here, the translator actually functions as $\mathbf{L_2}$, performing linguistic synthesis of the output text. The source data are not affected in the least, and the inverse transformation remains possible. A language is similar: it allows for both synthesis and analysis of texts, without deforming the meaning or the text processed.

 This is no more than a simile! It is not at all implied that a human translator or the language functions exactly as presented.

Finally, the next metaphor seems the most revealing. A lecturer comes to class with an approximate sketch of his talk: he has cue cards and small sheets of paper on which are written formulas, schemas, key points, and crucial examples. The language of these raw sketches is irrelevant; there can even be no natural language at all. The sketch is a representation of the informational content of the lecture-to-be. Having an occasional look at his notes, the lecturer constructs (in his mind) linguistic meaning, which he expresses through the text of his lecture. Getting from linguistic meaning to linguistic text, our lecturer is carrying out linguistic synthesis. The members of his audience, listening to and understanding the lecture, perform the inverse operation—linguistic analysis.

A caveat:

 The informational content of a sentence (or of a sequence of sentences) and its linguistic meaning are by no means the same entity. This important distinction will be made more precise later (see *2.3.4*, p. 36).

Now, if a natural language **L** is a particular correspondence between meanings and texts, we have to accept Assumption 2.

Assumption 2

> The goal of a linguist studying (= describing) language **L** is to construct a system of rules that specifies the same correspondence between meanings and texts of **L** that **L**'s speakers have.

Such a system of rules is a functional model of **L**—or, more precisely, a model of **L** of the Meaning-Text type: a Meaning-Text model [= MTM].

1.1 WHAT IS NATURAL LANGUAGE AND HOW TO DESCRIBE IT?

It seems convenient to separate this model into two major submodels: a lexicon, which stores **individual** rules, each dealing with **one** lexical unit [= LU] of **L**, and a grammar—a system of **general** rules, each dealing with **a class of** linguistic units.

- **Lexicon.** The lexicon of **L** is a structured collection of LUs of **L**. Formally speaking, an LU constitutes an individual rule of **L**—rule that specifies a correspondence between a signified (= a lexical sense) and a signifier (= the stem of the LU) allowed under particular context conditions (= the description of the LU's cooccurrence). An LU is a lexical item of one of two types:

  – A lexeme, or a word taken in one well-defined sense (see *5.2.3*, Definition 10, p. 135); for instance: $\text{TABLE}_{(N)}^1$ 'piece of furniture...', $\text{TABLE}_{(N)}^2$ 'list of pieces of information arranged in rows or columns...', $\text{SLEEP}_{(V)}\text{I.1}$ 'rest one's mind and body...', $\text{SLEEP}_{(V)}\text{I.2}$ 'have enough beds for n people to sleep in', $\text{SLEEP}_{(V)}\text{II}$ 'have sex with Y', ...). In this book, lexemes are printed in SMALL CAPITAL LETTERS and supplied (when needed) with lexicographic numbers, which identify the intended sense.

  – An idiom, or a non-compositional set expression; for instance, ⌐BALL-PARK FIGURE⌐ 'rough estimate', ⌐JUMP DOWN [N_Y's] THROAT⌐ 'criticize or scold Y overhastily', ⌐ALL THUMBS⌐ 'clumsy'. Idioms are printed between raised semi-brackets.

  The full lexicon of a natural language numbers about one million (= 10^6) LUs.[3] (On the very special role of lexicon in the Meaning-Text approach, see Section *5.4*, p. 151*ff.*)

- **Grammar** (semantics + syntax + morphology + phonology). The grammar of **L** is a structured collection of **L**'s grammatical rules of all levels. The full grammar of a language includes about one thousand (= 10^3) rules; this number comes from my own experience with the description of various languages.

1.2 Illustrations of some basic notions

The very abstract ideas about meanings and texts expounded in the opening remarks and, in particular, in the chapters that follow may be better grasped if the reader is supplied with specific linguistic examples. To this end, I will illustrate four basic notions: informational content, linguistic meaning, linguistic text, and language.

Consider the production of three synonymous sentences in three different languages: English, Russian, and Korean. These sentences convey the same informational content and have (more or less) the same linguistic meaning, but they differ from each other tremendously.

☞ In order to make the illustration understandable, I drastically simplify the linguistic representations and the rules, preserving, however, their essence (if not the form). All relevant notions get no more than a very approximate characterization; for a fuller description, the reader is kindly asked to consult the corresponding sections and/or the Subject Index.

Informational content

(1) | A ghoulish scene in a Northern city: a homeless beggar is found dead after a very cold night.

Linguistic meaning

(2) 'one–1→beggar←1–die–2→cold2'

☞ 'cold2' stands for a particular sense of the noun COLD: 'low temperature of the air; cold weather'.

What is called in LMT *linguistic meaning* is, in fact, a **representation of linguistic meaning**; this representation is known as **semantic structure**. A semantic structure is a formal expression, a **graph**. Its nodes are the **meanings** of words of a language. Meanings are conventionally enclosed in semantic (= single) quotes: thus, *die* is an English word, and 'die' denotes its meaning, whatever the latter may be. (I use English words to denote meanings simply because this book is written for English-speaking readers.) The arcs of the meaning graph carry numbers of the **argument positions** of a given **predicate** (all this will be explained later, in *3.2.2*, p. 47, and for the time being, a minimum of understand-

1.2 ILLUSTRATIONS OF SOME BASIC NOTIONS   7

ing is sufficient). A **predicate** is a meaning that has open slots for other meanings, which are called its **arguments**; thus, 'die' is a predicate with two arguments and, consequently, two **argument positions**, X and Y: 'X dies from Y', while 'one' has one argument position: 'one X'.

One of the possible literal readings of the meaning representation above is *The beggar died from the cold* [= 'cold2']; this is fully understandable and grammatically correct sentence, but not what an English-speaking journalist would write.

Linguistic texts

(3) a. *Eng. The beggar+Ø   froze   to death+Ø.*
                    SG   freeze-PAST   SG

   b. *Rus. Nišč +ij   zamërz   +   Ø +Ø*
          beggar SG.NOM dead.freeze-PERF PAST MASC.SG

   lit. 'Beggar dead.froze'.

   c. *Kor. Kəči+ka   el   +e   čʰuk +ess + ta*
          beggar SUBJ freeze CONV   die   PAST DECLARATIVE

   lit. 'Beggar freezing died'.

☞ The symbol "+" stands for the border between elements (= linguistic signs) that compose a wordform—that is, between morphs, elementary segmental signs, which will be defined later, see *5.2.2*, p. 121. In English, **-Ø** is a zero suffix, opposed to the **-s** of the plural; in Russian, the first **-Ø** is the zero suffix of the past tense opposed to the -l after a vowel, and the second **-Ø** is a zero suffix opposed to **-a** and **-o**, respectively, of the feminine singular and the neuter singular. CONV in Korean represents a converb—a verbal form similar to the English **-ing**-form, and SUBJ is a grammatical case used to mark the syntactic subject.

These three short texts, each one sentence long, express the meaning (2), but in very different ways. Thus:

– English and Russian, but not Korean, obligatorily express the number of dead beggars: in this case, one. Korean leaves this information implicit (were the number of victims more than one, it could optionally be indicated—by the suffix **-tɨl**).

8   1. THE PROBLEM STATED

- English, but not Russian and Korean, obligatorily expresses the definiteness of **the** dead beggar: he was mentioned in a previous sentence.
- Korean, but not English and Russian, obligatorily marks the sentence as a statement by the declarative suffix on the Main Verb.
- Russian and Korean, but not English, mark their syntactic subject with a grammatical case: Russian uses the nominative (= the case of naming), and Korean, the subjective (= the case marking syntactic subjects).

All these and a huge amount of other details must be taken into account in order to ensure the transition from (2) to (3a), (3b) and (3c). To simplify my task and alleviate the efforts of the reader, I will consider not the actual sentences in (3), but their syntactic structures.

(4) Syntactic structures of sentences in (3)

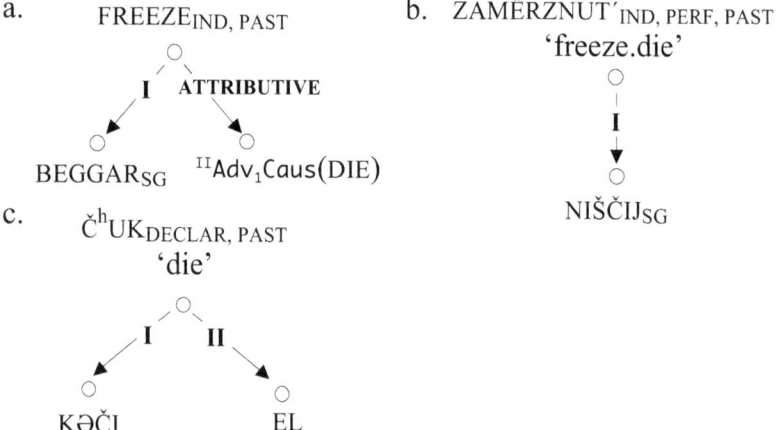

Comments

1. Roman numbers I and II stand for **deep-syntactic actants**: roughly speaking, I corresponds to the syntactic subject and its transforms, while II represent the "strongest object"—in the first place the Direct Object, but not only the DirO.

2. In (4a), the phrase *to death* is encoded by the lexical function $^{II}Adv_1Caus$—i.e. '[this] causing death', which is a modifier of the verb FREEZE (lexical functions are explained in detail in *4.2*).

1.2 ILLUSTRATIONS OF SOME BASIC NOTIONS 9

3. In (4c), the verb EL 'freeze' appears as syntactic actant II of the verb Čʰ UK 'die' ('X dies of Y').

4. The three languages make use of all three logically possible lexical expressions for the combinations of the meanings 'die' and 'freeze':

> in (4a), 'freeze to.death', where 'freeze' is realized by a syntactically dominant lexeme (FREEZE), and 'die' by a syntactically dependent expression (*to death*);
> in (4b), 'freeze.die', where 'freeze' and 'die' are realized together by a derived verb (ZA+MËRZNUT′);
> in (4c), 'die by.freezing', where 'freeze' is realized by a syntactically dependent expression (*ele* 'freezing'), and 'die' by a syntactically dominant lexeme (Čʰ UK-).

There are no other possibilities! Thus, French says *mourir de froid* lit. 'die from cold'—that is, the Korean way, while German does it the Russian way, with the derived verb ERFRIEREN 'freeze.die' (from FRIEREN 'freeze').

The tree-like structures in (4) are what we call **Deep**-Syntactic Structures; to completely grasp their formalism requires much additional knowledge (see *3.2.3*, p. 52*ff*). For the time being, however, full understanding is not necessary.

Anticipating a future discussion, I would like to emphasize that the syntactic structures of sentences are described in *LMT* in terms of **dependency** formalism (see *5.5*, p. 170*ff*)—rather than in terms of phrase-structure, or constituent, formalism, more familiar to many. The dependency technique is intimately related to the spirit of our approach: from Meanings to Texts— that is, from semantic networks to dependency trees to morphological strings.

The transition from the syntactic structures in (4) to real sentences is obvious enough even for an unprepared reader—basically, words must be ordered linearly and inflections added where necessary. I can leave these details aside and concentrate on the passage from (2) to (4)—more specifically, from the semantic structure to the deep-syntactic structure of the future sentence.

> The rules that describe this passage are specific to a particular language.

Languages

A natural language is a logical device that can go from a meaning to all the texts that express it (and, of course, vice versa). This device consists of a set of formal rules, and I will give a few specimens of these rules here, namely some (but not all!) of the rules necessary for the (2) ⇔ (4) passage above. These rules can be divided into two subsets: (i) rules dealing with **individual** lexical units of **L** that constitute the lexicon of **L**, and (ii) rules dealing with **classes** of lexical units and smaller linguistic signs (i.e., morphs and morphological operations) that constitute the grammar of **L** (see the end of Subsection *1.1*). The interface between the lexicon and the grammar of **L** is the set of deep-syntactic structures of sentences of **L**, as exemplified by (4).

‖ Language **L** is the sum of **L**'s lexicon and **L**'s grammar.

In what follows, the three languages will be described—quite partially, each represented by just five rules (out of perhaps a million—that is, ≈ 0.0001%).

Lexicon: lexical semantic rules

Under the Meaning-Text approach, the lexicon of a language **L** is recorded and formalized in what is known as an *Explanatory-Combinatorial Dictionary* [ECD], see *5.4*, p. 151*ff*. I will give the relevant parts of the lexical entries of an ECD for the verbs meaning 'X freezes' and 'X dies from Y' and for the noun meaning 'beggar' in the three languages in question. (The semantic actant slots 'X' and 'Y' are the same in all three.)

1.2 ILLUSTRATIONS OF SOME BASIC NOTIONS

English	Russian	Korean
'cold2←1–affect–2→X' ⇔ **FREEZE**, verb	'cold2←1–affect–2→X' ⇔ **MËRZNUT'**, verb	'cold2←1–affect–2→X' ⇔ **EL**, verb
$\begin{array}{\|c\|} X \Leftrightarrow \mathrm{I} \\ \hline 1.\ \mathrm{N} \end{array}$	$\begin{array}{\|c\|} X \Leftrightarrow \mathrm{I} \\ \hline 1.\ \mathrm{N_{NOM}} \end{array}$	$\begin{array}{\|c\|} X \Leftrightarrow \mathrm{I} \\ \hline 1.\ \mathrm{N_{SUBJ}} \end{array}$
Constraint 1 if 'X←1–die', then FREEZE–ATTR→ $^{\mathrm{II}}\mathrm{Adv}_1\mathrm{Caus}(\mathrm{DIE})$	Constraint 1 if 'X←1–die', then ZAMËRZNUT'	Constraint 1 if 'X←1–die', then ČʰUK–II→EL
'X←1–die–2→Y' ⇔ **DIE**, verb	'X←1–die–2→Y' ⇔ **UMERET'**, verb	'X←1–die–2→Y' ⇔ **ČʰUK**, verb
$\begin{array}{\|c\|c\|} X \Leftrightarrow \mathrm{I} & Y \Leftrightarrow \mathrm{II} \\ \hline 1.\ \mathrm{N} & 1.\ \mathit{from}\ \mathrm{N} \end{array}$	$\begin{array}{\|c\|c\|} X \Leftrightarrow \mathrm{I} & Y \Leftrightarrow \mathrm{II} \\ \hline 1.\ \mathrm{N_{NOM}} & 1.\ \mathit{ot}\ \text{'from'}\ \mathrm{N} \end{array}$	$\begin{array}{\|c\|c\|} X \Leftrightarrow \mathrm{I} & Y \Leftrightarrow \mathrm{II} \\ \hline 1.\ \mathrm{N_{SUBJ}} & 1.\ \mathrm{V}\text{-}e \end{array}$
Constraint 1 if 'Y' = 'cold2', then FREEZE–ATTR→ $^{\mathrm{II}}\mathrm{Adv}_1\mathrm{Caus}(\mathrm{DIE})$ $^{\mathrm{II}}\mathrm{Adv}_1\mathrm{Caus}$: *to death*	Constraint 1 if 'Y' = 'cold2', then ZAMËRZNUT'	
'beggar' ⇔ **BEGGAR**, noun	'beggar' ⇔ **NIŠČIJ**, noun	'beggar' ⇔ **KƏČI**, noun

Comments

1. The Arabic numbers **1** and **2** stand for the first and second semantic actants, the Roman numbers **I** and **II**, for deep-syntactic actants, and the expression $^{\mathrm{II}}\mathrm{Adv}_1\mathrm{Caus}$, for a particular lexical function, as explained above. "⇔" means 'corresponds', **ATTR** denotes the deep-syntactic relation of modification (to be explained in *3.2.3*, p. 56*ff*); shading shows, as already noted, the context of a rule.

2. The underscoring of a semanteme (in a Sem-structure) indicates the communicatively dominant semanteme, which represents, in a reduced form, the whole structure; thus, 'cold2←1–affect–2→X' is 'X is affected by the cold2' rather than 'the cold2 that affects X'. See *3.2.2*, Fig. 2, p. 49.

3. The meaning 'die' occupies an important place in the lexicon of a language (for obvious reasons). As a result, the cause of death (Sem-actant Y = 2 of 'die') is most often expressed idiomatically, which has to be indicated in the corresponding lexical entry. Thus, the lexical entry for DIE carries the following constraint:

«if 'Y' = 'cold2', then FREEZE–ATTR→^{II}Adv$_1$Caus(DIE)»;

this tells us that the meaning 'die from cold2' is expressed in English as *freeze to death*. A similar constraint for UMERET' in a Russian dictionary signifies that 'die from cold2' corresponds to one derived verb ZAMËRZNUT' 'die from cold2'. The real lexical entry for UMERET' includes more constraints of this type:

Y = 'external physical agent'	: //*pogibnut'*	'die a violent dead'
Y = 'submerging in liquid'	: //*utonut'*	'drown'
Y = 'lack of air'	: //*zadoxnut'sja*	'suffocate'
Y = 'brutal fall'	: //*razbit'sja*	'be killed in a fall'

Grammar

Grammemic semantic rules

Grammemic semantic rules ensure the correspondences between **semantemes** (or configurations of semantemes) and **grammemes**. Semantemes are semantic units of a language—roughly, the meanings of its lexical units, while grammemes are values of its inflectional categories, such as SINGULAR/PLURAL, PRESENT/PAST/FUTURE, etc.

Implementation of the semanteme 'one' (= *Rus.* 'odin', *Kor.* 'han')

	English	Russian	Korean
'one' ○ 1 ↓ ○ 'Y' ⇔	L('Y')$_{(N)SG}$	L('Y')$_{(N)SG}$	—

Structural semantic rules

Structural semantic rules map semantic dependencies on deep-syntactic dependencies.

1.2 ILLUSTRATIONS OF SOME BASIC NOTIONS

Implementation of Sem-dependency 1

	English	Russian	Korean
'X' ↓1 'Y' ⇔	L('X')$_{\text{(V, intrans)FIN}}$ ↓I L('Y')	L('X')$_{\text{(V, intrans)FIN}}$ ↓I L('Y')	L('X')$_{\text{(V, intrans)FIN}}$ ↓I L('Y')

If a semanteme 'X' that is a predicate is manifested by an intransitive verb L('X') in the finite form ("L" stands for a concrete lexical unit), the Sem-actant 1 of 'X' becomes the deep-syntactic actant I of this verb (that is, roughly, the syntactic subject).

☞ Semantic actant 1 is realized as deep-syntactic actant I with intransitive verbs in the three languages considered here. However, some languages show a correspondence Sem-actant 1 ⇔ DSynt-actant II with special (= "impersonal") transitive verbs. For instance, consider the meaning 'Pete vomits' and its realization in Russian:
'Pete←1–vomit' ⇔ Rus. PETJA←II–RVAT' ⇔ *Petju*$_{\text{ACC}}$ *rvët* lit. 'It vomits Pete', where PETJA is a direct object.

Now, to drive home the idea of a language as a system of rules, I will show how the language rules apply to a initial semantic structure to produce the corresponding sentences. Let me do it for English.

In its present state, the Meaning-Text model **does not deal with the actual procedure** of rule applications;[4] therefore, all linguistic rules are written in such a way as to be applicable in any order. Take the very first English lexical rule. Applying the rule 'cold2←1–affect–2→X' ⇔ FREEZE (see p. 11, English) to the Sem-structure of (2), we obtain

(i) 'X'←1–FREEZE

In (2), 'X[←2–affect–1→cold2]' is 'beggar', and 'beggar←1–die'; thus, Constraint 1 to the rule applied—**if** 'Y' = 'cold2', **then** FREEZE–ATTR→^{II}Adv$_1$Caus(DIE)—is satisfied, which gives (ii):

(ii) FREEZE–ATTR→^{II}Adv$_1$Caus(DIE)

Filling in X = BEGGAR and implementing the Sem-dependency **1**, we get (iii):

(iii) BEGGAR←I–FREEZE–ATTR→^{II}Adv$_1$Caus(DIE)

Add the definiteness, the singular and the past (not described here) and take the value of ^{II}Adv$_1$Caus(DIE) from the entry for DIE; the result is (iv)—that is, sentence (3a):

(iv) *The beggar froze to death.*

A reader who, at this juncture, feels sufficiently excited can try for himself to apply the rules of Russian and Korean and thus better grasp what a linguistic functional model—more precisely, an MTM—is.

In this way, we have seen a minuscule fragment of each of the three languages. That is what modern synchronic linguistics is about: developing such fragments into full-fledged models of languages. Such models are one of the primary goals of the science of language.

1.3 The structure of this book

The exposition that follows is organized thus:

Chapter *2*, based on Assumptions 1 and 2, introduces the notion of a 'functional model'.

Chapter *3* offers a short outline of a particular Meaning-Text model. I will examine the levels of representation of linguistic expressions (called, for short, linguistic representations), give examples of these representations and introduce rules for a transition from representations of level *n* to representations of level *n+1*; these rules constitute the modules of an MTM.

Chapter *4* considers links between non-observable semantic phenomena of natural languages and observable cooccurrence facts, allowing me to better justify the modeling techniques of the Meaning-Text approach. More specifically, I will dwell on the notion of lexical function.

Chapter 5 presents a trend in modern linguistics based on functional modeling of natural languages—namely, Meaning-Text linguistics. Its central feature is that it does not simply study and describe observable linguistic expressions and units composing them as such, but targets the **process of their production** by the Speaker, who starts from the meaning of a linguistic expression to produce its physical form. A couple of research topics in the Meaning-Text framework will be sketched out.

The book has three Appendices: a phonetic table (pp. 182–183), a table of possible combinations of the three types of linguistic dependency, and a list of languages mentioned in the book, with an indication of the family to which they belong. There is also a Subject and Name Index, which is in fact a glossary, including a minimal explanation of the terms used (pp. 229–253). This glossary is meant to come to the rescue of the reader faced with an unknown concept.

 All technical terms are printed, on their first mention (and often on subsequent mentions, too) in Helvetica font. All of these are included into the Subject and Name Index. So you know where to look for help!

Additional remarks, which develop some tangential points, are reserved for the endnotes, referred to by numbers; minor remarks are relegated to footnotes.

1.4 Limitations accepted

Given the nature of the present undertaking—an introduction to the science of linguistics that seeks to eschew the over-technical whenever possible—some major limitations are inevitable:
- I cannot provide all requisite references, too numerous for this small book. In particular, I will not compare the Meaning-Text approach to other linguistic theories, models and approaches. MTM was launched in Moscow in the 1960s – 1970s, in close collaboration and interaction of the present writer with, in the first place, A. K. Žolkovskij, Ju. D. Apresjan and L. N. Iordanskaja. It is not by chance

that many of my considerations and proposals coincide with those coming from these colleagues and friends.

- Nor can I introduce systematically and consistently all the relevant notions and formalisms. This would require much more text—that is, developing this book into a multi-volume treatise, inaccessible to an uninitiated reader. (Chapter 5, p. 109*ff*, gives some references to in-depth studies carried out within the framework of Meaning-Text approach.) I try to make do with additional explanations presented as endnotes, while supplying minimal explications for the terms in the body of the text. I rely heavily upon concrete examples and the subject index. The impossibility of rigorous deductive-logical exposition entails repetitions and, on the other hand, insufficient clarity (what I have to explain to a non-linguist will seem overly pedantic to a linguist, and a linguist might object to what he perceives as over-simplification). I have, however, no choice in this matter.

- *LMT* addresses an educated English reader, not necessarily a linguist; therefore, my illustrations are drawn, for the most part, from the English language. Other languages are discussed only where the phenomenon in question is not represented (or insufficiently represented) in English.

Chapter 2

Functional Modeling in Linguistics

In this chapter, three points will be discussed: the concept of "model" as a research tool (*2.1*), then a more specific type of model, a functional model (*2.2*), and finally, an even more specific type of model, a linguistic functional Meaning-Text model (*2.3*).

2.1 A model as a means of study and description

Models play a crucial role in all sciences. If, for any reason, the researcher cannot directly observe the inner structure of the entity or phenomenon P under examination (such is the case of human language: it cannot be directly observed), he has recourse to a model of this P. Studying the behavior of P "from the outside," he constructs a model **M** of P [= **M**(P)], trying to obtain the maximum similarity between the behavior of P and that of the model **M**(P). He can then scrutinize the inner structure of **M**(P), which is fully available, since the researcher has created **M**(P) himself. Where the behavior of P and that of **M**(P) are sufficiently similar, findings about **M**(P) can be applied to P. In an analogous way, if P is too complex or if the available data on P are too unwieldy and/or unclear, the researcher can work with an approximate model of P, which allows him to establish important regularities of P's behavior—to the extent, of course, that they are reflected in the model. Such is the situation in cosmology and geophysics, in molecular biology and atomic physics, in meteorology, neurology and sociology. In a certain sense, Science is the construction of models.

Take a simple example. Geophysicists strive to learn what exactly is happening in the Earth's liquid core; this is necessary, in particular, because the processes in the core fundamentally impact the Earth's magnetic field. However, the scientists cannot reach the Earth's core for direct observations: inhuman temperature and no less inhuman pressure block their way. Therefore, they have to limit their study to some observable manifestations of what is happening inside the Earth's core. However, based on this raw factual data, they can formulate hypotheses about the internal structure of the core: they postulate for it such a structure that—in light of known physical laws—would determine the observable phenomena available for us. In the same way science is studying the processes inside the Sun or the history of the Universe, starting with the Big Bang.

As always, when direct observation of the internal structure of some entities and phenomena is impossible, the only technique available is modeling these entities and phenomena.

Since Galileo, modern science has progressed by way of modeling. Rosenblueth & Wiener 1945 explicitly and clearly stated the necessity of formal modeling for all sciences. Twenty years later, their idea was taken up and reformulated by Auger 1965: 4: "There is no scientist who does not permanently think in terms of models—although many do not admit this to others and, sometimes, to themselves" (translation is mine—IM).

In this respect, linguistics is no different from other sciences. A natural language **L** is a very complex system of rules encoded in the brain of **L**'s speakers. This system is not available for immediate observation; at any rate, "pure" linguists (like myself) cannot reach it, since they do not know how to open human skulls or implant electrodes into the brain.* Facing this impossibility, we have to turn to linguistic models; for us, there is simply no other way.

Modern synchronic linguistics sets itself the task of constructing models of human languages. Although this task is far from always be-

---

* Neurologists can in principle try to directly observe linguistic phenomena in the brain. In this domain, some important results have been achieved and we can expect significant headway to be made in the near future (for modern neurological methods of linguistic research—concerning, in particular, meanings—see, for instance, Krifka 2011). A general overview of neurolinguistics is to be found in Ahlsén 2006.

ing explicitly formulated, today's linguists basically do exactly this: they develop linguistic models.

The idea of modeling came into linguistics in the late 1950s; it had two major sources:

- One of these is generative-transformational Chomskyan linguistics, since a formal grammar of language **L** proposed in this approach as the main tool of linguistic research is simply **L**'s model.[5]
- The other source is machine translation research, very active in the early 1960s. A rule-based machine translation system requires a formal representation of the facts of at least two languages, and such formal representations are linguistic models or fragments thereof.

The same period saw the first theoretical outlines of the notion of "model" as applied to natural language; thus, the edited volume Nagel *et al.* 1962 gives quite serious consideration to linguistic modeling. Later J. Molino (1985: 29) wrote: "Morphology—like other parts of language and the language as a whole—can be described only by way of models" (translation is mine—IM). Nowadays, the active use of models seems to be solidly anchored in modern linguistics. My proposals, therefore, are not isolated: they are part of a widespread trend in linguistic studies.

Now, the question arises: what type of linguistic model is the most appropriate?

2.2 Functional models

To better understand what we are talking about, we need to resolve the ambiguity and vagueness inherent in the noun MODEL. The three senses of MODEL that are relevant here can be illustrated with the following utterances:

(5) a. *The painter's model was his wife.*
    b. *a paper model of a plane*
    c. *Bohr-Rutherford model of the atom*

☞ I will ignore other uses of the noun MODEL such as in *Toyota model 1999, follow the Swedish model*, or *model millionaire* vs. *millionaire model* [O. Wilde], etc.)

All these uses of the noun MODEL correspond to the same situation: there are two entities, X and Y, one of which, say X, is intentionally created by a person in such a way as to possess some properties of Y that are relevant in the given context. In the situations corresponding to the examples in (5), these entities are: a painting$_X$ (= a portrait) presenting a person$_Y$; a toy$_X$ resembling a plane$_Y$; mathematical equations$_X$ describing the atom$_Y$. We see here a binary anti-symmetrical relation 'be a model [of]'. To sharpen the notion 'be a model', the following three explanations are needed.

- First, let us distinguish two basic senses in which the term *model* is used. Under *model* represented by a painter is understood the given entity (actually, a person or a pet) Y, while the painter's creation, X, is a painting representing Y. But the *model* of a plane and that of the atom correspond to an inverse relation: Y is the given entity to be modeled, and we call *model* the entity X—that is, an artificially manufactured representation of Y.[6] In *LMT*, the term *model* will be used only in the second sense: *model of Y* is '**entity X created by the researcher** [to represent entity Y under analysis in a form better fit for observation and exploration]'.

- Second, consider an expression of the form *X, model of Y*. One can see the following important difference between its possible realizations: *the model of a plane* denotes a physical object, while *Bohr-Rutherford model of the atom* is a set of symbolic expressions—a system of equations. Thus, we have to distinguish concrete (= physical) and abstract (= symbolic) models. In this book, the term *model* will be understood exclusively as an **abstract system of symbolic expressions**.

- Third, the model of a plane reminds one of a plane—at least, in its perceivable form, even if it cannot fly; such a model is called structural. A structural model of Y is developed on the basis of direct observations of Y's structure, measuring and reproducing Y's components, etc. But the Bohr-Rutherford model of the atom does not at all resemble an atom: it merely represents its behavior, or functioning; this is a functional model. In linguistics, it is only a **functional model** of language that is aimed at.

Now I can further refine the notion of abstract functional model of language **L**.

Definition 2: Functional model of Y

> A system of rules (= logical device) X is called a functional model of the entity or fact Y if and only if [= iff] X is constructed by the researcher based on observation of Y's behavior in such a way that X reflects Y's behavior as closely as possible.

☛ Note that Chao 1962 presents over 40 (forty!) interpretations of the term *model* in linguistics; therefore, my attempt at resolving the vagueness and ambiguity of this term is not misplaced.

A functional model can satisfy the researcher's needs only if he is interested in the functioning, or behavior, of the entity studied; such is the case of language and linguistics. In this respect, functional models possess two important properties:

1) A functional model X represents its object Y as a "black box"— that is, as an object that has an observable behavior and can be manipulated by the researcher (at least, to certain extent) externally, but cannot be opened so as to reveal its inner workings.

2) A functional model X does not in principle guarantee the accuracy or even the correctness of the description of Y obtained through this modelling: it ensures only some approximation of the truth. We construct a functional model based on our observations of some effects (= perceivable effects of Y's behavior), from which we deduce possible causes. However, it is well known that a given effect can be due to very different causes. Therefore, some well-established facts can, generally speaking, correspond to mutually exclusive causes. This is the drawback with functional modeling. The positive side, however is this:

The better we study the object Y—namely, the more particularities of its behavior we take into account—the closer we approach the real state of affairs. One isolated effect can correspond to many different causes, but a complex structured system of effects corresponds, with a high probability, to one complex system of causes. In other words, the more complex the system of observed effects, the less numerous its possible causes. In the case of functional models, this means that while one observed fact could correspond to several postulated "deep" descriptions, a complex system of observed facts can likely be covered by only one such description.

Nevertheless, a researcher working with functional linguistic models must always keep in mind two simple truths. First, one good counterexample is sufficient to compromise a functional model (that is, to demonstrate its inadequacy, at least partially): a functional model is easily falsifiable, in the sense of K. Popper. On the one hand, this makes functional models legitimate and valuable research tools in linguistics. But, on the other hand, it is, in principle, impossible to rigorously prove the correctness of a functional model: its hypothetical nature is an inherent trait that linguists have to meekly accept. Second, there is a fundamental difference between functional models in physics and other nature-based hard sciences, on the one hand, and functional models in linguistics, on the other:

> Physical sciences are buttressed by a fundamental physical theory of the universe, so that any model proposed by a physicist must "fit" into this theory; this drastically reduces the set of possible models and makes them more reliable. The science of language does not have anything similar: there is no fundamental theory of the human brain, or at least of mental behavior, that could be a solid framework for linguistic models. As a result, today's linguistic models are still far from the level of reliability achieved by physical models.

Now, having sketched out the limited character of linguistic models in general, I can proceed to the central object of this book: a particular functional linguistic model—the Meaning-Text model.

2.3 The Meaning-Text model: a global functional linguistic model

This section is central to Chapter 2. After some introductory remarks (*2.3.1*), I will present the three basic postulates of the Meaning-Text approach (*2.3.2*), five formal properties of Meaning-Text models (*2.3.3*) and, finally, two pillars of this approach: linguistic meaning and paraphrasing (*2.3.4*); this is followed by a short insight into what will be discussed in the rest of the book (*2.3.5*).

2.3.1 Introductory remarks

I started work on Meaning-Text models [= MTM] in Moscow in the middle of 1964, together with Aleksandr Žolkovskij; later Jurij Apresjan joined us (Žolkovskij & Mel′čuk 1965, 1966, 1967; Apresjan *et al.* 1968, Apresyan *et al.* 1969; Mel′čuk 1974, Mel′čuk 1973). More colleagues took part in this research in the years that followed; I will limit myself to my own subsequent work: Mel′čuk 1981, 1988, 2012, 2013, 2015.

First, the theoretical framework of such models model, Meaning-Text linguistic theory, will be introduced. To simplify the presentation, a number of abbreviations and symbols are used; see the Table of Abbreviations and Notations, p. 226*ff*. The reader will find any unfamiliar terms in the glossary at the end of the book.

2.3.2 Three postulates of the Meaning-Text theory

The Meaning-Text methodological approach to natural language is based on the following three postulates.

- Postulate 1 specifies the OBJECT OF OUR DESCRIPTION; it expresses my general conception of natural language.
- Postulate 2 specifies the EXPECTED RESULT OF OUR DESCRIPTION; it expresses my conception of linguistic research.

- Postulate 3 specifies the LINK BETWEEN LANGUAGE AND ITS PROPOSED DESCRIPTION; it expresses my conception of the essential properties of natural language that have to be reflected in its description in an immediate and explicit way.

Postulate 1: A natural language is a "Meaning-Text" correspondence.

> A natural language is a finite system of rules that specifies a many-to-many correspondence between an infinite but countable set of meanings and an infinite but countable set of texts.

(A set is countable if and only if its elements can be numbered by natural numbers; this guarantees the discreteness of these elements.)

In an MTM, linguistic meanings appear as formal symbolic objects, called semantic representations [= SemR], as do linguistic texts, the corresponding formal symbolic objects being phonetic representations [= PhonetR]. Postulate 1 can be rewritten as follows:

(6) $\{SemR_i\} \Leftrightarrow \{PhonetR_j\} \mid i, j > 0$

PhonetR is simply a phonetic transcription; I do not have to discuss this notion here—it is well known. See, for instance:

IPA [= International Phonetic Alphabet; http://en.wikipedia.org/wiki/International_Phonetic_Alphabet]

or

APA [= American(ist) Phonetic Alphabet; http://en.wikipedia.org/wiki/Americanist_phonetic_notation]

Each language needs, of course, its own set of phonetic symbols, which are taken from a common pool.

SemR is a semantic transcription; from the viewpoint of its content, it is specific for each language, while formally, it is universal. I will return to this later.

The infinite set of correct SemRs for a given language **L** is given by a rather simple formal grammar (based on combinatorial properties of semantic elements). This set is the input for an MTM of **L**; its output is, of course, the infinite set of correct PhonetRs of **L**.

Informally, **text** (in the terminological sense) is the "external"—that is, phonetic or graphic—side of speech, while **meaning** (also in the terminological sense) is its "internal"—that is, mental—side. In a rigorous formulation, the meaning of a sentence S is the invariant of the set of all sentences S_i that have the same meaning as S—that is, of the set of paraphrases of S. The invariant of a set is the entity that all the elements of this set have in common. In our case, the semantic invariant of a set of synonymous paraphrases is represented by one of the paraphrases that satisfies a series of conditions and is represented in a particular way. (For more on SemR, see *3.2.2, p. 46ff.*)

Postulate 2: The main tool for the description of languages is a Meaning-Text model.

> Correspondence (6)—{SemR$_i$} ⇔ {PhonetR$_j$} is described by a logical device (= a system of rules), which is a Meaning-Text model.

An MTM takes as its input any of the possible SemRs of language **L** and produces as its output the corresponding PhonetRs; this operation is linguistic **synthesis**. The MTM is supposed to carry out linguistic synthesis in the same way as **L**'s speakers do—that is, it must reproduce, as exactly as possible, the correspondence that a speaker of **L** uses, when he wants to express a given meaning. And, of course, an MTM must also be capable of performing the inverse operation—linguistic **analysis**: taking as its input any PhonetRs of **L** and producing at the output the corresponding SemRs.

Formally speaking, the Meaning ⇒ Text and Text ⇒ Meaning transitions are fully equivalent. However, from the viewpoint of a linguist who is developing an MTM, as well as that of the users of the model, this is not so.

> Language prioritizes the Speaker as the first and necessary participant of a speech act rather than the Addressee, who is the second and optional participant. More precisely, it prioritizes the

production of speech that carries a given meaning—that is, linguistic synthesis, rather than the understanding of speech—that is, linguistic analysis. The activity of the Speaker is more linguistic than that of the Addressee.

The production of a text for a given meaning that the Speaker wants to put in words requires from the latter only his linguistic knowledge and abilities. However, the Addressee needs additional skills, if only because of the multiple ambiguities of many texts. In order to extract the encoded meaning from the text received he needs not only a full mastery of the language, but also various encyclopedic data and logical skills which allow him to grasp "what this speech is about." We have many facts that show that Language itself prioritizes the Speaker (over the Addressee); here are some of these:

- Any language has a special verb meaning 'produce speech' = 'speak', but none, as far as I know, has a verb meaning 'understand speech': to express the idea of understanding speech, languages use the same verb they use for understanding anything at all. (Sporadically, other verbs are used: for instance, 'hear', 'know' or 'be able'; however, none of these is specific to understanding speech.)

- The expression for 'speak language **L**' is quite often phraseologized, while the expression for 'understand language **L**' is, as a rule, free. For instance, French has the phrase *parler français* ⟨*anglais, russe, …*⟩ 'speak French ⟨English, Russian, …⟩', which is phraseologized: the noun FRANÇAIS 'French language' is used without an article—adverbially, so to speak. On the other hand, the phrase **comprendre français* '[to] understand French' is ungrammatical (the asterisk " * " before a linguistic expression X means that X is incorrect), since the correct expression is *comprendre le français* lit. 'understand the French', with the noun FRANÇAIS 'French language' duly taking the definite article; this phrase is quite non-idiomatic—that is, it is free (= non-phraseologized).

- Natural language is extremely "egocentric" in the sense that a great number of linguistic signs encode the viewpoint of 'I'—that is, the viewpoint of the Speaker, the person who says *I* in a given speech act. But the viewpoint of 'you'—that is, that of the Addressee, the person whom the Speaker calls *you* in a given speech act—is never encoded as a matter of course in linguistic signs. This egocentricity is manifested in many different ways in the lexicon and the grammar of a language; there is plenty of evidence, some of which I now give.

Language's Egocentricity in the Lexicon

Here are three examples that illustrate the egocentricity of the lexicon.

1) So-called shifters (R. Jakobson): I 'person who says *I*' (= the Speaker), HERE 'at the spot where the Speaker says *here*', TODAY 'day when the Speaker says *today*', MOM (without modifiers) 'the mother of the Speaker', etc. The meaning of a shifter word necessarily includes a direct reference to the Speaker.

2) Expressive words, which express the attitude of the Speaker toward their denotation. I can quote, for instance, derogatory names of ethnicities ("ethnic slurs"):

Arab	*raghead*	Japanese person	*Jap*
Chinese person	*Chink*	Jew	*kike*
Frenchman	*frog*	Pakistani	*Paki*
German	*Kraut, Hun*	Pole	*Polack*
Italian	*wop*	Russian	*Russky*
Italian, Spaniard or Portuguese	*Dago*	Spaniard	*Spic*

What indeed does the noun CHINK mean? 'Chinese person, **I hating and/or having a low opinion of the Chinese**'. The boldfaced component conveys an unwarranted opinion of the Speaker about ALL Chinese, which makes the term so offensive.[7] Quite a similar case is the contrast between the neutral term PROSTITUTE, which simply denotes a trade, and offensive nouns WHORE, HARLOT, STRUMPET, which mean 'prostitute, **I hating and/or having a low opinion of the prostitutes**'.

Each language has a set of such "propaganda words," whose meaning includes the component ≈ '[X,] **I having a negative attitude towards Xs**'.[8]

3) **Signalative lexical expressions**, which demonstrate the Speaker's attitude either towards the situation he is talking about or towards his own utterance (concerning its content as well as its form): WOW!, OH MY GOSH!, UNFORTUNATELY, TO TAKE AN EXAMPLE, etc. These are **lexical** signalatives.

Language's Egocentricity in the Grammar

4) In many languages, the 1st person singular [= 1SG] of the verb (that is, the verb form referring to the Speaker) has a host of particularities, semantic and formal.

A semantic particularity of the 1SG forms

Each language has performative verbs. A **performative verb**—or, more generally, a performative verbal expression—denotes such an action that to carry it out it is necessary and sufficient to utter this expression in the 1SG in the present indicative: thus, in order to swear (take an oath), you have to say *I swear*; in order to marry a couple—if you have the right to do so—you have to say *I declare you husband and wife*; etc. A performative verbal expression can be performatively used only in the 1SG in the present indicative: if you said *I swear!*, you have sworn, but if you uttered *I swore* or *He swears that he'll come* you simply described what a particular person said.

Formal particularities of 1SG forms

– Alutor marks the Direct Object on the governing verb—in all moods and all tenses, in all persons and all numbers—with a suffix. However, there is a single exception: if the Subject is of the 3rd person, a DirO of the 1SG (= 'me') is marked with a prefix. Thus,

'He beat up us two'	⇒	*na+tkəplə+**mək***
'He beat up us many'	⇒	*na+tkəplə+**lamək***
'He beat up you$_{SG}$'	⇒	*na+tkəplə+**γət***
'He beat up you two'	⇒	*na+tkəplə+**tki***, etc.

But

'He beat up me'	⇒	***ina**+tkəpl+i*, etc.

– In Bantu languages, a verb in the 1SG has a negative prefix different from the negative prefix in all other persons and numbers. Thus, in Swahili, all verbal forms are negated by the prefix **h(a)-**, which precedes the Subject noun class marker. But all the forms of the 1SG take the prefix **si-**, which cumulatively expresses negation and 1SG Subject (i.e., **ha-**+**ni-** ⇒ **si-**):

'You$_{SG}$ read'	⇒	*u* +Ø +*som*+*a*
'They read$_{PAST}$'	⇒	*wa*+*ku* +*som*+*a*
'We will read'	⇒	*tu* +*ta* +*som*+*a*
'You$_{SG}$ do not read'	⇒	*h* +*u* +Ø +*som*+*i*
'They did not read'	⇒	*ha* +*wa* +*ku*+*som*+*a*
'We will not read'	⇒	*ha* +*tu* +*ta* +*som*+*a*, etc.

But

'I read'	⇒	*ni* +Ø +*som*+*a*
'I read$_{PAST}$'	⇒	*ni* +*ku* +*som*+*a*
'I will read'	⇒	*ni* +*ta* +*som*+*a*, etc.
'I do not read'	⇒	**si** +Ø +*som*+*i*
'I did not read'	⇒	**si** +*ku* +*som*+*a*
'I will not read'	⇒	**si** +*ta* +*som*+*a*, etc.

5) For a verb denoting a psychological or physiological state ('be afraid', 'be sure', 'be cold', 'need'), Japanese allows only the first-person singular form in the declarative mood in the present, because—from a Japanese viewpoint—only I myself can know whether I am afraid or sure of anything, that I am cold or that I need something: 'I'm afraid / I'm cold / I need' ⇒ *Watasi*+*wa kowai / samui / hosii*. However, 'Taro is afraid / Taro is cold / Taro needs' ⇏ *Tarō+*wa kowai / samui / hosii*.⁹ In all other persons and in the plural the verb takes the suffix **-gar** 'looking as if': *Tarō*+*wa kowa*+*gat*+*te i*+*ru* lit. 'Taro looking.as.if.afraid there.is'.

6) In any language, **parenthetical constructions** show special behavior: they cannot be negated or interrogated—for instance, *Alan, as is known, is good for this job* vs. **Alan, **as is not known**, is good for this job* or **Alan **(as is known?)** is good for this job*. This is explained by

the fact that a parenthetical is not descriptive: it does not characterize a particular extralinguistic situation, but expresses a certain internal state of the Speaker, in this case, a conviction. The meaning of a parenthetical includes the meaning 'I' (= the Speaker). In other words, parentheticals are **signalatives**, which were introduced in Item 3 above, but they are **grammatical** rather than lexical—because they are freely built syntactic constructions.

Many more examples of this type could be be adduced, but those that have been provided seem to be sufficient to demonstrate the priority of the Speaker and thus buttress the chosen direction of linguistic description: from meaning to text.

An important caveat

The primacy of the Speaker is not limited to the prominence of 1SG forms. In some languages, it is 2SG that is privileged (in the person hierarchy, in politeness strategies, etc.). But remember that 2SG—that is, the Addressee—is, so to speak, nominated by the Speaker and is 100% his creature.

Postulate 3: The sentence and the word are basic units of linguistic description

> The description of the $\{SemR_i\} \Leftrightarrow \{PhonetR_j\}$ correspondence (see (6), *2.3.2*, p. 24) requires two intermediate levels of linguistic representation:
>
> > syntactic representation [= SyntR], reflecting the specific properties of sentences,
>
> and
>
> > morphological representation [= MorphR], reflecting the specific properties of words.

(Under *word* is here understood a **wordform**—that is, a word taken in one well-defined sense and in one concrete grammatical form; see Mel'čuk 1993–2000, vol. 1: 167*ff* and 2012: 30.)

The sentence and the word are, respectively, the maximal and the minimal speech entities. Being present in all languages, they are **universal**.

At the same time, they are autonomous: they, and only they are consciously perceived by speakers as well-formed entities of their language.

- **Sentence.** A sentence is a maximal complex of linguistic signs, defined by a particular language-specific "sentence" prosody, within which language rules operate: roughly speaking, they are not applicable beyond the limits of the sentence. Syntactic organization, communicative organization, word order, lexical cooccurrence, agreement and government—all these phenomena are describable within the frame of a sentence.

- **Word.** A word is the smallest linguistic sign available to the linguistic conscious awareness of speakers. The word is the domain of applicability of the rules for inflection and derivation, as well as for phonemic alternations (like *sing ~ sang*, *foot ~ feet* or *life ~ lives*).

In order to represent as exactly as possible both the particularities of sentences and those of words, Meaning-Text theory postulates two intermediate levels of linguistic representation between the representations of meanings and texts: the syntactic and the morphological levels. (By the way, the recognition of these two levels—that of the sentence and that of the word—corresponds to the tradition, followed, as far as I know, by all linguistic schools.)

It follows from Postulates 1–3 that the MTM has the following general structure:

(7) General Structure of the Meaning-Text Model

$$\{SemR_i\} \Leftrightarrow \{SyntR_k\} \Leftrightarrow \{MorphR_l\} \Leftrightarrow \{PhonetR_j\}$$

semantics   **syntax**   **morphology + phonology**

☞ The names of the major components, or modules, of the model are in boldface.

2.3.3 Main formal properties of a Meaning-Text model

A Meaning-Text model [= MTM] has the following five general formal features.

1) A MTM is not a generative system: it does not generate anything (in the mathematical sense of the term *generate*: 'specify a set by indicating the properties of its elements'). Rather, it is an equative, or transductive, system: it associates with each SemR all the PhonetRs that can express it in the given language, and vice versa: for each PhonetR it specifies all possible SemRs. **The MTM establishes correspondences.** More specifically, the MTM establishes correspondences between linguistic representations of adjacent levels:

- The model takes as its input a representation $R(n)$ of level n, just as one takes, for instance, a culinary recipe in order to cook a clam chowder, or the architect's plan of a house to start building the house itself.
- The model links with this initial representation $R(n)$ all possible representations $R(n+1)_i$ of level $n+1$, constructing them in accordance with $R(n)$, but without modifying it.
- The model selects (ideally) one of $R(n+1)_i$, which is—from a linguistic viewpoint—the best fitted to the situation spoken in and/or about.

Thus, a MTM is not a transformational system either, since the initial representations manipulated by a MTM are not affected. A MTM behaves like a normal speaker of a language, who neither engages in generating sets of grammatically correct sentences, nor in distinguishing between grammatical and ungrammatical sentences. He simply says what he needs—that is, he expresses some specific meanings he wants to communicate to his addressee. A MTM does the same: it "translates" a given meaning into a corresponding text, or performs an inverse "translation" of a text into a meaning. That is why an MTM can be qualified as a transductive (= translative) model.

The preceding paragraph should not be construed as meaning that an MTM does not allow for transformations—operations that, if applied to a linguistic representation of a given level, produce an equivalent representation of the same level. On the contrary:

2.3 THE MEANING-TEXT MODEL

– The MTM widely uses **paraphrase** transformations both in semantics and syntax; for instance:

Equivalent transformations of semantic structures

'John died of starvation' ≡ 'John starved to death'
'John crossed the street on foot' ≡ 'John walked across the street'
'rains are common in this region'≡ 'rains happen frequently in this region'

Equivalent transformations of deep-syntactic structures

APOLOGIZE ≡ OFFER AN APOLOGY
REMEMBER FOREVER ≡ NEVER FORGET
BUY A BOOK FOR 10 DOLLARS ≡ PAY 10 DOLLARS FOR A BOOK

– Alternation transformations are common in morphology: these can be meaningful, such as *sing ~ sang, spring ~ sprang, foot ~ feet* and *louse ~ lice*, or meaningless, such as *leaf ~ leaves* and *wife ~ wives*.

2) A MTM is a multimodule system: it consists of six autonomous mechanisms (= submodels, or modules, see *3.1*, Figure 1, p. 43). Each of these has its own organization; they function independently of each other and communicate through corresponding linguistic representations, which thus appear as interfaces. A linguistic representation R($n+1$) produced as the output of the module n is the input of the module $n+1$. But each module of the MTM is developed and described separately from all the other modules—in order to reflect as exactly as possible the specific properties of the language component modeled by the given module.

3) A MTM is a global and integral system: it is aimed at describing language **L** as a whole. All the modules of a MTM, including the lexicon of **L** and its grammar, must be perfectly in harmony with each other, since they are called upon to closely collaborate in the process of text synthesis.

4) A MTM is based on paraphrasing—that is, on the synonymy of sentences. The linguistic competence of speakers is their ability to con-

struct for a given meaning 'σ' all the texts T_i('σ')—all paraphrases possible for this meaning—and select the one that is the best for the given situation in the given context. (For paraphrasing and its role in linguistic modeling, see Milićević 2007 and Mel'čuk 2012: Chapters 8 and 9.)

5) A MTM is semantically centered: it presupposes a linguistic description that proceeds from the semantic representation of a family of sentences. This SemR is, as shown below, the invariant of a family of more or less synonymous paraphrases written in a well-defined formalism.

2.3.4 Two central notions of the Meaning-Text approach: linguistic meaning and paraphrasing

The notion of linguistic meaning, which is so important in our framework, can be illustrated as follows. Consider sentence (8a)—the formulation of a simple arithmetic problem:

(8) a. *A schoolkid Mike bought two exercise books, and another schoolkid, Al, bought three; how many exercise books do Mike and Al have together?*

To understand the meaning of this sentence in its role as an exam question the student reduces it to the formula (8b):

b. $2 + 3 = ?$

However, formula (8b) is by no means the linguistic meaning of sentence (8a), even if English allows us to use here the word MEANING and say that the formula "$2 + 3 = ?$" is—in some sense—the meaning of sentence (8a). I am talking here, however, not about the English noun MEANING (or an equivalent word of a different language), but about a technical term linguistic meaning: it means 'information that can be extracted from a linguistic expression by using exclusively one's linguistic knowledge'. It is impossible to perform the "translation" (8a) ⇔ (8b) based only on English; therefore, (8b) cannot be considered to be the linguistic meaning of (8a).

The same arithmetic problem can be formulated in English using a number of different sentences:

(9) a. *Mike, a schoolkid, purchased two exercise books, and his pal Al bought three; how many exercise books do the boys possess?*
   b. *A young student called Michael bought exercise books in the quantity of two, while another boy, by the name of Alex, bought them in the quantity of three; what is the total number of the exercise books these boys bought?*
   c. *Michael, a young student, has two exercise books, while his friend Alex has three; calculate the quantity of exercise books both kids own.*
   d. *Two exercise books were acquired by a schoolboy Mike, and three more by his classmate Al; give the number of all the exercise books bought.*

Varying the words and their arrangements, it is possible to construct thousands of similar paraphrases. Each semantic "chunk" in these sentences has several possible expressions:

Mike ~ Michael and *Al ~ Alex* : 4 variants
*young/little/*Λ *{schoolkid ~ schoolboy ~ student ~ boy ~ kid}*
: 15 variants

☞ The symbol Λ stands for the empty set (= 'nothing', 'zero').

called ~ by the name of ~ Λ : 3 variants
buy ~ purchase ~ acquire : 3 variants
have ~ possess ~ own : 3 variants
two ~ couple ~ pair ~ in the quantity of two : 4 variants
three ~ in the quantity of three : 2 variants
give ~ tell ~ calculate : 3 variants
number ~ quantity ~ how many : 3 variants

These variants allow for all possible combinations, which gives us

$4 \times 15 \times 3 \times 3 \times 3 \times 4 \times 2 \times 3 \times 3 = 116\,640$ sentences,

without counting possible additional variation. (See below, p. 204, a similar exercise with multiple paraphrases.) All these sentences can be obtained from each other without having recourse to anything but English; no other knowledge is required. Therefore, all these sentences—plus (8a), which started it all—have the same linguistic meaning. They are synonymous: they are paraphrases of each other. Their meaning is strictly the only thing all of them have in common in spite of their "physical" differences: this meaning is their invariant. In order to be able to manipulate this invariant formally we have to represent it formally, by means of a well-defined symbolic notation. Such a notation will be shown below: it is a **semantic network**. For now, let us assume that the set of paraphrases given above can be specified by what strikes me as the simplest and most explicit, namely:

(10) *A schoolboy named Michael bought two exercise books, another schoolboy named Alex bought three exercise books; say what is the number of exercise books that Michael and Alex bought.*

We consider sentence (10), formalized and symbolized in a particular way (see *3.2.2*) to be the linguistic meaning of the whole family of paraphrases specified by means of (8a) and (9). Linguistic meaning is somehow encoded in the brains of speakers—of course not by Latin letters or similar symbols, but by electronic and chemical configurations that are **isomorphic** to our semantic notation.

The arithmetical—that is, non-linguistic—expression (8b), which can, of course, be read in English (*What is two plus three?*), reflects the generalized informational content of the paraphrases now under discussion. This reflection is intentionally incomplete: it represents only the information that the user considers necessary and sufficient for his task. The informational content of linguistic expressions—a discrete mental reflection of real-world situations in the human psyche—will be called a **conceptual representation**.

> One conceptual representation can and very often does correspond to several linguistic meanings.

Thus, the problem (8b) can be expressed by a completely different linguistic meaning—that is, by a completely different family of paraphrases, for instance:

(11) a. *Kate has three kids, and her sister Luce two; how many kids do both sisters have?*
  b. *Kate is the mother of three children, while her sister Luce has two daughters; compute the number of kids the two sisters have.*
  c. *Kate gave birth to three kids, and Luce, her sister, to two; what is the quantity of kids both of them have together?*

In what follows, where reference is made to meaning, linguistic meaning is to be understood; the modifier *linguistic* is accordingly omitted henceforth.

2.3.5 General characterization of the Meaning-Text approach

At this juncture, I can switch to a more detailed characterization of a concrete Meaning-Text model. At the same time, I will consider the particular linguistic approach that has grown out of the research carried out around the MTM—Meaning-Text linguistics. This will be done in Chapters *3*, *4* and *5*.

Dear reader! I have to warn you that in the chapters that follow the presentation is much more technical than it has been until now. The reason for this is that linguistics cannot simply use a natural language as its tool for describing natural languages—this would result in imprecisions and confusions, leading to a logical mess. Like any other hard science, linguistics needs a formalized notional apparatus and corresponding terminology—or, in other words, a special linguistic metalanguage. Only such a metalanguage can ensure commensurable descriptions that can be easily translated into each other.

However, formalisms tend to frighten unaccustomed people away. In order to facilitate the perusal of *LMT* by educated non-specialists, I will take special pains to lead the reader through by the hand. More specifically, I will apply a rule of thumb commonly followed by good lecturers: "First, tell the audience what you will be talking about; then talk about this; and finally, remind them of what you were talking about." Therefore, I will explain now, in the simplest and most approximate terms, what you will be reading in the following chapters. Something to this effect was already said (*1.2*), so that I will repeat myself; but, as everybody knows, *Repetitio mater studiorum* (if your Latin is a bit rusty, this means 'Repetition is the mother of studies').

Chapter *3* characterizes one particular Meaning-Text model.

- The **linguistic representations** of sentences are introduced:
– the semantic representation, which reflects, in a formalized way, the meaning of the given sentence S (as well as that of all the sentences synonymous with S);
– the syntactic representation, which reflects the structure of S in terms of lexical units and relations between them;
– the morphological representation, which reflects the structure of S in terms of actual words linearly ordered and supplied with a corresponding prosody;
– and the phonic representation, which reflects the sound side of S.

Starting with the syntactic level, two sublevels are distinguished within each level: deep-syntactic and surface-syntactic sublevels; ditto for higher levels (which are closer to the text): deep-morphological and deep-phonic (= phonemic) sublevels *vs.* surface-morphological and surface-phonic (= phonetic) sublevels. A deep sublevel is geared toward meaning and is designed to preserve all relevant semantic distinctions; a surface sublevel is geared toward text and is intended to reflect all relevant formal distinctions.

- The **transition** between the representations of two adjacent levels is carried out by a module of a Meaning-Text model. Each module accepts, as its input, a representation of the sentence and produces, as its output, all corresponding representations closer to the surface (carrying, of course, the same meaning)—and vice versa.
- All the steps through which linguistic synthesis passes are examined in some detail.

Chapter *4* covers the two main dimensions for the description of natural languages:

– the paradigmatic axis, on which the Speaker chooses one of several competing linguistic units: a word, a grammatical signification, or a syntactic construction;
– the syntagmatic axis, on which the Speaker combines the selected units according to the grammar rules of **L** and thus constructs sentences.

In other words, the speaker's linguistic activity under synthesis can be fully reduced to these two operations: the **selection** of units and the **combination** of units. Therefore, lexical selection and lexical cooccurrence are discussed in more detail. Using linguistic illustrations, I will try to demonstrate how the observable cooccurrence of words helps verify and sharpen the hypotheses about their non-observable meanings.

The notion of lexical function [= LF] is also introduced. LFs are the main tool for the description of restricted lexical cooccurrence, which we see in such phrases as *utmost pleasure, high pressure, heavy rain, deep despair, huge success, strong coffee*, etc., where the adjective meaning 'high degree [of N]'—that is, an intensifier—is selected as a function of N.

Four topics are discussed in Chapter 5.

- The **advantages of the Meaning-to-Text approach** according to which the linguistic phenomena are studied and described strictly from the synthetic viewpoint are demonstrated by two short case studies:
– Spanish glides (linguistic sounds that have neither properties of vowels nor of consonants: [i̯] *bien* 'well' and [u̯] *bueno* 'good');
– Russian binominative verbless constructions (*Kukuruza$_{NOM}$ segodnja—èto kolbasa$_{NOM}$ zavtra* lit. 'Corn today—this [is] sausage tomorrow').
- The paramount **importance of a rigorous notional apparatus** for linguistics. Three groups of linguistic notions are introduced, which play a crucial role in linguistic research: sign/word, grammatical voice, and the ergative construction.

- The **central place of a monolingual lexicon** of a new type—the *Explanatory-Combinatorial Dictionary* [= ECD]; two Russian lexical entries are given in full.
- **Linguistic dependencies**; three major types of dependencies are examined—in particular, syntactic dependencies. (This is, probably, the most technical section in *LMT*.)

Remember that there is an alphabetical index with a glossary at the end of the book; therefore, dear reader, as soon as you face an unknown term (such as glide or suppressive), don't panic: take a deep breath and look it up in the index.

Chapter 3

An Outline of a Particular Meaning-Text Model

As a detailed illustration, I will consider a particular version of the Meaning-Text model, on which I have been working myself for about half a century. First, the distinction between deep and surface (sub)levels of linguistic representations is established (*3.1*); second, linguistic representations of a sentence at all the levels are given (*3.2*); third, each MTM module is exemplified by a few rules (*3.3*). In this way, it is possible to show the reader all the steps of linguistic synthesis: from a given meaning to one of the texts that express it. (For more details on Meaning-Text models and, in particular, on the semantic representation of sentences, see Mel'čuk 2012.)

3.1 Deep and surface sublevels of linguistic representations

All levels of linguistic representation, with the exception of the semantic level, are split into two sublevels: deep [= D-] and surface [= S-]. Each deep sublevel—deep-syntactic, deep-morphological and deep-phonic—is oriented towards meaning: its task is to express all meaning-related distinctions that are relevant on their respective levels. Each surface sublevel—surface-syntactic and surface-morphological—is oriented, on the other hand, towards text (i.e., towards the surface-phonic, or phonetic, representation): its task is to express all formal distinctions that are relevant on the respective level.

Having introduced the dichotomy "deep *vs.* surface (sublevels)," we obtain for each sentence a set of seven representations. The structure of the Meaning-Text model can be now presented in more detail:

3. AN OUTLINE OF A PARTICULAR MEANING-TEXT MODEL

(12) Detailed Structure of the Meaning-Text Model

$$\{\text{SemR}_i\} \Leftrightarrow \{\text{DSyntR}_{k1}\} \Leftrightarrow \{\text{SSyntR}_{k2}\} \Leftrightarrow \{\text{DMorphR}_{l1}\} \Leftrightarrow$$

    semantics   deep   surface   deep
                      syntax   syntax   morphology

$$\Leftrightarrow \{\text{SMorphR}_{l2}\} \Leftrightarrow \{\text{DPhonR}_{j1}\} \Leftrightarrow \{\text{SPhonR}_{j2}\}$$

    surface   phonology
    morphology

The names of the linguistic representations in (12) seem self-explanatory, except for the two phonic levels.[10]

- DPhonR is a **deep-phonic**, or **phonological**, representation [DPhonR = PhonolR]: it reflects only semantically loaded phonic distinctions.
- SPhonR is a **surface-phonic**, or **phonetic**, representation [SPhonR = PhonetR]: it reflects articulatory/acoustic distinctions relevant for the production of physical sounds, or **phones**, of language **L**.

Figure 1 presents the same information as contained in (12), but in a more graphic form. It shows all the modules of the Meaning-Text model in their relation to linguistic representations at all levels: the modules of the model and the levels of representation are set out in a vertical direction, starting from the deepest (= semantic) level and moving up from below—that is, to the closest-to-surface (= phonetic) level.

The Meaning-Text model consists of six modules mediating between each pair of representations; if for the moment we ignore the difference between the deep and surface sublevels, what is represented here corresponds to the four major divisions of linguistics:

    semantics (meanings) + syntax (sentence) +
    + morphology (word) + phonology (sound)

Each module is named according to its input representation. Thus, the Semantic module takes as its input a SemR and constructs for it all the DSyntRs that carry the same meaning as the initial SemR; then the rules of the Deep-Syntactic module are applied to a DSyntR and construct all the SSyntRs that this DSyntR can implement; etc.

3.2 LINGUISTIC REPRESENTATIONS IN A MEANING-TEXT MODEL

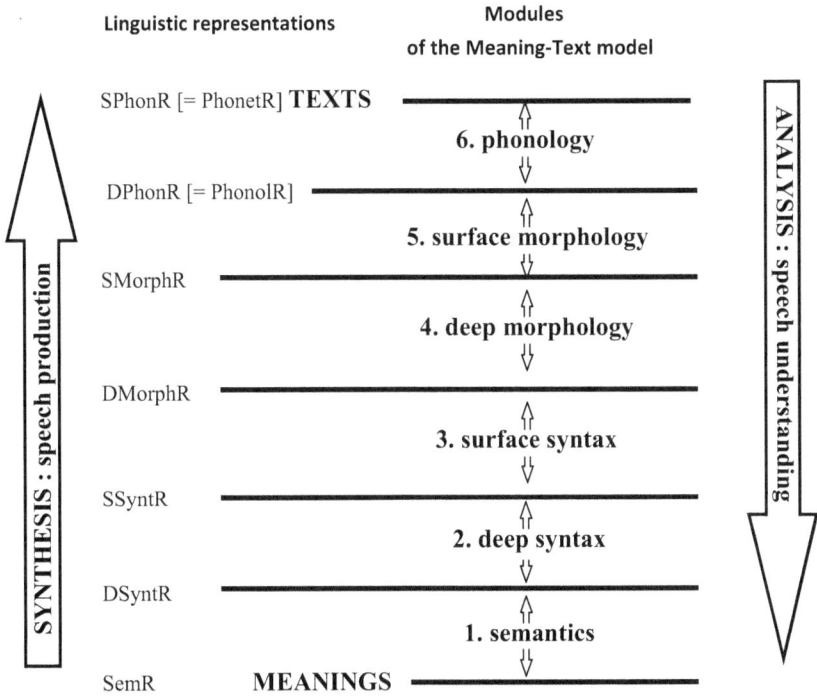

Figure 1: Levels of Linguistic Representation and Modules of the Meaning-Text Model

3.2 Linguistic representations in a Meaning-Text model

After a general characterization of linguistic representation (*3.2.1*), the basic structures of "pre-phonic" linguistic representations are examined: the Sem-structure (*3.2.2*), the DSynt-structure (*3.2.3*), the SSynt-structure (*3.2.4*), the DMorph-structure (*3.2.5*) and the SMorph-structure (*3.2.6*); then conceptual representation is introduced (*3.2.7*).

3.2.1 Introductory remarks

The MTM presupposes seven representations of a sentence (or a part of a sentence), as shown in Fig. 1 above. Each representation is a set of

44   3. AN OUTLINE OF A PARTICULAR MEANING-TEXT MODEL

formal objects called structures [= -S]. Thus, the SemR includes four structures:

- Semantic structure [= SemS] reflects the propositional ("objective") meaning of the expression under description; it constitutes the core of the SemR, its basic structure, upon which the three other structures are superimposed (they contribute additional relevant information). Semantic structure will be illustrated below, so that no example is needed here.

- Semantic-communicative structure [= Sem-CommS] reflects the communicative ("subjective") meaning of the expression. Metaphorically, it specifies the Speaker's route through the initial SemR: it indicates, for example, what he wants to speak about and what exactly he wishes to say; what he believes to be known to the Addressee and what will be new to him; what to move to the foreground and what, on the contrary, to push behind the scene. This structure operates with such oppositions as "Rheme (what to say) ~ Theme (what to say this about)," "Given ~ New," "Foregrounded ~ Backgrounded," etc. (Mel'čuk 2001). Thus, sentences (13a) and (13b) have the same Sem-structure, but different Sem-Comm-structures, shown, respectively, in (14a) and (14b):

(13) a. *John built the cabin last year.*
    b. *The cabin was built (last year) by John.*

(14) a.

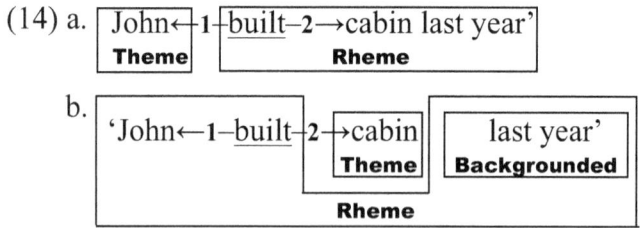

- Rhetorical structure [= RhetS] reflects the expressive, or stylistic, goals of the Speaker: whether he wants to be neutral, formal, ironic, poetic, vulgar; communicate dispassionately, appeal to the emotions or cause laughter; etc.

- Referential structure [= RefS] encodes the links of the elements of the SemR—that is, of semantemes—with their referents in the ex-

3.2 LINGUISTIC REPRESENTATIONS IN A MEANING-TEXT MODEL

tralinguistic universe (on referents of a linguistic sign, see *5.3.2*).*
More precisely, the RefS indicates:

(i) the referential status of the given semanteme (see Padučeva 1985: 79*ff*);
(ii) if it is referential, its referent;
(iii) the coreferentiality of semanteme configurations (coreferential semantemes have the same referent).

This kind of information is, strictly speaking, not about language; yet it is necessary to ensure the correctness of linguistic expressions. This can be illustrated by the following four examples.

Example 1: the indicative *vs.* the conditional

(15) a. *John is looking for a student who **can** run computer programs.*
vs.
b. *John is looking for a student who **could** run computer programs.*

Sentence (15a) is appropriate if the Speaker presupposes that such a student exists (the meaning 'student' in the initial SemR has a referent), and sentence (15b), if the Speaker does not presuppose the existence of such a student.

Example 2: in Russian, the long *vs.* short form of an adjective as the syntactic predicate (E. Padučeva's observation)

(16) a. *Podobnye dovody očen′ ubeditel′**ny*** [short form]/
očen′ ubeditel′nye*** [long form]
'Arguments of this type are very convincing'.
vs.
b. *Èti dovody očen′ ubeditel′**ny*** [short form]/*očen′ ubeditel′**nye***
[long form]
'These arguments are very convincing'.

---

* These links are, of course, specified not for genuine physical referents—that is, entities and facts of the real world, but for their mental reflections, or, in our context, for their conceptual representations. However, here, this subtlety is not material.

Adjectives cannot be used as a copular attribute in the long form, if the subject does not have a concrete individual referent, but denotes a class of entities, as in (16a).

Example 3: in Russian, the verb LJUBIT´ 'love' vs. the verb NRA-VIT´SJA 'like' (T. Bulygina's observation)

(17) a. *Ja ljublju ètot sup lit. 'I love this soup'
   [a statement about a particular entity; the correct expression is Ètot sup mne nravitsja 'I like this soup'].
   vs.
   b. Ja ljublju takoj sup 'I love the soup of this type'
   [a statement about a class of entities].

The verb LJUBIT´ 'love' in this sense requires its Direct Object to be non-referential and denote a class of entities.

Example 4

(18) *When **Tchaikovsky** arrived in the United States, the **composer's** name was widely known.*

The coreferential elements are in boldface.

Linguistic representations of other levels are organized in a similar way: each is a set of several structures. The full picture is thus rather complex. I will sacrifice precision and, in what follows, will consider only one structure per representation—namely, its basic structure.

3.2.2 The semantic structure of a sentence

A semantic representation is an ordered quadruplet (the basic structure is in boldface):

$$\text{SemR} = \langle\, \textbf{SemS}\,;\, \text{Sem-CommS}\,;\, \text{RhetS}\,;\, \text{RefS}\,\rangle$$

The core of a SemR is the semantic structure [= SemS], which represents the meaning of a family of synonymous sentences. Formally, it is a connected directed labeled graph (a set of labeled nodes, or vertices, linked by labeled arcs), known as **network**.

➤ NODES (= vertices) of a semantic network are labeled with the names of semantic units of language **L**, called semantemes. A **semanteme** is the meaning of a semantically full lexical unit of **L**; in this book semantemes are meanings (= separate senses) of full English words. Semantemes are divided into (semantic) predicates, including quasi-predicates, and semantic names.

In logic and linguistic semantics, a **(semantic) predicate** is a meaning that cannot be described without reference to some other meanings, called its **arguments**; it is, so to speak, a binding meaning that binds together other meanings. Thus, it is impossible to explain what 'sleep' is: one has to explain the expression 'X sleeps', where 'X'—the sleeper—is the argument of the predicate 'sleep'. Predicates are distinguished by the number of their possible arguments, or **places**: 'sleep' is a one-place predicate, 'see' a two-place one ('X sees Y'), 'communicate' has three places ('X communicates Y to Z'), 'compare'—four places ('X compares Y with Z according to W'), etc. As empirically established by Apresjan 2010: 303*ff*, in natural language a predicate expressed by a single lexeme can have maximally six arguments: for instance, 'X exiles Y from Z to W for reason P for the time T'. A predicate denotes a fact: an event, an action, a state, a property, a relation, etc. When speaking of linguistic units—that is, of a predicate semanteme or a lexeme expressing a predicate semanteme—the arguments of the corresponding predicate are called **Sem-actants** of this semanteme/lexeme. To put it differently, 'argument of the predicate σ' is the same as 'semantic actant of the semanteme σ or the lexeme L(σ)'.

 This terminology is convenient, since it allows for a systematic comparison of semantic, deep-syntactic and surface-syntactic actants, as we will see below.

A **semantic name** [= Sem-name] is a stand-alone meaning: its denotation is an entity—that is, an object, a being, a place, a substance, etc. ('tree', 'fox', 'sea', 'air', etc.); a semantic name cannot have actants.

A **quasi-predicate** is, in a sense, a meaning intermediate between a predicate and a name. A quasi-predicate denotes an entity, like a Sem-name, but has actants like a Sem-predicate: these actants are borrowed from the situation in which the denotation of the quasi-predicate is supposed to be used. For instance, 'hospital' denotes an entity—a building, with the corresponding equipment and staff; but this meaning has actants: staff X of a hospital treat patients Y (*children's*$_Y$ *hospital*) for medical problems Z (*cardiac*$_Z$ *hospital*).

➤ ARROWS (= arcs) of a semantic network are labeled with numbers of semantic dependencies (= semantic relations); these numbers do not carry meaning, but are purely indexical—they correspond to arguments of the given predicate: 'P'–2→'α' means that 'α' is the second argument of the predicate 'P'; thus, 'Mary←1–see–2→John' ≡ 'see(Mary, John)'.

Let me now give an example of a semantic structure. We have already seen a simple enough Sem-structure in *1.2*, p. 6, (2). The SemS below is more complex; it specifies the meaning of a family of synonymous sentences, one of which is sentence (19):

(19) *Orwell is sure that his political activity improves his work.*

☞ 1. The underscoring of the semanteme '<u>sure</u>' marks it out as the communicatively dominant node of this SemS. This indication is part of the semantic-communicative structure [= Sem-CommS] of the paraphrases of the given family. The communicatively dominant node in the SemS 'σ' is a meaning '<u>σ</u>$_1$' such that 'σ' can be reduced to '<u>σ</u>$_1$' with loss, but without deformation, of information. As a rule, '<u>σ</u>$_1$' is the generic component of 'σ'.

2. 'work6' [in accordance with *LDOCE*] stands for 'something ... that is produced by a painter, writer, or musician, etc.'.

3. The symbol "α" is an abbreviation for the meaning 'than Orwell's works were before'.

The SemS of Figure 2 can also be realized by sentences (20), among others:

(20) a. *Orwell does not doubt the positive impact of his political activity on the quality of his writings.*
b. *Orwell has no doubt that his activity in politics makes his work better.*

3.2 LINGUISTIC REPRESENTATIONS IN A MEANING-TEXT MODEL   49

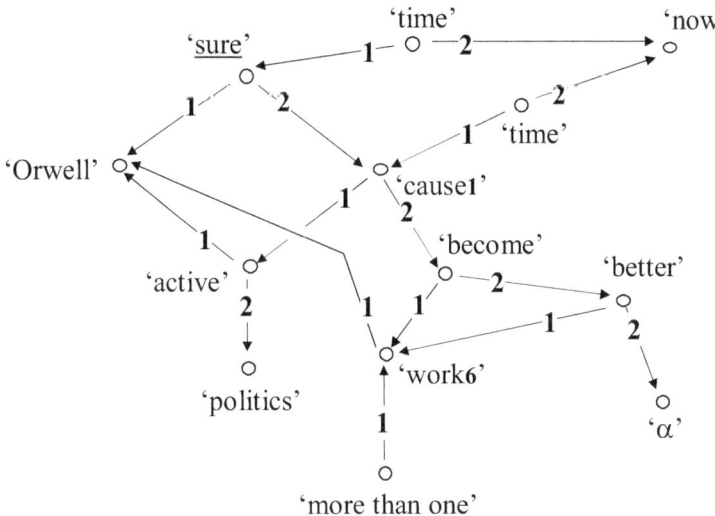

Figure 2: The Semantic Structure of Sentence (19)
and of All Other Sentences Having (Almost) the Same Meaning

c. *Orwell is in no doubt concerning the beneficent influence of his being politically active on his literary production.*
d. *Orwell is certain that the fact that he is active in politics heightens the quality of his literary creations.*
e. *That his writings improve as a result of his being politically active does not cause Orwell any doubts.*
f. *Orwell believes, without a shadow of a doubt, that his political activities positively influence his literary work.*
g. *Orwell is convinced that the quality of his literary creations improves due to his political activities.*
h. *It is Orwell's conviction that his literary production becomes better thanks to his political engagement.*

It is known that a sentence that is sufficiently (but far from extraordinarily) complex can have tens of thousands or even tens of millions of paraphrases (this was shown above, in *2.3.4*, p. 35; see also Žolkovskij & Mel'čuk 1967: 179–180, Mel'čuk 1981: 31–32, 2012: 87–89).[11] The examples in (20) demonstrate again the synonymic wealth and flexibility of natural language, which an MTM sets out to reflect.

The following two points are especially important for the subsequent discussion.

– The SemS and paraphrasing

A SemS, as just mentioned, presents the meaning not of a particular sentence, but that of a whole family of more or less synonymous sentences—in other words, of paraphrases. Paraphrasing essentially underlies the Meaning-Text approach and, at the same time, is its testing ground: a MT-model has to ensure the construction of all possible paraphrases for a given meaning that are recognized by the speakers as grammatically correct and carrying the meaning in question.

– The SemS and the informational content of a text

When speaking about meaning in *LMT*, we are speaking exclusively about linguistic meaning—that is, the meaning that can be extracted from a text of language **L** only on the basis of the mastery of **L**, without the participation of common sense, encyclopedic knowledge, logic, etc.

Sentences (21a) and (21b) have different linguistic meanings and thus are not synonymous:

(21) a. *The price of milk doubled.*
 b. *The price of milk grew 100%.*

(21a) and (21b) are, of course, informationally equivalent and have the same conceptual representation. However, in order to be able to see this, you have to know arithmetic—which is a non-linguistic skill. Similarly, (22a) and (22b) are not synonymous although they are also informationally equivalent:

(22) a. *twenty to eight* '7: 40'
 b. *Fr. huit moins vingt* lit. 'eight minus twenty' = '7: 40'

In other words:

> SemRs represent purely LINGUISTIC meanings; as a result, they are "domestic"—specific to concrete languages—rather than universal.

The full model of linguistic behavior presupposes one more level of representation of the contents of the text: **conceptual representation**

[= ConceptR], which has already been mentioned and will be briefly characterized below, in Subsection *3.2.7*, p. 66.

The crucial delimitation between "domestic" SemSs and "international" ConceptSs now established, we can have a closer look at the properties of SemSs. The SemS in Figure 2 is written in a formal semantic language; it constitutes the "semantic transcription," which was mentioned above. As with any language, natural or formal, semantic language is specified by its lexicon (= a set of its basic units) and grammar (= a set of rules that describe the ways of combining basic units into well-formed expressions).

➤ In the Meaning-Text approach, the lexicon of the semantic language designed for the description of natural language **L** includes almost all the semantemes of **L**.

☞ The adverb *almost* reflects the fact that the signifieds of certain lexical units [= LUs] of **L** are not included in the semantic language. In the first place, these are the signifieds of all structural (≈ grammatical) LUs; there are some other kinds of signifieds in this category as well.

The Meaning-Text approach presupposes a separate semantic language for each natural language **L**. This constitutes a major difference with the semantic theory of Anna Wierzbicka (see, e.g., Wierzbicka 1999), aiming at the elaboration of a universal semantic language, whose lexicon consists of **semantic primitives** (or **semantic primes**)—elementary, or indecomposable, meanings. Wierzbicka's primitives are supposed to be identical for all languages.

➤ The grammar—that is, the syntax—of the semantic language of the MTT, is the syntax of semantic networks. A network (in the sense of graph theory) is a formal "carrier" for expressions based on the language of predicate calculus. As mentioned above, arcs (= arrows) of this network represent "predicate→argument" relations:

a network of the form 'x←1–P–2→y' ≡ the predication 'P(x, y)'

The expressions of this form cover the meanings of an infinity of sentences and phrases: *John likes Mary* (where 'x' = 'John', 'y' = 'Mary',

52   3. AN OUTLINE OF A PARTICULAR MEANING-TEXT MODEL

and 'P' = 'like'), *John depends on Mary, John's love for Mary, Mary's betrayal by John*, etc.

A sentence implementing the SemS of Figure 2— for instance, sentence (19)—is constructed in several steps. First of all, the semantic module of the MTM produces the corresponding DSyntR, which contains, along with other structures, the DSyntS in Figure 3, next page.

 While a SemS carries the common meaning of a rather large family of synonym-ous sentences, a DSyntS describes, most often, a particular sentence or several sentences featuring only minor surface-syntactic differences. The structures of all levels closer to the surface each describe, as a rule, one individual sentence.

3.2.3 The deep-syntactic structure of a sentence

Deep-syntactic representation is an ordered quadruple of the following form (boldface, as before, identifies the basic structure):

DSyntR = ⟨ **DSyntS** ; DSynt-CommS ; DSynt-ProsS ; DSynt-AnaphS ⟩.

Here:

- DSyntS is, of course, Deep-Syntactic Structure.
- DSynt-CommS stands for Deep-Syntactic-Communicative Structure; it shows the division of the DSyntS in communicative areas, which (roughly) correspond to Sem-Comm-areas.
- DSynt-ProsS is Deep-Syntactic-Prosodic Structure, which specifies all semantically loaded prosodemes of the sentence (declarative, expressive, interrogative, etc.).
- DSynt-AnaphS, or Deep-Syntactic-Anaphoric Structure, indicates the coreferentiality of the LUs building up the DSyntS of the sentence—that is, the LUs that refer to the same extra-linguistic element). It is responsible for pronominalization—in particular, for the introduction of substitute pronouns such as HE, SHE, IT, THEY, THIS, ..., WHICH/WHO.

3.2 LINGUISTIC REPRESENTATIONS IN A MEANING-TEXT MODEL 53

The core of a DSyntR is a **deep-syntactic structure** [= DSyntS]; it describes the organization of the sentence in terms of its LUs, the grammemes attached to these LUs and the deep-syntactic relations [= DSyntRels] that link the LUs; only the DSyntS is considered in this book: see Figure 3.

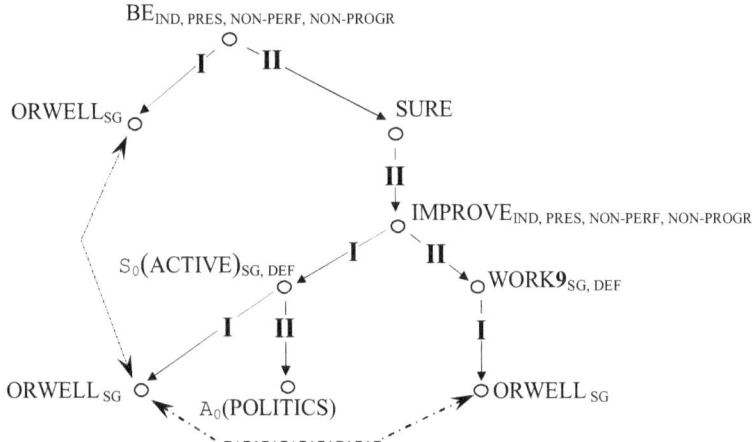

☞ 1. This diagram shows coreferential links using dashed two-headed arrows (the lexeme ORWELL refers three times to the same person). The specification of coreferential links is part of the DSynt-AnaphS.
2. The lexeme WORK9 [http://www.oxfordlearnersdictionaries.com/us/definition/american_english] stands for 'the set of all works6' (see Fig. 2).
3. S_0(ACTIVE) is a lexical function: a deadjectival noun (ACTIVITY); A_0(POLITICS) is another lexical function: a denominal adjective (POLITICAL).

Figure 3: The Deep-Syntactic Structure of Sentence (19)

The DSyntS of a sentence S is a linearly unordered **dependency tree** of S (see Glossary, p. 235).

➤ NODES (= vertices) of a DSyntS are labeled with the names of semantically full lexical units [= LUs] of the sentence represented; these LUs are supplied with semantic **grammemes** —that is, semantically full inflectional values, such as number and definiteness in nouns, or mood, tense, perfectivity and progressivity in verbs; for instance:

– the lexeme $\text{DIGIT}_{\text{PL, DEF}}$ (= *the digits*);

- the idiom ⌐STEP ON THE GAS¬$_{\text{COND, PRES, PERF, NON-PROGR}}$ (= *would have stepped on the gas*).
- **Deep lexical units.** The DSynt-tree of *S* contains all and only full LUs of *S*. Structural LUs of all types are banned from DSyntS— auxiliaries, articles, governed prepositions and conjunctions, as well as substitute pronouns (HE, SHE, etc.). Under synthesis, the DSyntS presents the sentence before pronominalization: the DSyntS of Figure 3 features, instead of the pronouns HE and HIS, their source: the noun ORWELL.

The full LUs, also called **deep** LUs, are of four types:

1) "Normal" full lexemes.

2) Idioms—that is, non-compositional phrasemes ⌐KICK THE BUCKET¬, ⌐BEAT AROUND THE BUSH¬, ⌐TOOTH AND NAIL¬, ⌐PIECE OF CAKE¬, etc. An idiom is represented in the DSyntS by a single node, since an idiom is but a single LU, in spite of being a multiword expression. (On compositionality/non-compositionality of complex linguistic signs, see 5.2.2, p. 130; idioms are shown by raised semi-brackets ⌐ ¬.)

3) **Lexical functions** [= LFs] (or, more precisely, the applications of LFs), which describe **semantic derivatives** and compositional phrasemes—collocations:[12]

$S_0(ADMIRE)$ = *admiration*   vs. $S_0(LEGITIMATE)$ = *legitimacy*
$S_1(ADMIRE)$ = *admirer*   vs. $S_1(THREATEN)$ = *threat* [something that threatens]
$Adv_2(RISK)$ = *at the risk* [*of* N] vs. $Adv_2(THREATEN)$= *under threat* [*of* N]
pay [Oper$_1$] *ATTENTION*   vs. *use* [Oper$_1$] *CAUTION*
play [Oper$_1$] *an important* [Magn] *ROLE* vs. *have* [Oper$_1$]
  a vital [Magn] *SIGNIFICANCE*
take [Oper$_2$] *an EXAM*   vs. *undergo* [Oper$_2$] *a TEST*, etc.

On LFs, see below, 4.2, p. 90*ff*.

4) **Fictitious lexemes** (shown by special quotes « »), which represent semantically full syntactic constructions; such a construction carries a meaning similar to the meanings of LUs. Thus, the English con-

3.2 LINGUISTIC REPRESENTATIONS IN A MEANING-TEXT MODEL   55

struction V–**subj**→N$_X$, where V$_{IRREALIS}$ + N$_X$,* ("the Main Verb in the irrealis whose subject follows it") means 'if':

Had Mary$_X$ *loved us, she would come* ≡ **If** *Mary had loved us...,*
Were I *rich, I would buy the house* ≡ **If** *I were rich...*

In a DSyntS, this construction is represented by the fictitious lexeme «IF»:

if Mary had loved ... ⇔ IF–II→LOVE$_{IRREALIS, PAST}$–I→MARY

vs.

had Mary loved ... ⇔ «IF»–II→LOVE$_{IRREALIS, PAST}$–I→MARY

The meaning of a fictitious lexeme may or may not coincide with the meaning of a genuine lexeme of the language. Thus, «IF» ≡ IF (in the corresponding sense of IF), but «IF» can only be used with the irrealis form of the verb, while the genuine IF also takes the indicative.[13]

All deep LUs are introduced into the DSyntS by semantic-lexical rules of the semantic module; see *3.3*, rule **R**^{Sem} 2, p. 72.

- **Deep grammemes.** The name of a lexeme that can be inflected is supplied with all the semantic grammemes it expresses. (A semantic grammeme has a semantic source—it corresponds to a semantic configuration in the initial SemS.) In English, a noun has in the DSyntS the grammemes of definiteness (DEF ~ INDEF ~ NON-DEF) and of number (SG ~ PL). A verb is accompanied by grammemes of mood (IND ~ IMPER ~ SUBJ ~ IRREAL ~ COND), tense (PRES ~ PAST ~ FUT), perfectivity (PERF ~ NON-PERF), and progressivity (PROGR ~ NON-PROGR).

  All deep grammemes are introduced into the DSyntS by semantic-grammemic rules of the semantic module; see *3.4*, rule **R**^{Sem} 4, p. 73.

- ➤ ARROWS (= arcs) of a DSyntS are labeled with the names of deep-syntactic relations [= DSyntRel]. Unlike the numbers of semantic relations, which are purely distinctive, the names of the DSyntRels denote the most general types of syntactic constructions.

---

* Our representation of this construction assumes the existence (in English) of the following five verbal moods: indicative (*John* **is** *quiet*) ~ imperative (*John,* **be** *quiet!*) ~ subjunctive (*He orders that John* **be** *quiet*) ~ irrealis (*If John* **were** *quiet, ...*) ~ conditional (*John* **would be** *quiet ...*); see Mel'čuk & Pertsov 1987: 169.

The DSyntRels are linguistically universal in the sense that they can be used to describe the DSyntSs of any language.

- All syntactic constructions known in world languages are divided into two major families: coordinate *vs.* subordinate constructions. The <u>coordinate constructions</u> are described by two DSyntRels: **COORD**(inative) and **PSEUDO-COORD**.

  NB: In previous publications, the **PSEUDO-COORD** DSyntRel (and the corresponding SSyntRel) was called ***quasi**-coordinative*. Here, an attempt is made at improving the terminology. Namely, the prefix *quasi-X* will be used, from now on, for an element that is not an X, but—under appropriate conditions—can be treated as an X, i.e., confounded with genuine Xs (for instance, quasi-elementary [sign], quasi-grammeme, quasi-morph). An element that is not an X and can never be confounded with Xs, but resembles X to a sufficient degree will be called *pseudo-X*. This modification concerns also such names of SSyntRels as **quasi-subjectival* ⇒ *pseudo-subjectival*, etc.

- The subordinate constructions are subdivided, in their turn, into weak-subordinate *vs.* strong-subordinate. The <u>weak-subordinate constructions</u> are described by the **APPEND**(itive) DSyntRel.

- The strong-subordinate constructions fall in two subsets: modifying *vs.* actantial DSyntRels.

The <u>modifying constructions</u> are described by the **ATTR**(ibutive) and **ATTR**$_{descr(iptive)}$ DSyntRels.

The <u>actantial constructions</u> are described by DSyntRels **I, II, ..., VI**, and **II**$_{DIR(ECT).SPEECH}$.

A deep-syntactic actant [= DSyntA] of a lexeme L is a syntactic dependent of L that expresses some of L's semantic actants. In the sentence *Because of this John reminded Mary about the exam in my presence* the lexemes JOHN, MARY and EXAM are DSyntAs of REMIND, since they are imposed by the meaning of the verb (*X reminds Y of Z*); however, the expressions *because of this* and *in my presence* are not the verb's actants, but freely added modifiers.

3.2 LINGUISTIC REPRESENTATIONS IN A MEANING-TEXT MODEL

An LU of a natural language has up to six DSynt-actants, which gives six actantial DSyntRels; there is an additional DSyntRel for Direct Speech (which functions as an object of the speech verb, as in *Micky shouted:*–II$_{dir.speech}$→*"Come over right away!"*).

These all add up to the 12 DSyntRels used in the Meaning-Text approach, which I will now exemplify.

Two coordinate DSyntRels

– **COORD**, as in MARY–**COORD**→JOHN–**COORD**→OR ANN ⇔
Mary, John or Ann

The **COORD** DSyntRel represents normal coordination, eihther without a conjunction or with one.

– **PSEUDO-COORD**, as in

IN–**PSEUDO-COORD**–[NEW YORK]→
ON–**PSEUDO-COORD**–[MANHATTAN]→AT JOHN'S ⇔
[*He stayed*] *in New York, on Manhattan, at John's*.

This DSyntRel represents syntactic constructions of elaboration, where, for instance, a prepositional phrase follows—necessarily without a conjunction—another such a phrase.

☞ In our examples, square brackets isolate the expressions that are irrelevant for the given example, but are needed in order to make it natural.

Ten subordinate DSyntRels

– One appenditive DSyntRel

APPEND, as in

SORRY,←**APPEND**–[I]–BE$_{IND, PRES, NON-PERF, NON-PROGR}$ BUSY ⇔
Sorry, [*I*] *am* [*busy*].

The **APPEND** DSyntRel subordinates such "extra-structural" elements as parentheticals and addresses to the Main Verb of the clause.

– Two modifying DSyntRels

ATTR, as in RED←**ATTR**–FLAG ⇔ *red flag*

MAN–**ATTR**→OF [GREAT COURAGE] ⇔ *man of* [*great courage*]

VERY←**ATTR**–INTERESTING ⇔ *very interesting*

DRIVE$_{(V)}$–**ATTR**→FAST ⇔ *[John] was driving [very] fast.*

The **ATTR** DSyntRel describes all types of modifier constructions (minus descriptive ones, see the next DSyntRel).

ATTR$_{descr}$ as in

MARY–**ATTR**$_{descr}$→TIRED [AND HUNGRY] ⇔ *Mary, tired [and hungry]*

The **ATTR**$_{descr}$ DSyntRel is used for so-called descriptive modifiers, which do not limit the denotation of the element modified, but simply qualify it.

– Seven actantial DSyntRels

I, as in JOHN←**I**–READ ⇔ *John is reading*; MY←**I**–TRIP ⇔ *my trip*;

TRANSLATION–**I**→BY JOHN ⇔ *translation [of this novel] by John*

II, as in BOOK←**II**–READ ⇔ *[John] is reading a book*:

JOHN←**II**–EXPULSION ⇔ *John's expulsion*

FOR–**II**→JOHN ⇔ *for John*

III, as in

BOOK←**II**–SEND–**III**→JOHN ⇔ *[Mary] sends a book to John*

IV–VI, as in

HUNDRED DOLLAR$_{PL}$←**II**–LEND–**IV**→MONTH ⇔

[Would you] lend [me] $$100 for a month?

ISTANBUL←**III**–MISSION–**IV**→MONTH ⇔
  ↘**V**→STUDY

a mission to Istanbul for a month to study Turkish

II$_{dir.speech}$, as in

WHISPER–**II**$_{dir.speech}$→COME$_{IMPER}$ ⇔

[John] whispered: "Come [back]!"

The DSynt-tree is linearly not ordered: the arrangement of its nodes on a plane—for instance, on paper—is irrelevant and is chosen for legibility. This is only common sense:

3.2 LINGUISTIC REPRESENTATIONS IN A MEANING-TEXT MODEL

> Since word order is one of the linguistic means used in natural languages for the expression of syntactic structures, it cannot be part of these structures.

Thus, in English, the anteposition of a prepositionless noun N to a finite verb marks its syntactic role as the subject, while N's postposition to a transitive verb indicates that N is the direct object: $Mary_{Subj}$ helps $John_{DirO}$.

Word order appears only in the deep-morphological structure of a sentence, closer to the text than a syntactic structure.

The same is true of two other linguistic means for the expression of the syntactic structure: syntactic prosody (roughly, phrasing) and syntactically-determined morphology (markers of agreement and government). These elements cannot be part of the syntactic structure; they also appear, for the first time, in the deep-morphological structure.

The deep-syntactic module of the MTM receives, as its input, a DSyntR of a sentence including its DSyntS—in our case, the DSyntS of Figure 3 (p. 56). For this DSyntR, the module constructs all possible SSyntRs, among them the SSyntR of sentence (19). The next Subsection presents the basic structure of this SSyntR—the SSyntS of sentence (19).

3.2.4 The surface-syntactic structure of a sentence

A Surface-Syntactic Representation is an ordered quadruple

SSyntR = ⟨ **SSyntS** ; SSynt-CommS ; SSynt-ProsS ; SSynt-AnaphS ⟩

Its component structures play the same roles as their deep counterparts, so that no special explanations are needed.

The core of an SSyntR is the Surface-Syntactic Structure [= SSyntS]; in the same way as the DSyntS, it characterizes the organization of the sentence in terms of its LUs (supplied with grammemes) and Surface-Syntactic relations between them, see Figure 4.

60   3. AN OUTLINE OF A PARTICULAR MEANING-TEXT MODEL

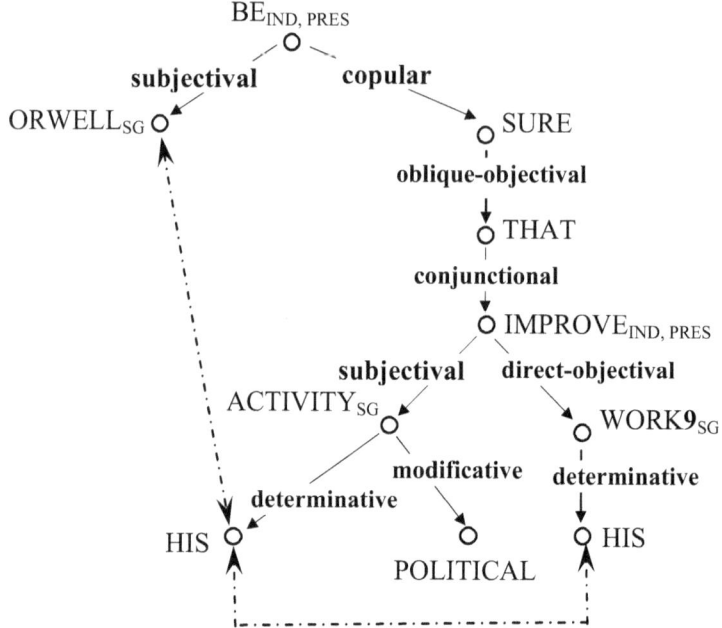

☞ As in the DSyntR, two-headed dashed arrows mark the relation of coreferentiality, this time between the substitute pronouns and their antecedents. (The noun or the adjective that is replaced by a pronoun is called its **source**; thus, the source of the two pronominal adjectives HIS in this diagram is the noun ORWELL.)

Figure 4: The Surface-Syntactic Structure of Sentence (19)

The other structures of the SSyntR are quite similar to their counterparts in the DSyntR and play the same role.

However, the DSyntS and the SSyntS are essentially different with respect to the labeling of the nodes and the branches.

➤ The NODES of the SSyntS are labeled with the names of **all** actual lexemes making up the sentence; they are supplied—as in the DSyntS—with semantically full inflectional values (= semantic grammemes). This means that:

• The SSynt-tree contains all the lexemes of the sentence. More precisely, in the SSyntS of a sentence:

– All structural words are present.

3.2 LINGUISTIC REPRESENTATIONS IN A MEANING-TEXT MODEL 61

- The substitute pronouns are shown (the SSyntS represents the sentence after pronominalization has been carried out: the SSyntS of Figure 4 contains two pronominal adjectives—two occurrences of HIS).
- An idiom is expanded into its full subtree, which, from now on, is treated by the SSynt-module exactly the same as all other parts of the SSynt-tree. For instance:

  DSyntS [one node]
  ⌈KICK THE BUCKET⌉ ⇔

  SSyntS [full subtree]
  KICK–**direct-objectival**→BUCKET$_{SG}$–**determinative**→THE

- The name of a lexical function taken together with its keyword is replaced with an element of its value (a genuine LU).

  DSyntS
  Oper$_1$(ATTENTION)–II→ATTENTION$_{SG, NON-DEF}$ ⇔

  SSyntS
  PAY–**direct-objectival**→ATTENTION$_{SG}$

☞ The grammeme NON-DEF attached to ATTENTION in the DSyntS disappears in the SSyntS because the grammemes of the category of definiteness are expressed analytically, by separate structural words, which appear as such in the SSyntS.

  Magn(ATTENTION)←**ATTR**–ATTENTION   ⇔
  CLOSE←**modificative**–ATTENTION

- A fictitious lexeme is "turned" into the corresponding construction—that is, into a SSynt-subtree:

  DSyntS   **SSyntS**
  «IF»–II→L$_{(V)}$ ⇔   L$_{(V)}$ | **SUBJ-INVERSION**

☞ The verbal top nod in the SSynt-tree is supplied with the reference to the **Subject-Inversion** rules, which, under linearization, produce the necessary word order (*Had he come on time, ...*)

- The inflectional characteristics of the lexemes remain incomplete: as in the DSyntS, only semantic grammemes are presented. Syntactic grammemes appear as the result of agreement or government (two major morphological dependencies, p. 172); therefore, they are present only in the DMorphS of the sentence, where they are inserted by the rules of the SSynt-module.

➤ The BRANCHES of the SSyntS are labeled with the names of surface-syntactic relations [= SSyntRels]. Unlike DSynt-relations, an SSyntRel denotes a particular syntactic construction of the language under consideration. The SSyntRels are specific to each language, as are phonemes, morphemes and lexemes. A language normally has a few dozen SSyntRels. As a brief illustration, here are a few English SSyntRels (for a full list, see Appendix II, p. 184*ff*).

Subordinate SSyntRels

Actantial SSyntRels

subjectival:

 I←subj–*got* [*old.*] | ***It***←subj–*is* [*useful to eat kiwis.*] |

 To←subj–[*eat kiwis*]–*seems* [*useful.*]

pseudo-subjectival:

 [*It*] *is*–[*useful*]–pseudo-subj→***to*** [*eat kiwis.*]

direct-objectival:

 eat–dir-obj→***kiwis***; *want*–dir-obj→***to*** [*eat kiwis*]

 say–dir-obj→***that*** [*kiwis are good*]

indirect-objectival:

 give–indir-obj→***Mary*** [*a kiwi*]; *give*–[*a kiwi*]–indir-obj→***to*** [*Mary*]

oblique-objectival:

 depend–obl-obj→***on*** [*circumstances*]; *threaten*–obl-obj→***with*** [*sanctions*]

copular:

 was–copul→***old***; *be*–copul→***useful***

comparative-objectival:

 larger–compar-obj→***than*** [*life*]

more–[*intelligent*]–compar-obj→***than*** [*Mary*]

[*John likes Mary*] *more*–compar-obj→***than*** [*he does Ann.*]

[*John likes Mary*] *more*–compar-obj→***than*** [*Ann does.*]

Non-actantial SSyntRels

determinative:

the←determ–*book*; ***our***←determ–*book*; ***this***←determ–*book*

modificative:

interesting←modif–*book*; ***German***←modif–*book*

possessive:

John's←poss–*book*; ***John's***←poss–*birth*; [*next*] ***week's***←poss–*party*

circumstantial:

runs–circum→***fast***; ***immediately***←circum–*left*;

[*John*] *works*–circum→***Fridays***.

[*John*] *lives*–circum→***in*** [*Canada.*]

[*John*] *shouted*–circum→***at*** [*the top of his voice.*]

[*Greece*] *fell*,–circum→***because*** [*part of it was intellectually paralyzed.*]

Coordinate SSyntRels

coordinative:

walks–coord→***swim***–coord→***runs*** ⇔ *walks, swims, runs*

walks–coord→***swims***–coord→***and*** [*runs*] ⇔ *walks, swims and runs*

pseudo-coordinative:

tomorrow–pseudo-coord→***at*** [*seven*]

Formally, a SSyntS is also (like a DSyntS) a linearly unordered dependency tree.

The SSynt-module of the MTM takes as its input the SSyntR of a sentence, which includes its SSyntS—for instance, that of Figure

4—and constructs for it all possible DMorphRs, which include, of course, the DMorphR of sentence (19); this is presented in Figure 5 in the next subsection.

3.2.5 The deep-morphological structure of a sentence

The deep-morphological representation [= DMorphR] of a sentence is the pair

$$\text{DMorphR} = \langle \, \textbf{DMorphS} \, ; \, \text{DMorph-ProsR} \, \rangle$$

The DMorphS is the **deep-morphological structure of the sentence**—an ordered string of all deep-morphological representations of individual wordforms that make up the sentence. (The DMorphR of a wordform is the name of the lexeme to which this wordform belongs supplied with all the relevant grammemes, semantic as well as syntactic; for instance, $\text{WRITE}_{\text{IND, PAST}}$ represents *wrote*, $\text{STRONG}_{\text{COMPAR}}$, *stronger*, $\text{WRITE}_{\text{IND, PRES, 3, SG}}$ specifies *writes*, and WE_{OBL}, *us*).

The other structure in the DMorphR of the sentence is the **deep-morphological-prosodic structure**, which specifies the division of the sentence into phonological groups (= phrases), as well as the stresses and intonational contours.

$\nearrow$ $\searrow$
$\text{ORWELL}_{\text{SG}}$ $\text{BE}_{\text{IND, PRES, 3, SG}}$ CONVINCED ||
 $\searrow$ $\searrow$ $\searrow$
THAT HIS POLITICAL $\text{ACTIVITY}_{\text{SG}}$ | $\text{IMPROVE}_{\text{IND, PRES, 3, SG}}$ HIS WORK_{SG} |||

☞ The vertical bars |, || and ||| represent the pauses of different length; the symbols "$\nearrow$" and "$\searrow$" stand for rising and falling intonation contours.

Figure 5: The Deep-Morphological Representation of Sentence (19)

The deep-morphological module of the MTM takes the DMorphR of the sentence, which includes its DMorphS, given in Figure 5, and constructs for it all possible surface-morphological representations, among which we find the SMorphR of (19); it is presented in Figure 6, next subsection.

3.2.6 The surface-morphological structure of a sentence

The SMorphS of sentence *S* is an ordered string of all wordforms of the sentence; its SMorph-ProsS is practically the same as its DMorphS (with minor adjustments). Each wordform appears as a set of its constituent morphemes:

{ORWELL}⊕{SG}   {BE}⊕{IND.PRES}⊕{3.SG}   {CONVINCED} ‖

{THAT}   {HIS}   {POLITICAL}   {ACTIVITY}⊕{SG} |

{IMPROVE}⊕{IND.PRES}⊕{3.SG}   {HIS}   {WORK}⊕{SG} ‖‖

☞ 1. Curly brackets denote a morpheme—a set of morphs that have the same signified and, roughly speaking, are distributed in a complementary fashion. Thus, the morpheme {PL} contains the following morphs: /s/, /z/, /ɪz/, /ən/ (*ox+en*), /aɪ/ (*alumn+i*), etc.

2. The name of a lexical morpheme is the name of the corresponding lexeme; the name of an inflectional morpheme is composed of the names of the grammemes it expresses.

3. The symbol ⊕ denotes the operation of linguistic union, see *5.2.2*, p. 129.

Figure 6: The Surface-Morphological Representation of Sentence (19)

In a language with rich morphology, grammemes are often distributed across morphemes in quite a capricious way.[14] The DMorphS features grammemes, while the task of the SMorphS is the most explicit reflection of inflectional morphemes (= sets of signs that express grammemes).

Starting with the SMorphR, where the SMorphS of Figure 6 is the basic structure, the SMorph-module of the MTM produces all possible deep-phonic representations that correspond to this SMorphS—in particular, the DPhonR of sentence (19). The DPhon-module of the MTM associates with this DPhonR the corresponding SPhonR—that is, the phonetic representation of (19); the "ceiling" of the model is thus reached. (The implementation of the SPhonR as a sequence of genuine linguistic sounds supplied with genuine linguistic prosodies is performed by a phonetic mechanism, which transgresses the limits of the MTM.)

I will not reproduce here the DPhonR and the SPhonR of sentence (19).

3.2.7 Prelinguistic Representation of the World: Conceptual Representation

In reality, the Speaker does not start constructing his sentence S from S's SemR (as I have been claiming up until now). The SemR of S is itself constructed on the basis of the information about the world that the Speaker wants to express or to communicate. In the Meaning-Text approach, this "prelinguistic" information is specified by a **conceptual representation** [= ConceptR]. Unfortunately, the ConceptR is not yet fully elaborated, so that I can only offer some general considerations here (see Mel'čuk 2001: 89, 154–155).

A ConceptR is supposed to specify a mental image of a real-world situation independently of the language, to the extent that this is possible. This is a discrete (= symbolic) representation of a reality perceived by the Speaker—the physical reality strained through the mental filters of the Speaker, but not yet adapted and fitted to the capacities and requirements of his language. An example will help.

Suppose a researcher wants a complete (but extremely limited) linguistic model capable of creating verbal portraits; more specifically, this model should be able to describe human faces, say, in English. The very first thing our researcher needs is a prelinguistic—that is, conceptual—description of possible faces based on a study of the human perception of facial traits and particularities, more or less independent from a specific language. This can be a list of all distinguishable parts of the face, with the indications of their parameters and the possible values of these parameters, see Figure 7 next page.* This ConceptR can give rise to several SemRs, which underlie, in particular, the English phrase (23a) and its Russian translational equivalent (23b):

---

* On linguistic description of human body—in particular, the human face—in English and Russian, see Iordanskaja & Paperno 1996.

NOSE
- Size : big
- Thickness :
- Form :
- Upper line : straight
- Color :
- Surface :

LIPS
- Size :
- Thickness : more than average
- Form :
- Color :
- Surface :
- Openness : small
- Expression :

CHIN
- Size : big
- Form : slightly rounded
- Surface :
- Expression : strong-willed

Figure 7: A (Partial) Conceptual Representation of the Face of a Person

(23) a. *his high-ridged, powerful nose, the full, open mouth, the hard, slightly rounded chin*
  b. *ego prjamoj krupnyj nos, polnye, slegka priotkrytye guby, tjažëlyj, nemnogo okruglënnyj podborodok*
  lit. 'his straight big nose, full, slightly open lips, heavy, a bit rounded chin'

Phrases (23a) and (23b) are, strictly speaking, not synonymous: their linguistic meanings are different. Thus, 'high-ridged [nose]' ≠ 'straight [nose]', 'powerful [nose]' ≠ 'big [nose], 'hard [chin]' ≠ 'heavy [chin]', etc. Nevertheless, these phrases are good equivalents, since they describe the same real entities—a nose, lips and a chin having the same appearance.

The difference between the SemRs of sentences (23a) and (23b) is similar to the difference between the meanings 'Sir Walter Scott' and

68 3. AN OUTLINE OF A PARTICULAR MEANING-TEXT MODEL

'the author of *Waverley*', which was discussed in detail by Frege and Russel. These meanings are different, but they refer to the same person. An identification of this writer corresponds to our ConceptR.

The proposed linguistic model—that is, the MTM—is but part of a larger and more general model that represents the entirety of linguistic behavior. This more general model can be called Perceived World ⇔ Speech model, see Figure 8.

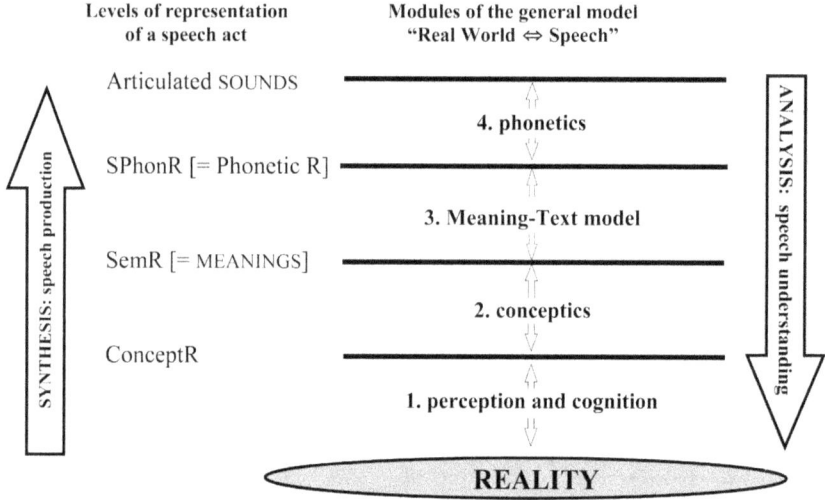

Figure 8: Levels of Representation and Major Modules of the World ⇔ Speech Model

A speech act can be described with respect to the following five levels (putting aside linguistically internal representation—that is, the representations used in the Meaning-Text model):

1. Real world, including the Speaker, with his knowledge (and illusions); more precisely, a **continuous** image of the world existing in the mind, which has been obtained via perception and memory.

2. Conceptual representation: a **discrete** image of the world in the Speaker's brain, selected by the Speaker.

3. Semantic representation (in the Meaning-Text model): a **discrete** representation of the meaning earmarked to be expressed by speech.

4. Phonetic (= surface-phonic) representation (in the Meaning-Text model): a **discrete** representation of the sounds to be produced.

5. Articulated sounds: a **continuous** acoustic phenomenon (back to the physical reality).

These representations are linked by four major modules:

- A transformer of a continuous representation of the world in the brain into its discrete conceptual representation. This psychic mechanism has no name as yet.
- A transformer of a conceptual representation of the world into a semantic representation—under the impact of the Speaker's language. This mechanism can be called conceptics.
- A transformer of a semantic representation into a phonetic representation. This is simply a Meaning-Text model.
- A transformer of a phonetic representation into real physical sounds. This is phonetics.

This is a framework for theoretical and experimental studies of languages.

3.3 The modules of the Meaning-Text model

3.3.1 Introductory remarks

The input to a Meaning-Text model is a SemR of a family of (quasi) synonymous sentences and its output consists of these sentences, in a phonetic transcription or standard spelling.

The MTM itself is functional in two senses of the term *functional*.

- On the one hand, the MTM is functional insofar as it models the FUNCTIONING of language: what speakers do and only what they do—namely, translating meanings into texts and vice versa (*2.2*, p. 21.)

– On the other hand, the MTM is functional insofar as it itself is organized as a FUNCTION (in the mathematical sense): this function associates with a given argument—a particular meaning 'σ' represented by a SemR—a value, which is a set of synonymous texts $\{T_i\}$ carrying this meaning. Symbolically:

(24) a. $\mathbf{f}_{language}('σ') = \{T_i('σ')\}$; this is linguistic synthesis.

The same function can be inverted and applied to a text T as its argument to produce, as its value, a set of meanings '$σ_j$':

b. $\mathbf{f}_{language}(T) = \{'σ_j'(T)\}$; this is linguistic analysis.

I believe that

> the study and description of natural languages is best done by models of this type.

To flesh out this statement, I will proceed to a more detailed characterization of the Meaning-Text model.

A Meaning-Text model consists of six independent modules; each of these implements the correspondence between linguistic representations of two adjacent levels. The Sem-module takes care of the correspondence between a given SemR and all DSyntRs that carry the same meaning. The DSynt-module does the same for a given DSyntR and all the appropriate SSyntRs. And so forth. Now I will go into more detail and give, for each module, a few rules selected in such a way as to show the transitions between the linguistic representations of sentence (19). I will, once again, follow the synthesis of this sentence, starting with the SemR of Figure 2—that is, exactly as this is performed by a Meaning-Text model.

1. All rules presented below as illustrations are drastically simplified; in particular, their conditions are not set out in detail.

2. The shading indicates the context of the rule: the elements of the rule that do not participate in the correspondence specified by it, but that control its applicability.

3.3.2 Semantic module

The rules of the Sem-module, or **semantic rules**, are classified under three rubrics: rules for semantic paraphrasing, rules for SemR ⇔ DSyntR transition, and rules for deep-syntactic paraphrasing.

☛ Illustrative rules are numbered arbitrarily—in order of appearance.

3.3.2.1 Semantic paraphrasing: rules of the form "SemR$_i$ ≡ SemR$_j$"

These rules, very numerous, give semantic decompositions of all decomposable semantemes; they are necessary to establish the equivalence (in this case, the equality) of SemRs. If applied from left to right, a Sem-paraphrasing rule expands the SemS being operated on, thus enlarging the depth of decomposition. Applied from right to left, it decreases the depth of decomposition and thus reduces the SemS.

Paraphrasing semantic rule: **R^{Sem} 1**

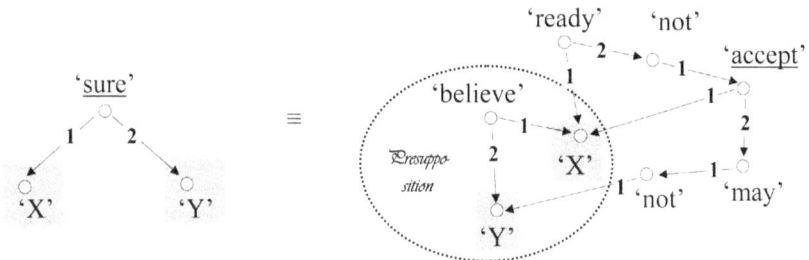

☛ Remember (*3.2.2*, Figure 2, p. 49), the underscoring of a node in a SemS (= 'sure') indicates its status as communicatively dominant—that is, as a meaning to which the meaning of the whole SemS can be reduced with losses, but without deformation. Presupposition is one of the Sem-communicative values that will be explained below; see Note 19, p. 209.

The semantic network on the right side of the rule is equivalent to the linear verbal expression '|[believing that Y,]| X is ready to not-accept that that it may be non-Y'. This expression is in fact the definition of the adjective SURE and is part of the dictionary entry for SURE in a dictionary of the ECD type, see Section *5.4*, p. 151*ff*. A linear verbal formulation of this semantic decomposition is given in Section *4.1*, (28a), p. 89.

3.3.2.2 Semantic transition: rules of the form "SemR$_i$ ⇔ DSyntR$_k$"

The left-hand part of a Sem-transition rule contains a semanteme, and the right-hand part—one of the three linguistic units allowed into the DSyntS: a lexical unit, a grammeme or a DSynt-branch. Accordingly, three types of Sem-transition rule are distinguished: lexical, grammemic (= inflectional), and structural. Thus, a Sem-transition rule describes the implementation:

- either of a semanteme (or a configuration of semantemes) by the corresponding LU (rule **R**^{Sem} **2** and **3**) or by the corresponding grammeme (rule **R**^{Sem} **4**);
- or of a specific Sem-dependency by the corresponding DSynt-dependency (rule **R**^{Sem} **5**).

<u>Lexical transition</u>

Sem-rule **R**^{Sem} **2**

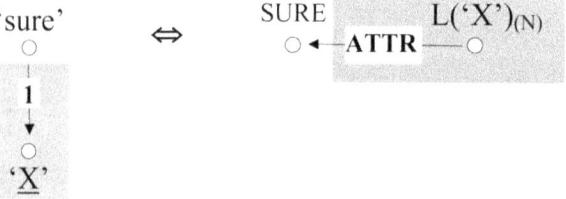

☞ In the right-hand part of the rule, L('X') stands for «lexical unit L that expresses the meaning 'X'».

The right subscript in parentheses accompanying the name of the lexeme L is a fragment of L's syntactics: L$_{(N)}$ means that L is a noun. On syntactics, see *5.2.2*, p. *124ff*.

Rule **R**^{Sem} **2** lexicalizes the semanteme 'sure' as the adjective SURE, but only if its Sem-actant 1 (⇔ 'X') is communicatively dominant, cf. the left-hand side of **R**^{Sem} **2**, where the meaning 'X' is underscored. In the transition from the SemS of Figure 2 to the DSyntS of Figure 3 this rule is, however, inapplicable, since in the initial SemS it is the semanteme 'sure' itself that is communicatively dominant, and not its SemA 1. Here one needs another lexical Sem-rule:

3.3 THE MODULES OF THE MEANING-TEXT MODEL

Sem-rule **R**^{Sem} **3**

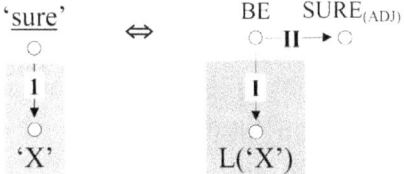

Since in English (as in all Indo-European languages) an adjective cannot be the top node of a Synt-tree, this rule introduces the copula verb BE governing SURE, thereby securing the well-formedness of the DSyntS being synthesized.[15]

☞ Sem-actant **2** (⇔ Y) of 'sure' (*sure of his charm*$_Y$, *sure to achieve*$_Y$ *his goal, sure that Mary is*$_Y$ *happy*) is syntactically implemented according to Sem-rule **R**^{Sem} **6**, see below.

 The union of Sem-rules **R**^{Sem} **1** (applied from right to left) and **R**^{Sem} **2/3** (applied from left to right) is, in point of fact, the central part of a lexical entry for the lexeme SURE: **R**^{Sem} **1** gives its lexicographic definition, or semantic decomposition, while rules **R**^{Sem} **2/3** specify its lexical and syntactic properties.

The number of "rule unions" of this form in a major global language—that is, the number of lexical entries—is, as was stated on p. 5, between half a million and a million. Sem-rules for lexical transition build up the *Explanatory Combinatorial Dictionary* [= ECD], which is the pivotal part of the semantic module of the MTM.

I will not consider other types of transition semantic rules, such as idiomatic Sem-rules, which introduce idioms as single nodes into the DSyntS, and constructional Sem-rules, which introduce fictitious lexemes, representing semantically loaded syntactic constructions.[16]

<u>Grammemic transition</u>

Sem-rule **R**^{Sem} **4**

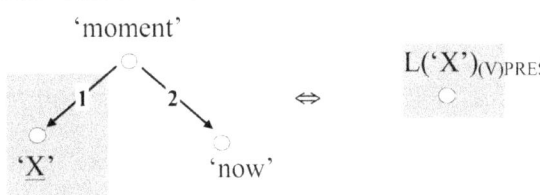

74   3. AN OUTLINE OF A PARTICULAR MEANING-TEXT MODEL

Rule $\mathbf{R}^{Sem}$ 4 tells us that the meaning 'moment of X is now' (= 'fact X takes place at the moment of this speech act') can be expressed in English by the grammeme PRES(ent), which must be attached to the verb that expresses 'X'—that is, to L('X')$_{(V)}$. This rule is applied twice in the process of synthesizing the DSynt-tree of Figure 3: it associates the grammeme PRES to the verbs BE and IMPROVE.

Rules of this type cover the semantics of the grammemes of **L** (in other words, they constitute the morphological semantics of **L**). The number of these rules depends on the complexity of **L**'s morphology; it varies between a couple dozen to a hundred or so ($10^1 \sim 10^2$).

Structural transition

This group of Sem-rules fulfills two tasks: they establish the top node of the DSyntS (see Mel'čuk 2001: 38–48) and construct its branches. They can be exemplified by rules $\mathbf{R}^{Sem}$ 5 – $\mathbf{R}^{Sem}$ 7.

Sem-rule $\mathbf{R}^{Sem}$ 5

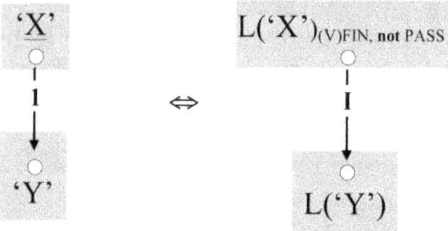

Sem-rule $\mathbf{R}^{Sem}$ 5 "translates" Sem-relation 1 as DSynt-relation I if the communicatively dominant meaning 'X' is expressed by a finite verb form not in the passive:

'kill–1→hunter' ⇔ HUNTER←I–KILL$_{FIN, not\ PASS}$ ⇔

The hunter kills [the wolf.]

This rule works for transitive verbs in the active voice and for intransitive verbs.

3.3 THE MODULES OF THE MEANING-TEXT MODEL   75

Sem-rule **R**^{Sem} 6

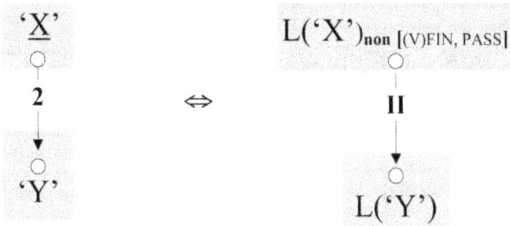

Sem-rule **R**^{Sem} 6 implements Sem-relation 2 by DSynt-relation II if the communicatively dominant meaning 'X' is expressed by a lexeme of any class but not by a finite transitive verb in the passive (see the next Sem-rule):

'kill–2→wolf' ⇔ KILL$_{NON\ PASS}$–II→WOLF ⇔ [*The hunter*] *kills the wolf.*

'sure–2→charms' ⇔ SURE–II→CHARM$_{PL}$ ⇔ *sure of* [*his*] *charms*

This rule covers all lexemes except for finite transitive verbs in the passive voice.

Sem-rule **R**^{Sem} 7

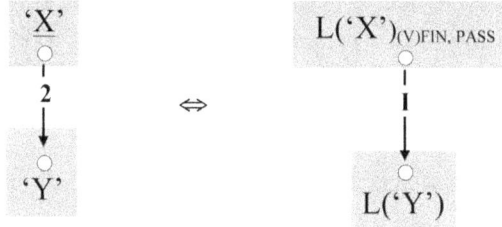

Sem-rule **R**^{Sem} 7 expresses Sem-relation 2 as DSynt-relation I if the communicatively dominant meaning 'X' is expressed by a finite verb form in the passive:

'kill–2→wolf' ⇔ WOLF←I–KILL$_{FIN,\ PASS}$ ⇔
  The wolf was killed [*by the hunter.*]

The grammeme PASS(ive) is introduced by a Sem-rule for grammemic transition, which takes into account the fact that the Sem-dependent, the meaning 'Y', is the **Theme** of the clause.

Two other major types of Sem-transition rules will not be considered here:

- rules responsible for the communicative structures, which, based on the initial Sem-CommS, construct the DSynt-CommS of the sentence;
- rules responsible for the formal well-formedness of the DSynt-tree obtained by the Sem-module.

3.3.2.3 Deep-syntactic paraphrasing: rules of the form "DSyntR$_{k_1}$ ≡ DSyntR$_{k_2}$"

These rules ensure the maximum possible number of DSynt-paraphrases—what can be referred to as **multiple semantic synthesis**; that is why they are included in the Sem-module. Two examples of such rules are given immediately below. The DSynt-paraphrasing system, elaborated in Žolkovskij & Mel'čuk 1967, is described in detail in Mel'čuk 2013: 137–197.

The DSynt-paraphrasing system is linguistically universal: it is based on lexical functions and, therefore, does not depend on a particular language. (For more on lexical functions, see *4.2, p. 90ff.*)

DSynt-paraphrasing Sem-rule: **R**^{Sem} **8**

$$L_{(V)} \circ \equiv \text{Oper}_i(S_0(L)) \circ {-}\text{II}{\to} \circ S_0(L)$$

This rule describes a semantic equivalence between a verb [= $L_{(V)}$] and a collocation whose base is an action noun [= S_0] of this verb, and the collocate is a "semi-auxiliary" verb [= Oper$_1$] of this action noun. Rules of this type are known as **fissions**; for instance:

(25) X *aids* Y ≡ X *comes to the aid of* Y
X *resists* Y ≡ X *puts up resistance to* Y
X *blunders* ≡ X *commits a blunder*
X *sighs* ≡ X *heaves a sigh*

DSynt-paraphrasing Sem-rule: **R**^{Sem} **9**

$$L_{1(V)} \circ {-}\text{II}{\to} \circ L_{2(V)} \equiv L_{2(V)} \circ {-}\text{ATTR}{\to} \circ \text{Adv}_i(L_{1(V)})$$

Rule **R**^{Sem} **9** specifies another semantic (quasi-)equivalence, this time, of the two deep-syntactic configurations; this is a **dependency reversal** (the lexeme that was the syntactic governor becomes the dependent, while the former dependent becomes the governor):

(26) X *hurried→to leave.* ≅ X *left→in a hurry.*
  X *used→to drink coffee.* ≅ X *usually←drank coffee.*
  X *continues→to drink coffee.* ≅ X *drinks–[coffee]→as much as before.*

3.3.3 Deep-syntactic module

Logically speaking, the rules of the DSynt-module, or **deep-syntactic rules**, are classified in the same way as the rules of the Sem-module: rules for deep-syntactic paraphrasing, rules for DSyntR ⇔ SSyntR transition, and rules for surface-syntactic paraphrasing. However, the DSynt-paraphrasing rules have already been characterized, and the SSynt-paraphrasing rules need not detain us here. Therefore, there will be no more discussion of paraphrasing rules: only DSyntR ⇔ SSyntR transition rules will be considered.

A DSyntR ⇔ SSyntR transition rule contains on its left-hand side a linguistic unit of one of the following three types: deep (= full) LU, deep (= semantic) grammeme, or deep-syntactic relation. Accordingly, transition DSynt-rules are of three major types: lexical, grammemic and structural.

DSynt-rules for **lexical transition** are divided, in turn, into four subtypes: lexemic rules, idiom rules, lexical-functional rules, and constructional rules.

<u>Lexemic transition</u>

The corresponding DSynt-rules are trivial: full lexemes of the DSyntS remain the same in the SSyntS.

Idiom transition

DSynt-rules for idioms enable the correspondence between the representation of an idiom in the DSyntS, where it labels a single node, and its fully developed surface-syntactic tree.

DSynt-rule $\mathbf{R^{DSynt}}$ 1

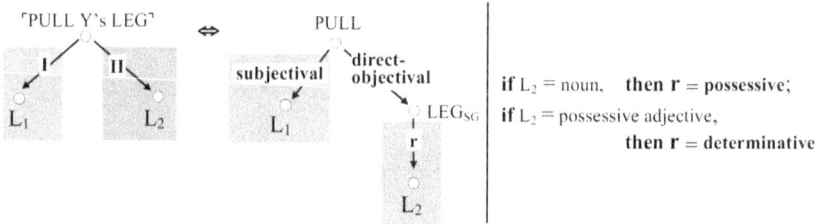

$\mathbf{R^{DSynt}}$ 1 expands the node of the idiom ⌐PULL Y's LEG¬ 'tell Y a harmless lie for the purpose of fun or entertainment' into its complete surface subtree.

Lexical-functional transition

The corresponding DSynt-rules compute the values of LFs using the information stored in the lexical entry for the LF's keyword (= the base of the corresponding collocation).

DSynt-rule $\mathbf{R^{DSynt}}$ 2:

$\text{Oper}_1(\text{ATTENTION})-\text{II}\rightarrow\text{ATTENTION}_{SG} \Leftrightarrow \text{PAY}-\text{II}\rightarrow\text{ATTENTION}_{SG}$

DSynt-rule $\mathbf{R^{DSynt}}$ 3:

$\text{Magn}(\text{ATTENTION})\leftarrow\textbf{ATTR}-\text{ATTENTION}_{SG} \Leftrightarrow$
$\text{CLOSE}\leftarrow\textbf{ATTR}-\text{ATTENTION}_{SG}$

☞ Lexical DSynt-rules must be written, of course, not for individual LUs, as in the above examples, but for the families of LUs of the same type—that is, in the form of rule schemata. However, in this text, I prefer to avoid abstract rule schemata to ensure better surveyability and easier understanding.

3.3 THE MODULES OF THE MEANING-TEXT MODEL

Constructional transition

DSynt-rules for constructions replace a fictitious lexeme that encodes a meaning-bearing syntactic construction with the surface-syntactic tree of this construction.

DSynt-rule **R**^{DSynt} 4

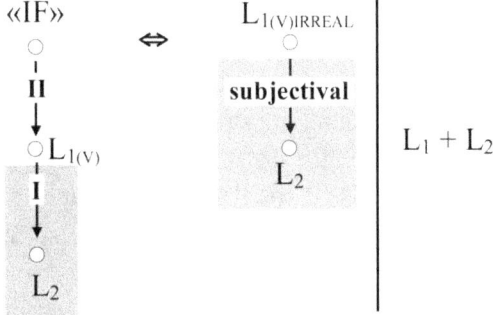

☞ The condition requires that in the morphological string the finite verb L_1 immediately precedes the subject L_2: *Were*$_{L_1}$ *John*$_{L_2}$ *around today, we would be safer.*

These, then, are the four subtypes of DSynt-rules for lexical transition. I now go on to consider the second and third major types of DSynt-rule.

Grammemic transition

DSynt-rules of this type replace, where needed, a deep grammeme by a surface grammeme.

DSynt-rule **R**^{DSynt} 5 (for plural-only nouns)

SCISSORS$_{(pl!)SG}$ ⇔ SCISSORS$_{(pl!)PL}$

☞ "!" means 'only': $N_{(pl!)}$ is a *plurale tantum*.

Here, the semantic singular ('one pair of scissors') is replaced with the necessary formal plural.

Structural transition

These DSynt-rules implement a DSynt-relation either with a structural word (such as a governed preposition) and the corresponding SSynt-branch or with a SSynt-relation.

80   3. AN OUTLINE OF A PARTICULAR MEANING-TEXT MODEL

DSynt-rule **R**^{DSynt} 6

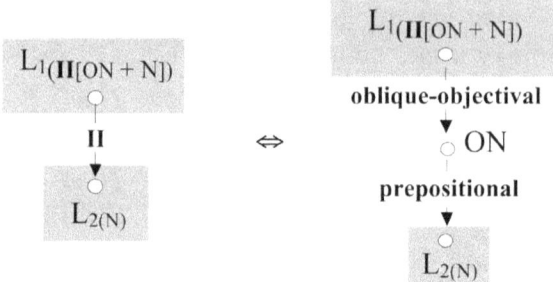

This rule describes the prepositional government of a family of lexical units, such as DEPEND [*on*], INSIST [*on*] and FEED [*on*]. More specifically, the subscript "(II[ON + N])"* of the LU L_1 indicates that L_1's DSynt-actant II is expressed by the preposition ON. The set of all such indications constitutes the government pattern of L_1.

A government pattern of an LU L specifies the means for the expression of L's DSynt-actants (see *3.2.3*, p. 56; Mel'čuk 2004). Thus, in English we help somebody, while in Russian, one helps **to** somebody (*pomogat' komu*); we wait **for** somebody, but in French, one waits somebody (*attendre quelqu'un*) and in German, **on** somebody (*auf jemanden warten*); etc. This information is supplied in the government pattern in the lexical entry for an LU, so that the structural transition DSynt-rules can select the appropriate preposition or grammatical case.

3.3.4 Surface-syntactic module

The rules of the SSynt-module carry out the following three operations on the SSyntS: linearization (≈ word order), morphologization (≈ inflection) and prosodization. Thus, this module:

– linearly arranges the lexemes of the sentence;
– attaches to them all grammemes (semantic grammemes, which come from the SSyntS, and syntactic grammemes, computed by this module); and

---

* This subscript is a feature of L_1's **syntactics**; on the syntactics of a linguistic sign, see *5.2.2*, p. 124*ff*.

– cuts the lexemic string so obtained into actual phrases, each supplied with its appropriate prosody (pauses, group and sentence stresses, intonational contours).

Accordingly, three types of SSynt-rules are distinguished: ordering, inflectional, and prosodic SSynt-rules.

Ordering SSynt-rules are subdivided into three groups: local, quasi-local, and global rules.

The left-hand part of a local ordering rule contains one SSynt-branch with both of its nodes; the ordering of the dependent element with respect to the governor is done taking into account only minimal, i.e. local, context.

Quasi-local and global ordering rules essentially use communicative information and wider context limited only by the borders of the sentence. These rules are too complex to be introduced here; hence, only local ordering rules will be illustrated.

<u>Local ordering</u>

SSynt-rule **R**^{SSynt} **1**

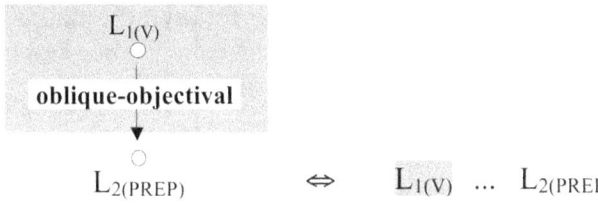

☞ The three dots " ... " indicate that the insertion of lexical material between L_1 and L_2 is allowed.

A British man has been found$_{L_1}$ dead outside a hotel in$_{L_2}$ eastern France. ~
In$_{L_2}$ eastern France, a British man has been found$_{L_1}$ dead outside a hotel.

R^{SSynt} **1** places a preposition (more precisely, the preposition together with its dependent noun and all the dependents of the latter—that is, the whole prepositional phrase) depending on a verb—either after its SSynt-governor, or before it: this is shown by the absence, on the right-hand side of the rule, of the symbol " + , " see the next rule. The final position of the preposition and its dependents with respect to the governing verb is determined by global word-order rules (which, as noted above, are not considered in *LMT*).

SSynt-rule **R**^{SSynt} **2**

$L_{1(PREP)}$
○
↓
prepositional   ⇔ $L_1 + ... + L_2$, $L_1 \Rightarrow №3(SSG_N)$, $L_2 \Rightarrow № 8(SSG_N)$ |
▼
○
$L_{2(N)}$
    if N = (pron, pers), **then** N_{OBL}

in_{L_1} *eastern France*$_{L_2}$

R^{SSynt} **2** 1) puts the preposition before the governed noun, 2) indicates the place of the preposition and that of the noun in the template of the Simple Syntactic Group of the noun [= SSG_N, see immediately below] and 3) if the N is a personal pronoun, adds to it the grammeme of the oblique case (*for me, without her*).

A Simple Syntactic Group is a device that facilitates the linearization of certain types of syntactic subtrees. The following remarks will explain the idea behind this.

– Generally speaking, an SSG for LUs $L_{(PoS)}$ of a given part of speech [= PoS] is a linear schema for positioning some direct dependents of $L_{(PoS)}$. Note, however, that for nouns, the SSG_N includes, along with fixed-position dependents of N, two of its possible direct governors—a coordinate conjunction and a preposition, which also occupy a fixed linear position with respect to $L_{(N)}$.

– The arrangement of the lexical classes in an SSG is not affected in any significant way by other elements of the clause in which $L_{(PoS)}$ and its immediate dependents appear, so that linearization can be performed according to a rigid schema: a linear pattern, see the SSG_N below.

– A syntactic group is called simple, because it does not contain any other syntactic group of the same type. Here are some examples of

3.3 THE MODULES OF THE MEANING-TEXT MODEL

a simple noun syntactic groups: *a month, for a month, or for all these three horrible months*, etc. (For **complex** syntactic groups, see below.)

Simple Syntactic Group of a Noun in English

1	2	3	4	5	6	7	8	9
CONJ$_{coord}$	PARTICLE	PREP	ADJ$_{quant}$	ADJ$_{det/poss}$	NUM	ADJ	N	Ψ$_{invar}$
but	*only*	*for*	*all*	*the/these/our*	*seven*	*interesting*	*examples*	*(13)*

☞ 1. Position 5 is reserved for an article or a demonstrative/interrogative/possessive adjective.
2. Position 7 actually allows for a string of adjectives, as in *expensive antique French book*. Special rules are needed to determine their linear order.
3. Position 9: Ψ$_{invar}$ is any un-English expression, such as a number written in digits, a symbol, a foreign word, etc.
4. Each position can be filled not only by one element of the corresponding class, but also by an SSG of a different type: an element with NOT (***not** only*, ***not** all*, ...), an adjective with its dependents (*a **hard to swallow** solution*), a noun with a preceding nominal modifier (***college** student*), etc.
5. The SSG$_N$ template must be supplied with a series of constraints on the cooccurrence of some elements in it; thus, the schema has to take care of the cases such as *all these* vs. *all of these, *this my book* vs. *this book of mine, three of my books, the first three moves*, etc.

As we see, the SSG$_N$ template has a maximum of 9 positions; the lexemes in the phrase *or for all these three horrible months* receive, according to the corresponding local ordering rules, the following position numbers:

OR – 1, FOR – 3, ALL – 4, THIS – 5, THREE – 6, HORRIBLE – 7, and MONTH – 8.

Such templates are also necessary for adjectives, verbs, and adverbs.

Several SSGs can be united to form a Complex Syntactic Group [= CSG], something like *because of my first disastrous marriage to this graduate of Harvard*, a CSG$_N$ built out of three SSG$_N$s: *because of my first disastrous marriage, to this graduate* and *of Harvard*. Uniting SSGs into CSGs is the task of quasi-local ordering rules. CSGs, which are saturated clause elements, are then manipulated by global ordering rules.

3.3.5 Deep-morphological module

A DMorph-rule associates a grammeme or a set of grammemes either to a morpheme, which is a set of synonymous elementary segmental signs called morphs, or to another type of -emic morphological signifier: a reduplicationeme (set of synonymous reduplications), an apophoneme (set of synonymous apophonies) and a converseme (set of synonymous conversions). A DMorph-rule tells us that this grammeme (or this given set of grammemes) is expressed in **L** by one sign, without specifying exactly which sign. (The selection of an appropriate sign to implement a morpheme is done by the SMorph-module.) Here are examples of rules of the "grammeme ⇔ morpheme" type.[17]

R^{DMorph} **1**
PAST ⇔ {PAST}   [in a finite verb: *answer+**ed***]

R^{DMorph} **2**
3, SG ⇔ {3.SG}   [in a finite verb: *seek+**s***]

R^{DMorph} **3**, Russian
PL, DAT ⇔ {PL.DAT}   [in a noun: *jablok+**am*** 'to.apples']

R^{DMorph} **4**, Latin
FEM, SG, ABL ⇔ {FEM.SG.ABL} [in an adjective:
  *pulchr+**ā*** 'from.beautiful.one$_{FEM}$']

Each of DMorph-rules R^{DMorph} 2 – R^{DMorph} 4 implements several grammemes with one morpheme; such a morpheme is called cumulative.[18]

3.3.6 Surface-morphological module

The SMorph-module contains two types of rule: morphemic rules, applicable to morphemes; and morphophonemic rules, applicable to morphs.

Morphemic rules

Morphemic SMorph-rules perform two operations:

– They select the appropriate concrete (allo)morphs for the morphemes obtained in the preceding step (and, of course, also all concrete allo-'s for all other -emes).
– They select megamorphs—non-elementary linearly indivisible segmental complex signs that each express several morphemes together.

Here are some examples.

R^{SMorph} **1**: selection of (allo)morphs

{3.SG} ⇔ /s/ | __{/C$_{[non-sibilant, voiceless]}$/}
     (*speaks, laughs, drops*)
    ⇔ /z/ | __{/C$_{[non-sibilant, voiced]}$/, /V/}
     (*stands, moves, calls, sues*)
    ⇔ /ɪz/ | __{/C$_{[sibilant]}$/}
     (*kisses, rushes, judges*)

R^{SMorph} **2** and **3**: selection of megamorphs

{BE}, {IND.PRES}, {1.SG} ⇔ /æm/ *am*
{BE}, {IND.PRES}, {3.SG} ⇔ /ɪz/ *is*

Morphophonemic rules

Morphophonemic SMorph-rules perform phonemic alternations inside morph signifiers. In a sense, they adapt morphs to the particular morphological and/or phonological context in which these morphs appear. For example:

R^{SMorph} **4**

/f/ ⇒ /v/ | __+/z/ **and** in a stem marked "f/v" in its syntactics
     (*life* ~ *lives*)

The number of D/SMorph-rules varies from language to language—between a few dozen and several hundred. (For more on the description of morphology in the Meaning-Text approach, see Mel'čuk 1997–2006.)

Chapter 4
Modeling Two Central Linguistic Phenomena: Lexical Selection and Lexical Cooccurrence

The time has come for an in-depth discussion of the application of the Meaning-Text approach to the description of real languages. I would like to consider two very general problems and to show how they are intimately related. The first one concerns **lexical semantics**—that is, the meaning of separate words; the second lies in the domain of **lexical cooccurrence**—the combination of words in text.

As we know from the work of Ferdinand de Saussure, Louis Hjelmslev and Roman Jakobson, the linguistic activity of the Speaker is implemented along two orthogonal axes:

- On the paradigmatic (= "vertical") axis the Speaker selects from all linguistic units he has stored in his brain those he needs in the given speech act. These units are in opposition to each other: either X, or Y, or Z, etc.; logically, this is exclusive (= strict) disjunction. The Speaker has to decide which of these units he will actually use.

- On the syntagmatic (= "horizontal") axis the Speaker combines the selected units with each other: X, and Y, and Z, etc.; logically, this is conjunction. Here the Speaker has to decide whether the units selected can be combined, and if so, then in what way (which one precedes and which one follows, what kind of modifications such and such unit has to or can undergo, etc.)

Figure 9 shows schematically the selection and combination of units to produce the sentences *Father is quite satisfied, Dad is absolutely happy, My old man is fully contented*, etc.

This is why when we speak of the lexicon, we must deal both with lexical selection (*4.1*) and lexical cooccurrence (*4.2*).

4.1 MODELING LEXICAL SELECTION (PARADIGMATICS)

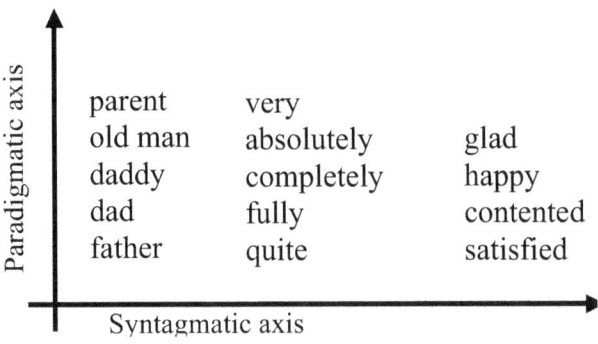

Figure 9. The two axes of speech activity

4.1 Modeling lexical selection (paradigmatics): semantic decompositions

The expressions *Orwell is sure that P* and *Orwell does not doubt that P* are synonymous:

1) They are mutually substitutable in an utterance without changing the meaning of the utterance—that is, *salva significatione*.*

2) Their negations are almost synonymous: *Orwell is not sure that P* ≅ *Orwell doubts that P* (the semantic difference between these two expressions will be explained below).

3) They are not factive—they do not presuppose the truth of P; both can be continued, for instance, as follows: ... *but in fact P is not true/P does not take place*.

The synonymy of these expressions is determined by particular correlations between the meaning of the adjective SURE and that of the verb $DOUBT_{(V)}$. What information is stored in the brain of an English speaker to allow him, without a split second's hesitation, to see the equality 'is sure' = 'does not doubt'? It is impossible to answer this

---

* The Latin phrase *salva significatione* literally translates as '[with] preserved meaning' and actually means 'so that meaning is preserved'; this is an absolute ablative construction $Adj_{ABL} + N_{ABL}$, also known as *Ablativus Absolutus*.

question through direct observation: we do not know how to see inside the brains of speakers to read the neurological encodings of words and their meanings. However, in line with what we have suggested above, we can propose a functional model of what happens.

Together with A. Zholkovsky, Ju. Apresjan, A. Bogusławski and A. Wierzbicka, I believe that the meaning of a word can and must be described in terms of simpler meanings—that is, decomposed. The **decomposition** of a meaning into simpler meanings is similar to the decomposition of living matter into cells, of any matter (including cells) into molecules, of molecules into atoms, of atoms into composite particles, and of composite particles into elementary particles.*

The idea of semantic decomposition, first developed in the 1960s by A. Bogusławski and A. Wierzbicka, is a natural fit with the prevailing scientific trends: for the description of an entity or a fact, science always proposes the identification of constituent elements and the establishment of links between them. (Semantic decompositions are examined in *5.3*, p. 142*ff.*)

Consider the following dataset ("#X" stands for 'linguistic expression X is pragmatically unacceptable'; ≡ and ≅ symbolize, respectively exact and approximate semantic equivalence, and ≠, the absence of such equivalence):

(27) a. *I believe that David is in Edmonton, but I am not sure of this.*
 b. *I am sure that David is in Edmonton, #but I don't believe this.*
 c. *I believe that David is in Edmonton, #but I doubt this.*
 d. (i) *I am sure that David is in Edmonton.* ≡
  (ii) *I don't doubt that David is in Edmonton.*
 e. (i) *I am not sure that David is in Edmonton.* ≅
  (ii) *I doubt that David is in Edmonton.*

For a speaker (or a computer) to be able to produce the sentences in (27), establishing their synonymy and pragmatical acceptability, it is

---

* Note, however, that the decomposition of a meaning is done in terms of simpler meanings, while the decomposition of matter into molecules and of the molecules in atoms etc. involves, on each step, entities of a different nature.

4.1 MODELING LEXICAL SELECTION (PARADIGMATICS)

sufficient to represent the meaning of the lexemes SURE and DOUBT$_{(V)}$ by means of the following decompositions, which actually are the **lexicographic definitions** of these lexemes:

(28) a. 'X is sure that P' = '|[believing that P,]| X is ready to not-accept [= reject] that it may be non-P'.
   b. 'X doubts that P' = '|[not believing that P,]| X is inclined to accept that non-P'.

☞ 1. The part of the definition that is included in special brackets ||[...]|| is presupposition.[19]
2. 'not believing that P' must be interpreted as 'it is not the case that X believes that P' rather than *'X believes that non-P'.

Using these definitions, one obtains for the sentences in (27) the following semantic decompositions (logical contradictions are shown by boldface):

(29) a. 'I believe that David is in Edmonton, but |[believing that David is in Edmonton,]| I am ready to accept [⇐ I am not ready to not-accept] that David may not be in Edmonton'.
   b. '|[**Believing that David is in Edmonton**,]| I am ready to not-accept that David may not be in Edmonton, but #**I don't believe that David is in Edmonton**'.
   c. '**I believe that David is in Edmonton**, but #|[**not believing that David is in Edmonton**,]| I am inclined to accept that David is in Edmonton'.
   d. '|[Believing that David is in Edmonton,]| I am ready to not-accept that David may not be in Edmonton'. = '|[Believing that David is in Edmonton,]| I am not inclined to accept that David may not be in Edmonton'.[20]
   e. '|[Believing that David is in Edmonton,]| I am ready to accept that David may not be in Edmonton'. ≈ '|[Not believing that David is in Edmonton,]| I am inclined to accept that David is in Edmonton'.

The sentences in (27e) are not fully synonymous: one intuitively feels that the second sentence, beginning with 'I doubt', expresses a higher degree of uncertainty than the first one with 'I am not sure'. This intuition is reflected in decompositions of (29e). Both sentences affirm that I accept ($\cong$ I am inclined to accept) that David is in Edmonton; however, the first one contains the presupposition that I believe that David is in Edmonton, while the second presupposes the absence of such a belief.

Thus, if one agrees with the proposed description of the meanings of SURE and DOUBT$_{(V)}$, it is possible to cover all the semantic facts presented in (27) fully, formally and consistently. The Meaning-Text approach is based on rigorous lexicographic definitions of the type shown in (28); these definitions are semantic decompositions—"molecular structural formulas" of meanings. They are drafted according to strict rules (Mel'čuk 2013: 283*ff*) and correspond to semantic equivalence rules of the Sem-module of the MTM (e.g., **R**^{Sem} **1**, p. 71). There are about one million ($\approx 10^6$) such rules, which correlates in an obvious way with the number of LUs in a language. The semantic decomposition of a meaning 'σ' constitutes the central part of the lexical entry for the LU L('σ') in the *Explanatory combinatorial dictionary* [= ECD], namely the lexicographic definition.

Along with the lexicographic definition of the head word L, L's lexical entry in an ECD contains a considerable amount of other types of information, most importantly, a detailed description of the cooccurrence patterns of L. Let me now turn to this new topic.

4.2 Modeling lexical cooccurrence (syntagmatics): lexical functions

Restricted lexical cooccurrence—capricious constraints on possible combinations of individual words that cannot be specified in terms of semantic or syntactic incompatibilities—creates well-known problems for lexicographic description and for linguistics in general. Anyone who had to grapple with a foreign tongue has learnt the hard way the extent to which lexical cooccurrence is whimsical and unpredictable. You *present* your COMPLIMENTS, but *offer* your APOLOGIES; you *fly into* a

4.2 MODELING LEXICAL COOCCURRENCE (SYNTAGMATICS)   91

RAGE, but you *sink into* DESPAIR; in Russian, you *fall into—vpadat'—* both RAŽ 'rage' and OTČAJANIE 'despair'. Something *fills* you *with* RAGE, but does not **drive* you *to* RAGE, while it can *drive* you *to* DESPAIR. You can be *completely* TIRED, but a Russian cannot: **soveršenno ustal*; Russians are *madly* (= *bezumno*) TIRED. One is *filthy* ⟨*stinking*⟩ RICH, but, amazingly, not **dirty* RICH. An American *takes* a STEP, but a Spaniard *gives* it (*dar un* PASO); a Frenchman and a Russian both *do* it (*faire un* PAS, *sdelat'* ŠAG). A DREAM [= 'images, feelings and thoughts that X experiences when asleep'] is *had* in English, but *done* in French (*faire un* RÊVE) and *seen* in Russian (*videt'* SON). A university course is *taught* in the USA, *given* in France (*donner un* COURS), and *read* in Russia (*čitat'* KURS). And so forth, *ad infinitum*!

These endless caprices have long been known; they are called collocations—phraseological expressions, or phrasemes, of a particular type. To describe them, the Meaning-Text approach makes use of the apparatus of lexical functions.

The notion of lexical function is based on the following fact: in most cases, individual lexical constraints on the cooccurrence of lexical units are related to the expression of quite special meanings. These meanings are very abstract (= general, poor) and not numerous: only few dozen. A stock example is the meaning 'very' ≈ 'intense', whose expression depends on the lexeme on which it bears semantically:

'very'(SLEEP$_{(V)}$) = *deeply, heavily, like a log, ...*
'very'(INJURED) = *badly, seriously* < *critically*
'very'(RAIN$_{(V)}$)   = *hard, heavily* < *cats and dogs*
'very'(RAIN$_{(N)}$) = *heavy* < *torrential*; *drenching, driving, soaking*
'very'(ALIKE)   = *as two peas in a pod*

☞ The symbol "<" is used to indicate a higher degree of intensity; the semicolon separates less synonymous expressions.

As one can see from these examples, the meaning 'intense(ly)' is expressed with the LU L_1 by a set of fairly synonymous LUs $\{L_{1-i}\}$, with L_2, by a set $\{L_{2-j}\}$, etc.; typically, $\{L_{1-i}\} \neq \{L_{2-j}\}$. Crucially, the choice between $\{L_{1-i}\}$ and $\{L_{2-j}\}$ cannot be described by any general rules, but has to be specified by lists; the choice is made as a function of L_1, L_2, etc.

Such a phenomenon is naturally described by means of a function (in the mathematical sense of the term) $\mathbf{f}_{'\sigma'}$: $\mathbf{f}_{'\sigma'}$ corresponds to the meaning 'σ' and associates with any x, on which 'σ' bears, all possible y_i that express 'σ':

$$\mathbf{f}_{'\sigma'}(x) = \{y_i\}, \text{ or } \mathbf{f}_{'\sigma'}(L) = \{L_i\}.$$

The LU L for which $\mathbf{f}_{'\sigma'}$ specifies the LUs L_i that express 'σ' as a function of L is the argument of the function $\mathbf{f}_{'\sigma'}$, and the set $\{L_i\}$ is its value. The above examples illustrate the function $\mathbf{f}_{'intense'}$. If we denote this function as Magn (*Lat. magnus* 'big, great'), we can write:

Magn(SLEEP$_{(V)}$) = *deeply, heavily, like a log, like a top, ...*
Magn(INJURED) = *badly, seriously < critically*
Magn(RAIN$_{(V)}$) = *hard, heavily < cats and dogs*
Magn(RAIN$_{(N)}$) = *heavy < torrential; drenching, driving, soaking, scudding*
Magn(ALIKE) = *as two peas in a pod*

Functions of this type are quite naturally called **lexical functions** [= LFs], since their arguments and the elements of their values are exclusively lexical units.

To avoid the infelicitous polysemy of the term *argument* (argument of a predicate ≠ argument of a lexical function), the argument of an LF $\mathbf{f}_{'\sigma'}$ will be called the **keyword** of $\mathbf{f}_{'\sigma'}$: in the above examples, the keywords are SLEEP$_{(V)}$, INJURED, etc.

A linguistic expression described by an LF $\mathbf{f}_{'\sigma'}$—an expression composed of the keyword L of $\mathbf{f}_{'\sigma'}$ and an element of $\mathbf{f}_{'\sigma'}$'s value $\{L_i\}$—is a **collocation** of L. L is called the **base** of the collocation, and the corresponding element of the value, the **collocate**.

4.2 MODELING LEXICAL COOCCURRENCE (SYNTAGMATICS)

The set of collocations of language **L** and the set of **L**'s expressions covered by LFs do not coincide:

- Some collocations are described not by LFs, but by the government pattern of L (see *5.4.3.2*, p. 158): for instance, in the collocations *health* INSURANCE (cf. *Fr.* ASSURANCE *maladie* lit. 'sickness insurance'), CONDEMN *to death/to life in prison* or *compassionate* LEAVE, the collocates correspond to the semantic actants of the base L; therefore, they are specified in the government pattern of L.
- Some LFs describe the derivatives of L rather than its collocates; see below.

All LFs share a conceptual core: **simple standard lexical functions**. Simple standard LFs have the following four important properties:

1) They are **linguistically universal**: the same simple standard LFs are valid for very different, and possibly all, languages—although the extent to which a given simple standard LF is "active" in a given language varies.

2) They are **not very numerous**: there are fewer than 60 simple standard LFs. Nevertheless, they are (almost*) sufficient to systematically describe not only most collocations in (or so I believe) most languages, but most derivations as well—see paradigmatic LFs below.

3) They are **systematic**: they maintain certain semantic-syntactic relations amongst themselves (for instance, Oper_1 is conversive with respect to Func_1; Fin is antonymous to Incep; etc.); and they can be united, according to simple general rules, to form complex standard LFs (such as IncepOper_1, AntiMagn, $\text{Caus}_1\text{Real}_1$, etc.).

4) They participate in **deep-syntactic paraphrasing** (see *3.3.2.3*, p. 76*ff*).

---

* This reservation is necessary since numerous collocations call for non-standard LFs.

Lexical functions have been described in detail in a series of publications (for the most recent overview, see Mel'čuk 2014: Ch. 14); here I will limit myself to a sketch.

LFs can be characterized according to the following three parameters:

– **Paradigmatic vs. syntagmatic LFs**. An element of the value of a paradigmatic LF $\mathbf{f}_{paradigm}(L) = \{L_i\}$ is used in the text **instead of** the keyword—replacing it, so to speak. An element of the value of a syntagmatic LF $\mathbf{f}_{syntagm}(L) = \{L_i\}$ is used in the text **together with** the keyword—in effect, completing it. Roughly speaking, paradigmatic LFs model (semantic) derivations, and syntagmatic LFs model collocations. A prime example of a paradigmatic LF is the action/state/property noun S_0: $S_0(discuss) = discussion$, $S_0(attack_{(V)}) = attack_{(N)}$, $S_0(sick) = sickness$, $S_0(capable) = capacity$, etc.; a prime example of a syntagmatic LF is the LF Magn, introduced above.

– **Standard vs. non-standard LFs**. The characteristic properties of standard (simple) LFs have just been formulated above. Non-standard LFs are characterized by four properties opposed to those just given:

1′) they are not language universal and have to be established for each particular language;

2′) they are numerous and cannot be theoretically foreseen, each having very few keywords (even just one keyword) and very few elements of the value (even just one element of the value);

3′) they are by no means systematic;

4′) they do not participate in DSynt-paraphrasing.

Here are three examples of non-standard LFs:

```
COFFEE
without dairy product                  : black [~]
NOSE
by expelling air through the N.
          X cleans it of mucus : blow [N_x's ~]
YEAR
having 366 days                        : leap [~]
```

4.2 MODELING LEXICAL COOCCURRENCE (SYNTAGMATICS)

As these examples demonstrate, a non-standard LF expresses a very specific meaning, which deprives it of having many keywords.

In what follows only standard LFs are systematically considered.

– Simple LFs *vs.* complex LFs *vs.* configurations of LFs.

Simple standard LFs are given by a list, a fragment of which is presented immediately below; for instance:

```
Anti (antonym)              [Anti(respect)   = despise]
Magn (intensifier)          [Magn(respect(N)) = deep, profound]
Incep (inceptive: 'begin')  [Incep(sleep(V)) = go to sleep]
Oper₁ (support verb)        [Oper₁(cold(N))  = have [ART ~]]
```

Complex standard LFs are built from simple LFs that are syntactically linked to each other, share the same keyword and are expressed by one lexical unit; for instance:

```
AntiMagn      [AntiMagn(respect(N)) = scant]
IncepOper₁    [IncepOper₁(cold(N))  = catch [ART ~]]
```
Magn(*apologize*) = *profusely*   vs.
         AntiMagn(*apologize*) = *perfunctorily*
Oper₁(*doubt*(N)) = *be* [*in* ~]   vs.
         IncepOper₁(*doubt*(N)) = *fall* [*into* ~]

Note that `AntiMagn` is an abbreviation for `Anti←ATTR–Magn`, while `IncepOper₁` stands for `Incep–I→Oper₁`. That is what I mean when I say that the simple LFs inside a complex LF are syntactically linked to each other.

A configuration of LFs consists of several LFs sharing the keyword and expressed by one LU, but not linked syntactically to each other; for instance:

[Bon₂ + Magn](*handshake*)   = *hearty* ('good and intense')
[Magn + IncepOper₁](*applause*) = *burst* [*in* ~]
                                   ('begin to produce intense applause')
[AntiMagn + Oper₁](*response*)   = *be muted* [*in* ~]
                                   ('give a mitigated response')

Each one of the simple and complex LFs inside a configuration of LFs is syntactically linked with the keyword; thus we have:

$[\text{Bon}_2 + \text{Magn}](L) = \text{Bon}_2(L)\leftarrow\text{ATTR}-L-\text{ATTR}\rightarrow\text{Magn}(L)$

$[\text{Magn} + \text{IncepOper}_1](L) =$
$\qquad\qquad \text{Magn}(L)\leftarrow\text{ATTR}-L\leftarrow\text{I}-\text{IncepOper}_1(L)$

I will now give a list of LFs; note, however, that it is purely illustrative and contains less than a fifth of the known LFs.

First, **paradigmatic LFs**, simple and complex.

1 – 3. LFs Syn (synonym), Anti (antonym) and Conv (conversive) play a special role in the LF system: they apply not only to LUs of a given language, but to other LFs as well. To put it differently, the following three semantic relations hold between LFs and complex expressions consisting of LFs (for the LFs appearing in the examples, see below):

- Synonymy, which means semantic equality—for instance, the following two expressions are synonymous:
  $\text{'L}_{(V)}\text{'} = \text{'S}_0(L_{(V)})\leftarrow\text{II}-\text{Oper}_1(S_0(L_{(V)}))\text{'}$.
- Antonymy, for instance, $\text{Fin} = \text{AntiIncep}$.
- Conversion, for instance, $\text{Labor}_{12}(L) = \text{Conv}_{132}\text{Oper}_1(L)$.

Syn, Anti and Conv can be loosely called "metafunctions."

Synonyms and antonyms are well known; I will say a few words about conversives.

The LF Conv_{ij} applies only to a lexical unit that expresses a predicate meaning and thus has semantic and deep-syntactic actants. "$\text{Conv}_{ij}(L_1) = L_2$" means that L_1 and L_2 have (roughly) the same meaning, but the DSynt-actants of one are permuted with respect to the same Sem-actants of the other as shown by the numerical subscript. Suppose that L_1's actants stand in the following relation: 'X' ⇔ I and 'Y' ⇔ II; then L_2 [= $\text{Conv}_{21}(L_1)$] shows an inverse relation between Sem- and DSynt-actants: 'X' ⇔ II, 'Y' ⇔ I. Thus, CONSIST = Conv_{21}(COMPOSE), as in *The team consists of five specialists* ≡ *Five specialists compose the*

4.2 MODELING LEXICAL COOCCURRENCE (SYNTAGMATICS)

team; similarly, WIN = Conv_{321}(LOSE): *John won two games against Pete* ≡ *Pete lost two games to John*.

These are examples of lexical conversions; many languages also have grammatical conversion: verbal voices. Thus, the passive form of a verb is a Conv_{21} of its active form:

John$_{\text{X'}\Leftrightarrow\text{I}}$ *wrote this novel*$_{\text{Y'}\Leftrightarrow\text{II}}$. ≡
This novel$_{\text{Y'}\Leftrightarrow\text{I}}$ *was written by John*$_{\text{X'}\Leftrightarrow\text{II}}$.

I continue with the list of paradigmatic simple LFs.

4. S_0 is the name of an action, a state, a property, etc.: S_0(*shoot*) = *fire*$_{(N)}$ [*They were shooting at us* ~ *Under their fire, we...*], S_0(*increase*$_{(V)}$) = *increase*$_{(N)}$, S_0(*many*) = ⌈*a lot*⌉, S_0(*equal*) = *equality*, S_0(*beautiful*) = *beauty*.

5. S_1 is the name of an agent—that is, of an entity that performs an action, is in a state, possesses a property, etc.: S_1(*shoot*) = *shooter*, S_1(*steal*) = *thief*, S_1(*influence*) = *factor*, S_1(*beautiful*) = [*a*] *beauty*.

6. S_2 is the name of a patient—that is, of an entity that undergoes an action: S_2(*shoot*) = *target*, S_2(*steal*) = *loot*$_{(N)}$, S_2(*laugh*$_{(V)}$) = *laughing stock*, S_2(*award*$_{(N)}$) = *recipient, holder*.

7. Able_1 is the "adjective of possibility" ('such that is capable of/ inclined to ...'): Able_1(*persist*) = *persistent*, Able_1(*rebellion*) = *rebellious*, Able_1(*afraid*) = *cowardly*, Able_1(*angry*) = *bad-tempered*.

Now, a few **syntagmatic LFs**, also simple and complex.

8. The adjective Bon [≈ 'good' = 'approved by the Speaker'; a clichéd praise]:

Bon(*contribution*) = *valuable*
AntiBon(*victory*) = *hollow; Pyrrhic*
Bon(*condition*) = *mint* < *superb*
AntiBon(*crime*) = *vicious*
Bon(*future*) = *brilliant, radiant*
AntiBon(*future*) = *bleak*

9-11. Semi-auxiliary (= light, or support) verbs Oper, Func and Labor. They are semantically empty in that they are selected not for their meaning, but are instead selected automatically as a function of the deep-syntactic role played by their keyword: `Oper` takes L as DSynt-actant II, `Func` takes L as DSynt-actant I, and `Labor` takes L as DSynt-actant III.

$\text{Oper}_1(order_{(N)})$ = give [ART ~]
$\text{Oper}_1(attention)$ = pay [~]
$\text{Oper}_1(responsibility)$ = bear [~]
$\text{Oper}_2(danger)$ = face [ART ~]
$\text{Oper}_3(order)$ = have [ART ~]

$\text{Func}_0(curfew)$ = is in place
$\text{Func}_1(aid)$ = comes [from N_X]
$\text{Func}_1(responsibility)$ = rests [with N_X]
$\text{Func}_2(danger)$ = threatens [N_Y]
$\text{Func}_3(ultimatum)$ = calls [for N_Z]

$\text{Labor}_{12}(list_{(N)})$ = put [N_Y on ART ~]
$\text{Labor}_{12}(applause)$ = greet [N_Y with ~]
$\text{Labor}_{32}(lease)$ = take [N_Y on ~]

☞ The numerical subscripts to the name of a support-verb LF specify, as with other LFs, the syntactic behavior of the LF actants. More precisely:

– **With Oper_i**, the subscript indicates which DSynt-actant of the keyword is the syntactic subject of this `Oper`: $\text{Oper}_1(exam)$ = give, while $\text{Oper}_2(exam)$ = take.

– **With Func_i**, the subscript indicates which DSynt-actant of the keyword is the first syntactic object of this `Func`: **Func_0**(curfew) = is in place [no object], **Func_1**(stress [language]) = falls [on N_X], **Func_2**(controversy) = surrounds [N_Y].

– **With Labor_{ijk}**, the subscripts indicate which DSynt-actants of the keyword are the subject, the first and the second syntactic object of this `Labor`: $\text{Labor}_{123}(inheritance)$ = receive [N_Y from N_Z in ~], $\text{Labor}_{213}(inheritance)$ = come [to N_X from N_Z in ~], $\text{Labor}_{321}(inheritance)$ = leave [N_Y to N_X in ~].

12. The preposition Loc_{in} expresses standard spatial or temporal localization with respect to the keyword:

$\text{Loc}_{in}(station)$ = at [ART ~] $\text{Loc}_{in}(country)$ = in [ART ~]
$\text{Loc}_{in}(street)$ = on [ART ~] $\text{Loc}_{in}(point)$ = at [ART ~]
$\text{Loc}_{in}^{temp}(year)$ = in [ART ~] $\text{Loc}_{in}^{temp}(month)$ = Λ [~] (next month)

Since in English the values of the LF Loc_{in} are not very rich, let me give here a small table of its possible values in four languages (Bierwisch 2011: 353).

	French	Dutch	German	Korean
in a pot	*dans*	*in*	*in*	*nehta*
in a case	*dans*	*in*	*in*	*kkita*
on a finger	*à*	*om*	*an*	*kkita*
on a cube	*sur*	*op*	*auf*	*kkita*
on a table	*sur*	*op*	*auf*	*nohta*
on the head	*sur*	*op*	*auf*	*ssuta*
on a hook	*à*	*aan*	*an*	*kelta*

The specification of LFs for the headword L constitutes an important part of the lexical entry for L in an *Explanatory Combinatorial Dictionary*, previously mentioned in *3.3.2.2*, p. 73; see also *5.4*, p. 151. A headword L, be it a lexeme or an idiom, is supplied with a list of LFs applicable to it, with their values and constraints on the selection of value elements. Thus, a lexical entry for L contains all the collocations where L appears as the base.

As already noted, LFs are linguistically universal: they ensure the systematic description of semantic derivatives and restricted lexical cooccurrence (that is, collocations) of any language in terms of the same formal means. Such a description facilitates the comparison of languages and the translation between them in this domain; LFs play the role of a very efficient interlingua. To illustrate, let us consider the values of two syntagmatic LFs—the intensifier Magn and the support verb Oper_1—for six structurally very different languages: English, Arabic, Chinese, German, Hungarian, and Russian. The keywords—that is, the arguments of these LFs—are semantically equivalent (or, at least, semantically very close).

English

```
Magn(rain(N))      = heavy
Magn(argument)     = cogent, convincing, strong < knock-down
Magn(applause)     = thunderous
```

Oper₁(*trip*) = *take* [ART ~]
Oper₁(*agreement*) = *reach* [ART ~], *come* [*to* ART ~]
Oper₁(*resistance*) = *offer* [ART ~]
Oper₁(*apologies*) = *present* [A₍poss₎(N_X) ~s]

Arabic

Magn(*maṭar* 'rain₍N₎') = *ġazīr* 'abundant', *qawijj* 'strong'
Magn(*ḥuǯǯa* 'argument') = *dāmiġa* 'striking', *qawijja* 'strong'
Magn(*taṣfīq* 'applause') = *ḥārr* 'hot'
Oper₁(*safar* 'trip') = *qāma* [*bi* ~] 'stand up to'
Oper₁(*ʔittifāq* 'agreement') = *tawaṣṣala* [*ʔila* ~] 'arrive at'
Oper₁(*muqāwamat* 'resistance') = *qāma* [*bi* ~] 'stand up to'
Oper₁(*ʔiʕiðarāt* 'apologies') = *qaddama* [ART ~_ACC] 'put forth'

Chinese (the symbols "¯, ´, `, ˇ " denote tones)

Magn(*yǔ* 'rain₍N₎') = *dà* 'big'
Magn(*lùnjù* 'argument') = *yǒulì-de* 'strong'
Magn(*zhǎngshēng* 'applause') = *léidòng* 'thunderous'
Oper₁(*lǚtú* 'trip') = *tàshang* [~] 'go on'
Oper₁(*xiéyì* 'agreement') = *dáchéng* [~] 'arrive at'
Oper₁(*dǐkàng* 'resistance') = *shíshī* [~] 'realize'
Oper₁(*qiànyì* 'apology') = *biǎoshì* [~] 'express'

German

Magn(*Regen* 'rain₍N₎') = *starker* 'strong', *Platz-* 'bursting'
Magn(*Argument* 'argument') = *gewichtiges* 'weighty', *schlagendes* 'striking', *unschlagbares* 'unbeatable', *unwiderlegbares* 'irrefutable'
Magn(*Beifall* 'applause') = *tosender* 'roaring'
Oper₁(*Reise* 'trip') = [ART ~_ACC] *machen* 'make'
Oper₁(*Übereinkunft* 'agreement') = [ART ~_ACC] *erzielen* 'obtain, reach'
Oper₁(*Widerstand* 'resistance') = [N_Y-DAT ART ~ACC] *leisten* 'deliver'
Oper₁(*Entschuldigung* 'apology') = [N_Y-ACC *um* ~_ACC] *bitten* 'beg, ask'

Hungarian (the symbols " ´, ˝ " denote long vowels; cz = /č/, gy = /ɟ/, ly = /j/, s = /š/)

    Magn(*eső* 'rain₍N₎')   = *zuhogó* 'torrential'
    Magn(*érv* 'argument')   = *komoly* 'serious'
    Magn(*taps* 'applause')   = *viharos* 'whirl-', *vas-* 'iron-'
    Oper₁(*utazás* 'trip')   = [~t]   *tenni* 'do'
    Oper₁(*megegyezés* 'agreement') = [~re] *jutni* 'arrive at'
    Oper₁(*ellenállás* 'resistance') = [~t]   *kifejteni* 'develop',
                                                  tanusítani 'demonstrate'
    Oper₁(*boczánat* 'pardon₍N₎') = [~ot] *kérni* 'beg'

Russian

    Magn(*dožd´* 'rain₍N₎')   = *sil´nyj* 'strong'
                                    < *prolivnoj* 'torrential'
    Magn(*dovod* 'argument')   = *veskij* 'weighty',
                                      ser´ëznyj 'serious',
                                      ubeditel´nyj 'convincing' <
                                      sokrušitel´nyj 'crushing'
    Magn(*applodismenty* 'applause') = *burnye* 'tempestuous',
                                      gromovye 'thunderous'
    Oper₁(*putešestvie* 'trip')   = *soveršit´* [~e] 'accomplish'
    Oper₁(*soglašenie* 'agreement') = *prijti*   [k ~ju] 'come to'
    Oper₁(*soprotivlenie* 'resistance') = *okazat´* [~e] ≈ 'demonstrate'
    Oper₁(*izvinenija* 'apologies') = *prinesti* [N_{Y-DAT}
                                      (*svoi* 'oneself's) ~*ja*] 'bring'

These examples demonstrate, once more, to what extent the values of LFs differ for semantically (almost) equivalent lexemes of different languages: applause, which is "thunderous" in English, is "hot" in Arabic, "thunderous" (as in English) in Chinese, "iron" in Hungarian, "roaring" in German, and in Russian, "tempestuous" (while "thunderous" and "hot" are also possible); let me add that in French intense applause is "fed" (*nourri*). LFs allow some order to be introduced into this chaos. The linguistic universality of LFs ensures a compact statement of the interlinguistic semantic correspondences between the values of a given LF for semantically equivalent keywords of different languages. It is practically impossible to do this in a different way. How, indeed, should one indicate in a Russian-English dictionary that the verb PRIOBRETAT' 'acquire' is translated as DEVELOP or FORM when the object is PRIVYČKA 'habit'? Or in an English-French dictionary that KICK can correspond to RENONCER 'renounce' if the object is HABIT? And this is necessary, since *priobretat' privyčku* ≡ *develop ⟨form⟩ a habit*, while *kick the habit* ≡ *renoncer à une habitude*. If the values of the same LF are specified in the lexical entries of the lexemes HABIT, HABITUDE and PRIVYČKA, the necessary correspondences are established mechanically, see Table 1.[21]

	HABIT	≡ Fr. HABITUDE	≡ Rus. PRIVYČK|A
IncepOper₁ ('begin to have')	acquire, develop, form [ART ~], get [into ART ~], take [to ART ~]	contracter 'contract', prendre 'take' [ART ~]	priobretat' 'acquire' [~u]
FinOper₁ ('cease to have')	drop [ART ~], get out, get rid [of ART ~]	abandonner 'abandon', perdre 'lose' [ART ~]	utratit' 'lose' [~u]
LiquOper1 ('cause to cease to have')	break [N_x of ART ~], wean [N_x] away [from ART ~]	détacher 'detach', détourner 'divert' [N_x de ART ~]	otučit' lit. 'unlearn' [N_{X-ACC} ot ~i]
Liqu₁Oper₁ ('cause oneself to cease to have')	break off, kick, shake off, throw off [ART ~]	se débarrasser 'get rid', se défaire 'rid oneself' [de ART ~], renoncer 'renounce' [à ART ~], rompre 'break' [avec ART ~]	otkazat'sja 'renounce', otučit'sja lit. 'unlearn oneself' [ot ~i]
CausFunc₁ ('cause to be at X')	instill [ART ~ in(to) [N_x]	inculquer 'inoculate' [ART ~ à N_x]	privit' 'inoculate' [N_{X-DAT} ~u]

Table 1: Several Lexical Functions and the Elements of their Values for Three Semantically Equivalent Lexical Units of Different Languages

4.3 Correlations between paradigmatic and syntagmatic aspects of lexeme behavior

The meaning and cooccurrence patterns of lexemes are essentially linked. The presence of these deep relations buttresses the hypotheses about the meanings of lexemes by taking into account the cooccurrence of lexemes in utterances. Let us consider three examples.

Example 1, Russian

(30) a. *Ja *očen' uveren, čto David v Èdmontone*
  'I am very sure that David is in Edmonton'. ~
  Ja absoljutno ⟨= soveršenno⟩ uveren, čto David v Èdmontone
  'I am absolutely ⟨perfectly⟩ sure that David is in Edmonton'. ~
vs.
b. *Ja očen' ⟨= sil'no⟩ somnevajus', čto David v Èdmontone*
  'I very much ⟨strongly⟩ doubt that David is in Edmonton'. ~
  Ja *absoljutno ⟨*soveršenno⟩ somnevajus', čto David v Èdmontone
  'I absolutely ⟨perfectly⟩ doubt that David is in Edmonton'.

Why do [*byt'*] UVEREN '[be] sure' and SOMNEVAT'SJA 'doubt$_{(V)}$' have an inverse cooccurrence with intensifiers (= values of the LF Magn)? The semantic decompositions of UVEREN and SOMNEVAT'SJA are identical to those of their English equivalents proposed in (28a-b), and they provide an answer to this question:

(31) a. 'X uveren, čto P' ('X is sure that P') =
  = '|[believing that P,]| X is ready to not-accept that it may be non-P'.
b. 'X somnevaetsja, čto P' ('X doubts that P') =
  = '|[not believing that P,]| X is inclined to accept that non-P'.

The central, or generic, component in the definition of UVEREN 'sure' is '**ready = gotov**'. An intensifier of UVEREN should bear on this component, but it is logically impossible to intensify a state of readiness: if you are ready, you are ready, period. You cannot say **očen' gotov* 'very ready', and therefore you cannot say **očen' uveren* 'very sure'. (The case of *very sure* will be considered at the end of this example.) But if you are **not** ready, you can be closer to or further from readiness, so that you can say *ne vpolne gotov* lit. 'not entirely ready' or *počti gotov* 'almost ready': the closeness to readiness is gradable. It is therefore not surprising that *ne vpolne/počti uveren* 'not entirely/almost sure' is a grammatical phrase. On the contrary, the affirmation itself (the corresponding speech act) can be intensified—not, of course, in the sense of 'very' or 'more', but in the sense of the Speaker's insistence on what he is stating: "**Absolutely**!" (what is known as rhetorical intensification). That is why the adverbs ABSOLJUTNO 'absolutely', SOVERŠENNO 'perfectly', TAK 'so' and NASTOL′KO 'to such a degree' cooccur with UVEREN (*On tak/nastol′ko uveren, čto Maša prava!* 'He is so/to such a degree sure that Masha is right!').

The verb SOMNEVAT′SJA 'doubt$_{(V)}$' presents a different picture. The central component in its definition is '**inclined** = **sklonen**', and this psychological state, of course, allows degrees: one can be more or less, a little or very inclined [to do Y], so that OČEN′ 'very' and SIL′NO 'strongly' cooccur with SOMNEVAT′SJA quite naturally, as well as SLEGKA 'slightly' and NEMNOGO 'a little'. (An interesting detail: the correctness of *On slegka* ⟨= *nemnogo*⟩ *somnevaetsja, čto* ... lit. 'He slightly ⟨a little⟩ doubts that ...' confirms the choice of 'inclined' over, for instance, 'ready', as the central component in the definition of SOMNEVAT′SJA: you cannot be *⟨slightly ⟨a little⟩ ready'.)

Now, at this point, an attentive reader might ask why this example uses the Russian lexemes UVEREN 'sure' and SOMNEVAT′SJA 'doubt$_{(V)}$' rather than the English SURE and DOUBT$_{(V)}$, if semantically they are identical ('uveren' = 'sure', 'somnevat′sja' = 'doubt')? The answer is as follows: because the English lexemes do not present the kind of clearcut picture one needs for a good illustrative example. In English, in spite of semantic incompatibility, you can say *very sure*! This is a case of a **phraseologized** rhetorical intensifier. (We have seen a case of a phraseologized negation in *4.1*, (27d-ii), p. 88.) A phrase with an intensifier is a **collocation** described by the lexical function Magn—that is, a phraseological expression; therefore, there is nothing astonishing for a particular language, in this case, English, to have an arbitrary, "countersemantic" coccurrence in such an expression. One sees this in other cases like the arbitrary cooccurrences *Rus. vpolne uveren* lit. 'entirely sure' vs. **polnost'ju uveren* lit. 'in.entirety sure', etc.

Example 2

The noun APPLAUSE is defined in *LDOCE Online* as 'the sound of many people hitting their hands together and shouting, to show that they have enjoyed something'; if we take out the superfluous components 'many' (even one person can applaud) and 'and shouting' (a crowd can applaud without vocalizing) and replace 'something' by 'somebody's acts' (you applaud somebody's having done something), this definition at first glance appears to be sound. However, what about these very frequent collocations: *frenetic ⟨frenzied, tempestuous, thunderous, ...⟩ applause* vs. *faint ⟨reluctant, scattered, subdued, ...⟩ applause*? They characterize the "degree" of applause that is proportional to the degree of satisfaction; but the above definition does not contain an explicit component that could receive gradation. Thus, the cooccurrence of the noun APPLAUSE with such adjectives as FRENETIC *vs.* RELUCTANT requires us to add to its definition the component characterizing the 'hitting': 'of a particular force and frequency'; this component will undergo gradation. But no sooner have we introduced this component than we discover another drawback of the traditional definition: it does not indicate that the force and frequency of hitting hands together is proportional to the degree of enjoyment. Here is the corrected definition:

'applause by X addressed to Y for Y's acts Z' = 'sound of X's hitting the hands together in order to show to Y X's approval/enjoyment of Y's acts Z, the force and frequency of this hitting being proportional to the degree of X's approval/enjoyment of Z'.

Example 3, Russian (Iordanskaja 2007)

(32) a. *Ivan **gorjačo** ugovarival*$_{\text{IMPERF}}$ *menja soglasit'sja*
   lit. 'Ivan passionately was.talking me into.accepting'.
   vs.
   b. *Ivan ***gorjačo** ugovoril*$_{\text{PERF}}$ *menja soglasit'sja*
   lit. 'Ivan passionately has.talked me into.accepting'.

What explains the different cooccurrence of two elements of the same lexeme, members of the aspectual pair UGOVARIVAT´ 'try to talk into…' and UGOVORIT´ 'have talked into…'? Consider the definitions of the verb in both aspects.

<u>Imperfective aspect</u>

'X ugovarivaet Y-a Z-it´' ('X is trying to talk Y into doing Z') =

'|[X wanting Y to Z, while Y does not want to Z,]|
    X is talking to Y with the goal that this cause1 Y to agree to Z'.

<u>Perfective aspect</u>

'X ugovoril Y-a Z-it´' ('X has talked Y into doing Z') =

'|[X wanting Y to Z, while Y does not want to Z, and X talking to Y with the goal that this cause1 Y to agree to Z,]|
    X has thereby caused2 Y to agree to Z'.

☞ 'Cause1' and 'cause2' are, respectively, semantemes of involuntary and voluntary causation: 'be the cause of' *vs.* 'be the causer of'.

The meaning of the perfective form UGOVORIT´ includes the meaning of the imperfective form UGOVARIVAT´; 'ugovorit´$_{PERF}$' (= 'have talked into') ≈ 'have caused2 by *ugovarivanie* ('trying to talk into')'. Now, the meaning 'ugovarivat´$_{IMPERF}$' (= 'try to talk into') is part of the presupposition in the meaning of 'ugovorit´'.* The adverb GORJAČO 'passionately', which describes the manner of talking, must semantically bear on the meaning 'talk' within both definitions. However, in 'ugovorit´$_{PERF}$' ('have talked into') this turns out to be impossible. Based on a wealth of similar data, Iordanskaja concludes that:

|| A modifier of a verb V cannot semantically bear on a component of V's definition if this component is part of the presupposition.

To put it another way, the presuppositions in the definition of L form a "no-go" zone that is outside the semantic scope of L's modifiers.

This conclusion can be buttressed by the following example:

―――――――
* This fact was noted in Apresjan 1980 [1995: 59].

(33) a. *The company made a **serious** accusation against the applicant.*
vs.
b. *The company ***seriously** accused the applicant.*

The incorrectness of (33b) is explained by the same principle.

ACCUSE, verb, transitive
'X accuses Y of Z in front of W' =
  '|[X believing that Z is bad,]|
   X tells W that Y is responsible for Z'.

The meaning of the modifier SERIOUSLY must reinforce the meaning 'bad', but 'bad' is within the presupposition—that is, inaccessible for external modification; as a result, sentence (33b) is ungrammatical. As for the noun ACCUSATION, since a noun cannot express a statement (or a judgment), a noun's definition is not divided into assertion and presupposition:

ACCUSATION, noun
'X's accusation of Y of Z in front of W' =
  'statement by which X accuses Y of Z in front of W'

The presupposition of ACCUSE remains inside of ACCUSE—it does not become a presupposition of ACCUSATION. Therefore, nothing prevents the correct use of the adjective SERIOUS to be felicitously used with ACCUSATION in (33a).

The restricted lexical cooccurrence of an LU L is in principle linked to L's meaning: the presence of a particular component in a particular position in the definition of L can condition the existence of the value of a given LF **f** for L and, at least in some cases and to some degree, the appearance of particular elements of **f**(L).

The three examples given above all illustrate correlations between L's meaning and L's **restricted** lexical cooccurrence; however, the same type of correlation exists between L's meaning and L's **free** cooccurrence, the latter correlations being even richer. Thus, the combinability/incombinability of L with numerals allows one to establish for the Russian noun KARTOŠKA 'potato' a sense—that is, a lexeme—'one tuber', which is absent from a quasi-synonymous KARTOFEL´ 'potato' (*tri kartoški* 'three potatoes' ~ *tri kartofelja). In an analogous way, one can see a semantic difference between English ONION and Russian LUK 'onion': *three onions* ~ *tri luka (ONION has the sense 'one bulb', while LUK does not; to count onions, Russian uses a noun GOLOVKA lit. 'little head': *Daj mne tri golovki luka* lit. 'Give me three little.heads of.onion!').

To sum up: Lexical cooccurrence is directly observable, while the components of a lexicographic definition are not. However, some of these components can be proven to exist precisely because of their necessary role in lexical cooccurrence. The MTM, as a functional model of natural language, should be able to reveal linguistic phenomena that are otherwise "invisible." These examples clearly demonstrate this ability.

Chapter 5
Meaning-Text Linguistics

It is now the opportune moment to discuss the substantive properties of Meaning-Text linguistics (its formal properties were characterized in 2.3.3, p. 31*ff*). The following topics are vital for a good understanding of this approach:

- The emphasis on the **passage from meaning to text**, rather than on text itself (5.1).
- A close attention to the **concepts used** and the corresponding terminology (5.2).
- Formal description of **meaning** (5.3).
- A central place for the **lexicon** (5.4).
- **Syntactic dependencies** rather than constituents (5.5).

Dealing with these topics, it is impossible to avoid some technicalities. I hope, however, that *ad hoc* explanations and examples will help the reader get through them unscathed; besides, readers have at their disposal a Subject and Name Index with a glossary, pp. 229–253).

5.1 Meaning-Text linguistics and the direction of linguistic description: from meaning to text

The Meaning-Text approach proposes that the linguist studies and describes linguistic phenomena not simply as he perceives them statically—as **texts**, but as the results of their production starting from their meaning—that is, dynamically, as **pairs** ⟨meanings, texts⟩. In other words, the right perspective for describing a linguistic expression (or a class of expressions) X is the description of the correspondence 'X' ⇔ X; the Meaning-Text principle is applied literally. Two examples, one taken from Spanish phonology (5.1.1), and the other from Russian syntax (*5.1.2*), will show to what extent the "static" (pure text) and the "dynamic" (meaning ⇒ text) descriptions can differ.

5.1.1 Example 1: Spanish "semivowels"

The set of Spanish phonemes (on phoneme, see Note 10, p. 203) is established virtually without problems. The only exception are so-called semivowels, [i̯] and [u̯], found, for instance, in such words as [bi̯én] *bien* 'well', [bu̯éno] *bueno* 'good', [péi̯ne] *peine* 'comb' and [neu̯mático] *neumático* 'pneumatic'.* Traditionally, they are considered to be allophones of the vowel phonemes /i/ and /u/, since the phones [i] ~ [i̯] and [u] ~ [u̯] are in a strict complementary distribution: the first (= vowel) appears under stress or not contiguous to another vowel, the second (= semivowel) appears not under stress and contiguous to a vowel. If we consider the distribution of Spanish sounds in a ready-made text, everything is OK. But as soon as we try to construct a functional model that produces Spanish wordforms—that is, to elaborate the morphological module of a Spanish MTM—the situation changes dramatically.

Spanish verbal forms have a variable stress, but the placement of stress is determined by a few simple rules that have no exceptions. In particular, in the singular of the present indicative the stress is always on the last vowel of the verbal stem: **bromé**+*o* 'I joke', **escój**+*es* 'you choose', **escríb**+*e* 's/he writes', etc. However, if we take, for instance, the verbs *bail*+*ar* 'dance' and *ahil*+*ar* 'go in single file' [the letter *h* is silent in Spanish], we run into a problem: what are their stems phonemically? If we accept the "monophonemic" treatment of the pairs [i] ~ [i̯] (that is, if we say that both are allophones of /i/) and [u] ~ [u̯] (both being allophones of /u/), the final edges of both stems look alike: /bail-/ and /ail-/, the last vowel in both is the phoneme /i/. However, in terms of the placement of stress, in the present indicative these verbs have different forms in the 1SG: [bái̯l+o] 'I dance', but [aíl+o] 'I go in single

---

* For the sake of simplicity, I ignore the fact that, depending on their position before or after a vowel, the semivowels in question each have two variants: more consonantic [j]/[w] or less consonantic [i̯]/[u̯].

5.1 THE DIRECTION OF LINGUISTIC DESCRIPTION

file' (*[baíl+o], *[áil̯+o]). If their phonemic structures were similar, these stems would have—according to the standard stress rule—the form *[baíl+o] and [aíl+o]; if we were to change the rule in order to obtain the correct form [báil̯+o], this rule would automatically produce the incorrect *[áil̯+o]. Spanish has a host of such verbal pairs:

agriar	'turn sour'	[áɣri̯o]	~ *aliar*	'ally'	[alío]
anestesiar	'anesthetize'	[anestési̯o]	~ *amnistiar*	'amnesty'	[amnistío]
anunciar	'announce'	[anúnθi̯o]	~ *rociar*	'sprinkle'	[r̄oθío]
arraigar	'become ingrained'	[ar̄ái̯ɣo]	~ *ahijar*	'adopt'	[aíxo]
cambiar	'change'	[kámbi̯o]	~ *enviar*	'send'	[embío]
envidiar	'be envious'	[embíði̯o]	~ *confiar*	'trust'	[komfío]
pairar	'drift'	[pái̯ro]	~ *ahincar*	'urge'	[aíŋko]
peinar	'comb'	[péi̯no]	~ *prohibir*	'prohibit'	[proíβo]
reinar	'reign'	[r̄éi̯no]	~ *rehilar*	'quiver'	[r̄eílo]

The situation with the semivowel [u̯] is identical. Under a "monophonemic" description of the pairs [u] and [u̯], the stems of such verbs as *atestiguar* 'testify' and *evacuar* 'evacuate' end in the same vowel phoneme: /atestigu-/ and /ebaku-/; but their 1SG forms differ again: [atestíɣu̯+o] 'I testify' *vs.* [eβakú+o] 'I evacuate' (*[atestiɣú+o], *[eβáku̯+o]). Such verbal pairs are also quite numerous:

averiguar	'find out'	[aberíɣu̯o]	~ *evaluar*	'evaluate'	[eβalúo]
defraudar	'deceive'	[defráu̯ðo]	~ *acentuar*	'accentuate'	[aθentúo]
fraguar	'forge'	[fráɣu̯o]	~ *graduar*	'graduate'	[graðúo]
incautar	'impound'	[iŋkáu̯to]	~ *actuar*	'act'	[aktúo]
menguar	'diminish'	[méŋgu̯o]	~ *continuar*	'continue'	[kontinúo]
paular	'chat'	[páu̯lo]	~ *aullar*	'howl'	[aúλo]
pausar	'interrupt'	[páu̯so]	~ *ahumar*	'smoke'	[aúmo]
restaurar	'restore'	[r̄estáu̯ro]	~ *aupar*	'hoist up'	[aúpo]

Therefore, if we consider the production (= synthesis) of Spanish verbal forms, we have to conclude that the phones of the pairs [i] ~ [i̯] and [u] ~ [u̯] belong, respectively, to two different phonemes. Examining contexts in which the phones [i̯] and [u̯] appear, we see that from a phonemic perspective these phones are **neither vowels nor consonants**:

they are glides. Thus, we obtain, for Spanish, four phonemes: the vowels /i/ ~ /u/ and the glides /j/ ~ /w/ (Mel'čuk 2006: 543*ff*). If all four of these phonemes are not included into the phonemic inventory of Spanish, it would not be possible to synthesize the observable phonetic forms of numerous verbs in the 1ˢᵗ person singular of the present indicative in a regular and predictable manner.

5.1.2 Example 2: Russian binominative sentences

Consider the following two Russian sentences:

(34) a. *Stolica Francii – Pariž* lit. 'Capital of.France—Paris'
      = 'The capital of France is Paris'.
   b. *Pariž – stolica Francii* lit. 'Paris—capital of.France'
      = 'Paris is the capital of France'.

Which noun is the syntactic subject in these sentences—STOLICA 'capital' or PARIŽ 'Paris'?

In both sentences both these nouns are in the nominative case, so that the sentences of this type are called **binominative**; Russian has no explicit copula in the present, and its word order is highly flexible. The question asked above has been fiercely debated for many decades, and several criteria have been put forth to determine the syntactic subject in a binominative sentence. Here are three of the most popular criteria:

1) Transformation of the sentence in the past tense, where the copula 'be' is necessary: the subject remains in the nominative, while the second element, the copular attribute, gets the instrumental.

2) The agreement of the copula in the past tense: it agrees with the subject, except when the subject is ÈTO 'this'. If the subject is ÈTO, the copula agrees with the attribute (just the opposite of English):

  Èto byl+$\emptyset_{MASC}$ Vanja   'This was Vania'.
vs. *Èto byl+a$_{FEM}$ Tanja*   'This was Tania'.
vs. *Èto byl+i$_{PL}$ Vanja and Tanja* lit. 'This were Vania and Tania'.

3) The subject is more referential than the attribute (Padučeva & Uspenskij 1979).

When applied to sentences in (34), all three criteria work well—namely, they identify PARIŽ 'Paris' as the subject, which corresponds to speakers' intuition: *Stolic+ej*$_{\text{(fem)INSTR}}$ *Francii byl+Ø*$_{\text{MASC.SG}}$ *Pariž*$_{\text{(masc)NOM}}$ 'Paris was the capital of France' (PARIŽ remains in the nominative with the copula in the past tense; the copula agrees with PARIŽ; and PARIŽ is more referential than STOLICA 'capital (city)'; **Stolic+a*$_{\text{(fem)NOM}}$ *Francii byl+a*$_{\text{FEM.SG}}$ *Pariž+em*$_{\text{(masc)INSTR}}$ 'The capital of France was Paris' is ungrammatical). However, in many types of sentence these criteria do not help. Thus, where is the subject in sentences (35)?

(35) a. *Xorošij urožaj – èto udobrenija* lit. 'Good crop—this fertilizers'. ≈ 'Good crops require/involve fertilizers'.
  b. *Udobrenija – èto xorošij urožaj* lit. 'Fertilizers—this good crop'. ≈ 'Fertilizers mean/ensure good crops'.

Changing these sentences into the past tense produces the following results:

(36) a. *Xorošij urožaj – èto byl+i*$_{\text{PL}}$ *udobrenija*$_{\text{PL}}$
   lit. 'Good crops—this were fertilizers'.
  b. *Udobrenija – èto byl+Ø*$_{\text{MASC.SG}}$ *xorošij urožaj*$_{\text{(masc)SG}}$
   lit. 'Fertilizers—this was good crop'.

The agreement of the verb does not give a strong indication as to what the subject is (as noted above, in the presence of ÈTO the copula agrees with the attribute); and it is difficult to say which one of the two nouns in (35) is more referential. In such cases, Russianists traditionally say that sentences of the type in (35) present a case of syntactic indeterminacy: it is impossible to identify the syntactic subject in them. If we consider sentences already in the text, such an answer can be tolerated (although having to accept defeat rankles some). However, if we want to describe the construction of such sentences starting from their semantic structure, such a solution becomes unacceptable: the Speaker knows quite well who is who and what is what in his meaning, and the output sentence must have a full correct syntactic structure for the Meaning-Text model to be able to construct and implement it. Therefore, we have to look for other ways to determine the syntactic subject of a sentence—based on the passage from its semantic to its syntactic structure.

Let me sketch out, in general lines, the production of the sentences in (35).

☞ In order to simplify, the adjective XOROŠIJ 'good' is omitted from the structures.

(37) a. SemS of sentence (35a)   b. DSyntS of sentence (35a)

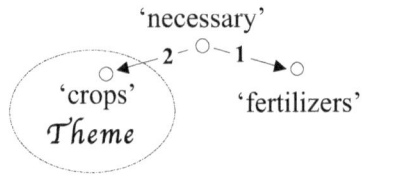 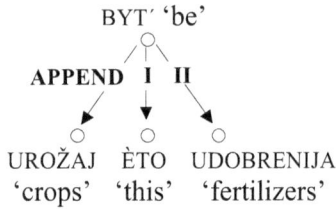

(38) a. SemS of sentence (35b)   b. DSyntS of sentence (35b)

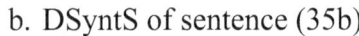
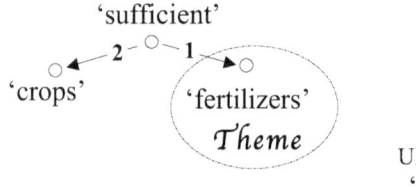 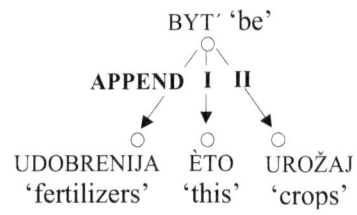

The first noun in these sentences is syntactically a **prolepsis**, and it expresses the (focalized) Theme of the sentence; the second noun is a copular attribute. The syntactic subject in both sentences is the pronoun ÈTO 'this'.

Note that, if, in the structures of (37) and (38), we replace the nouns UROŽAJ and UDOBRENIJA by the variables X and Y, we obtain the SemS ⇔ DSyntS semantic transition rules for the meanings 'necessary' and 'sufficient':

Dlja poezdki neobxodimo mnogo deneg
    lit. 'For trip is.necessary much money'. =
    'The trip requires much money/is very costly'. ≡
Poezdka – èto mnogo deneg lit. 'Trip—this much money'. =
    'The trip requires much money'.

5.1 THE DIRECTION OF LINGUISTIC DESCRIPTION

and

Učastie Lëni dostatočno dlja uspexa
  lit. 'Lyonya's participation is.sufficient for success'. =
  'Lyonya's participation is sufficient for success'. ≡
Učastie Lëni – èto uspex
  lit. 'Lyonya's participation—this success'. =
  'Lyonya's participation means/entails success'.

Let me now demonstrate how the MTM maps a semanteme 'σ' onto two radically different syntactic structures: 'σ' can be realized either through lexical or syntactic means. As 'σ', I take 'necessary' and 'sufficient', and the syntactic realizations are in Russian; the transition rules are given without communicative conditions.

(39) a.

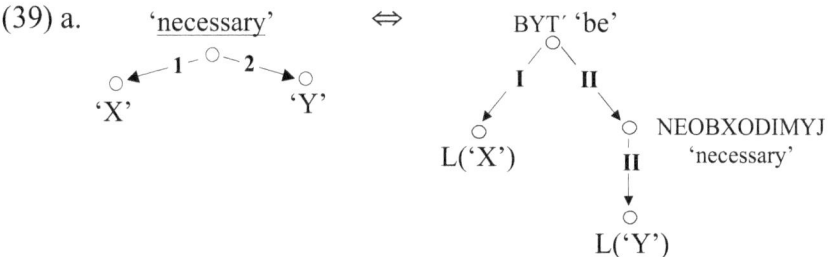

Udobrenija neobxodimy dlja xorošego urožaja
'Fertilizers are necessary for good crops'.

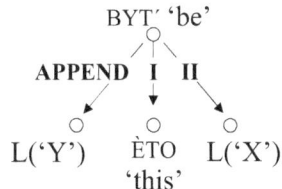

Xorošij urožaj – èto udobrenija
'Good crops require fertilizers'.

b.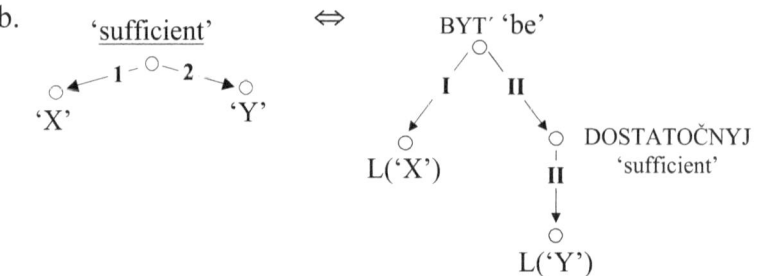

Učastie Lëni dostatočno dlja uspexa
'Lyonya's participation is sufficient for success'.

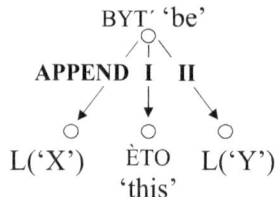

Učastie Lëni – èto uspex
'Lyonya's participation guarantees success'.

5.2 Meaning-Text linguistics and a linguistic conceptual apparatus

After some introductory remarks (*5.2.1*), three groups of linguistic notions are presented: linguistic sign (*5.2.2*), "word" (*5.2.3*) and the closely related terms case, ergative construction and voice (*5.2.4*).

5.2.1 Introductory remarks

Unlike all other sciences, linguistics has the following particularity:

> The object of linguistics and its main tool are the same—natural language.

Linguists use natural language in order to talk about natural language, the obvious result being conceptual confusions and logical incongruities. Because of this, the creation of a sufficiently formalized conceptual apparatus and the elaboration of a corresponding rigorous terminology is much more important for linguistics than for any other science (where the object of study and the language of description are completely different).

The Meaning-Text approach reserves pride of place to rigorously defined notions and unambiguous terms that express these notions. Developing a linguistic **metalanguage** ensures the unity of our field and allows different linguistic descriptions of the same phenomena to be compatible—that is, mutually translatable.

From its very inception in 1950s, the notional orientation of research in the Meaning-Text approach was based on the work of a group of French mathematicians who, in 1935, formed a scientific team under the pseudonym "Nicolas Bourbaki"; see Halmos 1957 and Queneau 1963. Bourbaki set out to create a unified formal apparatus and unified formal metalanguage for all of modern mathematics. Inspired by the ideas of "moderate Bourbakism" (I think that formalisms in linguistics are good only up to a point), I launched a project aimed at a system of linguistic notions: Mel'čuk 1975 and 1978. About 20 years of work produced a relatively complete, even if not exhaustive, deductive system of notions and a corresponding terminology for linguistic morphology: Mel'čuk 1993–2000. Starting with a handful of *indefinibilia* —concepts borrowed from logic and mathematics, but also from other domains of linguistics—this book proposes rigorous definitions for 249 morphological notions—such as linguistic sign, representability of signs in terms of other signs, wordform, lexeme, radical *vs.* affix, inflectional category and grammeme, case, voice, morph *vs.* morpheme, suppletion, reduplication, alternation, apophony, etc.

These notions have been constructed in accordance with the following three rules:
- A notion should be **defined deductively**—that is, as the most general subtype of the closest superordinate notion, its *genus proximum* 'the closest kind'. For instance, we want to define the notion of *phraseme*. A phraseme is 'a phrase which…'; therefore, all phrases

of a language must be exhaustively partitioned into phrasemes and non-phrasemes.

- The set of defining properties must **be minimal**, to ensure the minimal differences between notions: whenever possible, a single property distinguishing two notions. Thus, for phrasemes and non-phrasemes such a property is 'being constrained': a constrained phrase is a phraseme, a non-constrained phrase is a non-phraseme—that is, a free phrase.
- A notion must be based on **prototypical (= core) cases** of the phenomenon being defined (leaving aside, for the moment, marginal cases, which have to be taken into account by additional conditions).

It goes without saying that the definitions proposed satisfy all standard formal requirements imposed on all scientific definitions: a correct definition is 1) formal (= applicable automatically), 2) rigorous (= only contains terms that have been already defined or are indefinable), 3) necessary and sufficient (= specifies all defining properties and avoid all non-defining ones) and 4) saturated (= covers all entities/facts that intuitively correspond to the notion defined). For more details, see Mel'čuk 2006b.

5.2.2 Linguistic sign

The notion of the linguistic sign, which underlies the proposed conceptual system, goes back to the well-known definition by Ferdinand de Saussure (de Saussure 1916 [1962: 99]): "A linguistic sign is a psychic two-side entity «Concept ~ Acoustic image»." However, a bit further on the same page, «Concept» is replaced with «Signified», and «Acoustic image»—with «Signifier». I believe that these terms are more convenient by virtue of their more general character; therefore, the Saussurian definition of linguistic sign, restated by me in modern terms, reads:

‖ A linguistic sign is the pair ⟨Signified, Signifier⟩.

5.2 A LINGUISTIC CONCEPTUAL APPARATUS

At present, the bilateral character of linguistic signs is common knowledge. But before Saussure—and not infrequently, for a long time after him—the linguistic sign has been considered to be a unilateral entity: *sign* has been erroneously identified with what Saussure called *signifier*.

☞ In all probability, the confusion is explained by the meaning of the words *sign*, *signe*, *Zeichen*, ... in natural languages: as a rule, they denote what Saussure called *signifier*. This is a beautiful illustration of the idea that linguistics needs its own, well-defined metalanguage, different from a natural language. A similar situation with the term *word* is examined below, in *5.2.3*.

The notion of linguistic sign as the pair ⟨Signified, Signifier⟩ has played a role in linguistics similar to that played in modern mathematics by the notion of set, introduced by G. Cantor in 1883.

Nevertheless, the Saussurian notion of sign, while absolutely necessary, turns out to be insufficient:

‖ The pair ⟨Signified, Signifier⟩ does not completely specify the sign.

For instance, here is a pair ⟨Signified, Signifier⟩:

⟨'object X goes down under the surface of liquid Y'; /sínk/⟩

This pair is supposed to denote the lexeme [*to*] SINK, but it does not show that it is a verb, that its past form is *sank*, that it governs the preposition INTO (*The boat sank into the lake*), etc. Another pair of the same type

⟨'X constitutes connection between Y and Z'; /línk/⟩

denotes the lexeme [*to*] LINK, but again without showing that it is a verb, that its past form is *linked*, that it governs a noun N and the preposition WITH (*This train links Paris with Belgium*), that X is called [*a*] LINK, etc.

However, without this type of information the corresponding signs cannot be correctly used in utterances.

The unavoidable conclusion is that the linguistic sign needs a third component, containing all the data of this type. I called that component **syntactics** (Mel'čuk 1982: 26–28).

Now a definition of the notion 'linguistic sign' can be formulated—a definition comprising all the necessary components which, taken together, are sufficient.

Definition 3: Linguistic sign (Mel'čuk 1982: 40–41)
> A linguistic sign is an ordered triplet
> $$\mathbf{s} = \langle \text{Signified, Signifier, Syntactics} \rangle.$$

Notations: 's' stands for a signified, /s/ for a signifier, and Σ for syntactics.

The stem of the verb WRITE1 is, of course, a sign of English (an elementary segmental sign—a morph, see below):

write1 =
= ⟨'X forms symbols Y on surface Z with tool W', /rá¹t/,
$$\Sigma = \text{verb, transitive,} \mathbf{A}_{\text{PAST}}^{a^I \Rightarrow o^O}, \mathbf{A}_{\text{PART}}^{a^I \Rightarrow I}, \ldots \rangle$$

The phrase *write a capital N* is also a sign (but a **complex compositional sign**):

write a capital N =
= ⟨'X writes1 a capital N on surface Z with tool W', /rá¹təkǽpɪtəlén/,
$$\Sigma = \text{verbal phrase, intransitive,} \ldots \rangle$$

Let me demonstrate how the Meaning-Text approach develops the notions of the three components of a linguistic sign.

Signified. Most often, the signified of a sign is a chunk of meaning: 'book' (the sign **book-**), 'excellent' (**excellent-**), 'around the town' (**around the town**), 'Germany's unprovoked military invasion of Belgium's territory' (**Germany's aggression against Belgium**), etc. This is, however, not the only possibility; a signified of a linguistic sign can also be:

- empty, see below, (46), p. 126;
- a grammeme (or a set of grammemes): SG (the signs **-Ø, -us, -um,** …); PAST (**-ed, -t,** …); FEM, SG, DAT (the sign *Rus.* **-oj**, an adjectival suffix);

- a surface-syntactic relation [= SSyntRel]: L₁–**direct-objectival**→L₂, L₁–**modificative**→L₂, etc., expressed by a syntactic construction.

Signifier. Most often, the signifier of a sign is a string of phonemes, called a **segment**; a sign with a segmental signifier is called **segmental**. An elementary* segmental sign is called a **morph**. Morphs constitute the overwhelming majority of elementary signs of any language. Here are a few examples (morphs are separated by a "+" symbol):

(40) a. **money+less, re+enter+ed, key+Ø** vs. **key+s, down, Phew!**

  b. Alutor
  na + rrə   + tkəni+ɣəm 'I have nightmares'. =
  3.PL_SUB give.nightmares PRES 1.SG_OBJ lit. 'They [= spirits] give me nightmares'.

  c. German
  Spät+herbst+wald+es   'of [the] late-fall forest'
  late   fall   wood   SG.GEN

A signifier can also be empty, see (47), p. 127; furthermore, there is a host of non-segmental signs, which I will characterize now:

– suprafixes;

– reduplications, apophonies and conversions;

– syntactic constructions.

- **Suprafix** [= **Supr**] is a non-segmental sign whose signifier is a prosodeme.

(41) Chinantec: suprafixes that express the modality, the tense and the person-number in the verb.

Superscripts mark the tones: ^{H} (high), ^{M} (middle) and ^{L} (low); a combination of two tone symbols indicates a complex tone. The symbol " ´ " identifies a short intense syllable.

  a. *tá*^{ML} 'I am chopping'   vs. *tá*^{HL} 'I will chop'
  b. *ta*^{M} 'We are arriving' vs. *ta*^{H} 'Will we arrive?'

---

* A sign is called **elementary** iff it cannot be represented in terms of two or more other signs.

(41a) presents two suprafixes:

Supr$^{\text{DECLAR, PRES, 1, SG}}$ = ⟨DECL, PRES, 1, SG; ^{ML} ;
   Σ = suprafix, applies to Vs of the TÁ type, ...⟩
Supr$^{\text{DECLAR, FUT, 1, SG}}$ = ⟨DECL, FUT, 1, SG; ^{HL} ;
   Σ = suprafix, applies to Vs of the TÁ type, ...⟩

The first of these suprafixes expresses 1st person singular in the present of the declarative; this is shown by the middle–low tone on the verb. This suprafix applies to the verbs marked as "TÁ type" in their syntactics.

(41b) presents two other suprafixes:

Supr$^{\text{DECLAR, PRES, 1, PL}}$ = ⟨DECL, PRES, 1, PL; ^{M} ;
   Σ = suprafix, applies to Vs of the TA type, ...⟩
Supr$^{\text{INTERROG, FUT, 1, PL}}$ = ⟨INTERR, FUT, 1, PL; ^{H} ;
   Σ = suprafix, applies to Vs of the TA type, ...⟩

- **Reduplications [= Red], apophonies [= A]** and **conversions [= Conv]** are non-segmental signs which have as their signifiers the corresponding morphological operations.

Reduplication

(42) Dyirbal

'laugh'   *miyanday* ~ *miyamiyanday* 'laugh too much'
'wait'   *miḍul*   ~ *miḍumiḍul*   'wait too much'
'paint oneself' *gulgiṛibil* ~ *gulgigulgiṛibil* 'paint oneself too much'

                             radical **R**
                         ⎴⎴⎴⎴⎴⎴⎴⎴⎴⎴
Red$_{\text{TOO-MUCH}}$ = ⟨'too much'; /C$_1$V$_1$C$_2$(C$_3$)V$_2$Φ/ ⇒ /C$_1$V$_1$C$_2$(C$_3$)V$_2$**R**/;
   Σ = reduplication, applies to Vs, ...⟩

☞ /Φ/ stands for any string of phonemes.

5.2 A LINGUISTIC CONCEPTUAL APPARATUS

<u>Apophony</u>, or meaningful (= semantically loaded) alternation

(43) Yiddish: two apophonies that express the plural of the noun.

	SG	PL		SG	PL
'bank'	bank ~	benk	'day'	tog ~	teg
'neck'	haldz ~	heldz	'head'	kop ~	kep
'guest'	gast ~	gest	'bird'	foygl ~	feygl

	SG	PL
'brother'	bruder ~	brider
'son'	zun ~	zin
'cow'	ku ~	ki

$\mathbf{A}_{PL}^{a/o \Rightarrow e}$ = ⟨PL; {/a/, /o/} ⇒ /e/;
Σ = apophony, applies to Ns of **A** type, ...⟩

$\mathbf{A}_{PL}^{u \Rightarrow i}$ = ⟨PL; /u/ ⇒ /i/;
Σ = apophony, applies to Ns of **A** type, ...⟩

<u>Conversion</u> (morphological)

(44) Spanish: a conversion that produces the name of the tree from the name of a fruit.

'apple'	manzan+a	~	'apple tree'	manzan+o
'plum'	ciruel+a	~	'plum tree'	ciruel+o
'cherry'	cerez+a	~	'cherry tree'	cerez+o
'orange'	naranj+a	~	'orange tree'	naranj+o

Conv$_{TREE}$ = ⟨'tree bearing fruits Y'; fem ⇒ masc ; Σ = conversion, applies to N$_{('fruit', fem)}$, ...⟩

The marker of the meaning 'tree bearing fruits Y' is the substitution "fem ⇒ masc" in the syntactics of the name of fruit Y (this substitution automatically entails the replacement of the gender-marking suffix: **-a** ⇒ **-o**).

- **Syntactic constructions**, whose signifier is a particular configuration of parts of speech supplied with appropriate syntactic features (the signified is a syntactic dependency relation).

(45) Russian

$$\text{NUM} + ... + \text{N} \mid \textbf{AGREE(Num, N)}$$

☞ " ... " shows the possibility for inserting lexical material, e.g., adjectives; **AGREE(Num, N)** is a set of rules that describe the agreement of the numeral with the quantified noun and the governed forms of the noun.

This construction expresses the SSyntRel **quantitative**:

$$\text{SSyntRel}_{\text{QUANT}} = \langle L_1\text{–quantitative}\rightarrow L_2 \;;$$
$$\text{NUM} + ... + \text{N} \mid \textbf{AGREE(Num, N)} \;;\; \Sigma = ...\rangle$$

dvadacat' odin+$\emptyset_{\text{MASC}}$	*stol*$_{\text{(masc)}}$ +$\emptyset_{\text{SG, NOM}}$	'21 tables' ~
dvadacat' odn+a_{FEM}	*skam'*$_{\text{(fem)}}$ +$ja_{\text{SG, NOM}}$	'21 benches'
dv+a_{MASC}	*stol*$_{\text{(masc)}}$ +$a_{\text{SG, GEN}}$	'two tables' ~
dv+e_{FEM}	*skam'*$_{\text{(fem)}}$ +$i_{\text{SG, GEN}}$	'two benches'
pjat'	*stol*$_{\text{(masc)}}$ +$ov_{\text{PL, GEN}}$	'five tables' ~
pjat'	*skam*$_{\text{(fem)}}$ +$ej_{\text{PL, GEN}}$	'five benches'

Syntactics. The syntactics of a linguistic sign contains all and only information about this sign that is (i) necessary to its correct use in an utterance and (ii) cannot be naturally deduced by general rules either from its signified or signifier (that is, from this perspective, syntactics is, in most cases, arbitrary, being idiosyncratic to the **s** in question). Thus, the pragmatic incorrectness of the phrase #*drink honesty* follows from the incompatibility of these words' signifieds and therefore it should not be specified in their syntactics. The same is true of the phrase *a option: the correct form *an option* is determined by a general rule (*a* | __/C/, *an* | __/V/), which should not, of course, be placed in the syntactics of the noun OPTION.

Formally, syntactics is a set of syntactic features each of which has a particular set of values. A few examples of syntactic features follow:

1) Every sign has a feature defining its morphological type:

   {wordform, morph, morphological operation, supramorph, ...}

2) Every morph is specified for its morphological status:

   {radical; affix: prefix, suffix, infix, transfix, interfix}

5.2 A LINGUISTIC CONCEPTUAL APPARATUS

3) <u>Every radical</u>[22] is specified for the following kinds of syntactic information, none of which can be supplied by general rules:

  (i) Part of speech: {verb, noun, adjective, adverb, clausative[23]}

  (ii) Declension/Conjugation

  (iii) Government pattern

  (iv) Lexical functions

  (v) Possible alternations

  (vi) Stylistic label: {formal, informal, colloquial, slang, poetic, ...}

A radical of a noun must be also specified for its

  (vii) Gender/Noun class

(viii) Countability: {countable, non-countable}[24]

4) <u>Every affix</u> is specified as to:

  (i) The part of speech of the "hosting" radical:

    {nominal, verbal, adjectival, adverbial suffixes}

  (ii) Its linear position with respect to the "hosting" radical

  (iii) Any alternations that the affix triggers in the "hosting" radical

The syntactics of a linguistic sign is presented as a right subscript to the name of the sign in parentheses; for instance: $\text{FOOT}_{(N, A_{PL})}$, $\text{SLEEP}_{(V, A_{PAST}, \text{Magn: } profoundly, like\ a\ log)}$, etc.

Now an important statement can be formulated:

> Only the signs of **natural languages** have syntactics (in the above-defined sense.

The signs of formal languages—such as those used by mathematicians, computer scientists, physicists, chemists, etc.—do not have syntactics. They are used—that is, combined with other signs—according to their meaning (= their signified). In a natural language, on the other hand, the syntactics of its signs is arbitrary—in principle, it cannot be specified by general rules. Such is the gender of nouns in languages like French and Russian: we have *la* $\text{TABLE}_{(\text{fem})}$ 'the table' vs. *le* $\text{MEUBLE}_{(\text{masc})}$ 'the piece of furniture' in French or *odin* $\text{DIVAN}_{(\text{masc})}$ 'one sofa' vs. *odna*

KROVAT′$_{(fem)}$ 'one bed' vs. *odno* LOŽE$_{(neu)}$ 'one couch, bed [in former times]' in Russian, etc. A formal language never has anything similar. True, a symbol in this or that formal language might have complex enough rules of use, but these rules concern either the meaning or the form of the symbol. Take, for instance, the mathematical symbol of summing: $\sum_{i=1}^{n} i$. Let us put it into the standard form of a sign:

summing = ⟨'sum of *i* consecutive integers from 1 to n'; $\sum_{i=1}^{n} i$ ⟩

This symbol needs no syntactics.

> Natural language is the only semiotic system whose signs include syntactics as an integral component.

This formulation can be taken as another definition of natural language.

Interestingly, syntactics is the only component of a linguistic sign that can never be empty: so now is a good moment to turn to this new subject.

<u>A signified can be empty</u>: empty signs.

(46) a. Empty radicals

A good example of an empty radical comes from Eskimo. Eskimo renders a number of verbal meanings only by suffixes added to a noun: thus, 'buy' is expressed by the suffix **-si**, 'make [in the sense of 'manufacture']'—by the suffix **-lior**, etc.; the language has no corresponding verbs. To say 'buy N', you add the suffix **-si** to the noun N. Thus, 'tent' is **tupi-** in Eskimo; 'buy a tent' is **tupi+si-**, 'make a tent' is **tupi+lior-**, etc. Now, to denote the activity itself of buying and making things, Eskimo uses a "filler"—an empty nominal radical **pi-** and says **pi+si-** 'be busy buying things', **pi+lior-**'be busy making things', etc.

    Eskimo empty nominal radical
    pi- = ⟨Λ ; /pi/ ; Σ = radical, noun, ...⟩

  b. Empty affixes

    Spanish empty thematic elements [= Them.El]
    *habl+**a**+mos* '[we] speak' ~ *corr+**e**+mos* '[we] run'
                                ~ *dorm+**i**+mos* '[we] sleep'

5.2 A LINGUISTIC CONCEPTUAL APPARATUS

Them.El = ⟨Λ ; /a/ ; Σ = suffix, attaches to Vs of type "V-a", ...⟩
Them.El = ⟨Λ ; /e/ ; Σ = suffix, attaches to Vs of type "V-e", ...⟩
Them.El = ⟨Λ ; /i/ ; Σ = suffix, attaches to Vs of type "V-i", ...⟩

A signifier can also be empty: zero signs.

(47) a. Zero radicals

The zero radical of the demonstrative pronominal adjective in Kirundi

Kirundi has four demonstrative pronominal adjectives, three of which are presented in the table below—for 6 out of 12 noun classes:

Demonstrative adjective \ Noun class	I	II	III	IV	V	VI
'this—close to you$_{SG}$'	*uw+o*	*ab+o*	*uw+o*	*iy+o*	*iry+o*	*ay+o*
'this—close to him/her'	*u +rya*	*ba+rya*	*u +rya*	*i +rya*	*ri +rya*	*a +rya*
'that—far from us'	*u +riiya*	*ba+riiya*	*u +riiya*	*i +riiya*	*ri +riiya*	*a +riiya*

The form of a Kirundi demonstrative adjective consists of a **radical** (**-o, -rya** and **-riiya**)[25] and a **noun class** prefix, which marks the agreement of the adjective with the noun modified. However, the fourth demonstrative adjective, meaning 'this—close to me', presents a curiosity: **uwu, aba, uwu, iyi, iri, aya**, etc. Its forms consist of a noun class prefix, which is not followed (within the borders of the wordform) by anything. However, a prefix—by definition—must precede a radical; we conclude that these forms have a zero radical (a radical whose signifier contains zero phonemes):

$Ø_{1SG}$ = ⟨'this—close to me'; Λ ; Σ = radical, adjective, pronominal, demonstrative, ...⟩

b. Zero suffixes

Russian is rich in zero suffixes, for instance:

SG.NOM *róg+Ø* 'horn'   PL.GEN *rog+óv* 'of.horns';
ROG$_{(masc)}$ is a noun of second declension

SG.NOM *nog+á* 'foot'   PL.GEN *nóg+Ø* 'of.feet';
NOGA$_{(fem)}$ is a noun of first declension

SG.NOM = ⟨SG.NOM ; Λ ; Σ = suffix, attaches to masculine Ns of second declension, ...⟩

PL.GEN = ⟨PL.GEN ; Λ ; Σ = suffix, attaches to Ns of first declension, ...⟩

What is more, both the signified and the signifier of a sign can be simultaneously empty, which gives a rather paradoxical type of sign—a sign possessing syntactics only: empty zero signs. Good examples of this are the zero expletive and meteorological pronouns in Pro-Drop languages.[26] For instance:

(48) Spanish

    a. $\varnothing^{\text{expletive}}$ *Se vive bien aquí* lit. '[**It**] lives oneself well here'. = 'One lives well here'.
    b. $\varnothing^{\text{meteo}}$ *Llueve* '[**It**] rains'.

In such sentences, the Main Verb is in the 3rd person singular, but there is no "visible" subject—nothing that would correspond to the English IT in *It rains*. However, in the general case, in all other sentences, the grammemes of person and number are imposed on a Spanish Main Verb by agreement with its subject; therefore, we conclude that in (48) the verb agrees with a zero dummy subject $\varnothing_{\text{3SG}}$, corresponding to the non-zero dummies *Eng.* IT (*It rains*), *Fr.* IL (*Il pleut*) and *Ger.* ES (*Es regnet*):

$\varnothing_{\text{3SG}}$ = ⟨Λ ; Λ ; Σ = wordform, pronoun, 3, SG, ...⟩

This "amputee" sign, without an actual signified and an actual signifier, exists exclusively thanks to its syntactics.

For the overwhelming majority of linguistic signs, the signified, which is a configuration of semantemes, specifies the infinite set **D** of real entities or facts to which this sign points.* The set **D** is called the sign's denotation. Thus, the denotation of the noun SCREEN is the set of all imaginable screens, including those that do not as yet exist. But when the noun SCREEN appears in a specific utterance, for instance,

---

* Strictly speaking, a linguistic sign points to a mental image of an extralinguistic fact or entity, but I can ignore this subtlety here.

5.2 A LINGUISTIC CONCEPTUAL APPARATUS

in (49), it can specify one concrete element of the set **D**(SCREEN): sentence (49) means **the** screen which we were watching at the moment:

(49) *We could not take our eyes off the screen.*

This element is called the referent of the sign **s** in the given utterance.

☞ The denotation of a sign is the set of all its possible referents. The crucial distinction between the linguistic sign, its signified and its denotation/referent was established by G. Frege: Frege 1892.

I have already insisted on the importance of the referential status of a sign **s** for the description of **s**'s functioning in an utterance.

Having finished with the characterization of linguistic sign, I can conclude by emphasizing its importance for linguistics. The notion of linguistic sign underlies all morphological notions:

– a morph is an elementary segmental sign;
– a radical is a morph whose syntactics is mostly interlexemic (concerns the cooccurrence of wordforms in an utterance);
– an affix is a morph that is not a radical;
– a wordform is an autonomous minimal sign; for more, see Mel'čuk 1982 and 1993–2000.

All central notions of syntax—such as phrase, clause, sentence, syntactic structure, etc.—are stated in terms of wordforms and dependency relations between them: therefore, the notion of sign is no less vital to syntax than it is to morphology. Semantics and lexicology are entirely based on the notion of semanteme, which is the signified of a lexical unit, in particular, of a lexeme; a lexeme, in its turn, is a set of wordforms and phrases (= analytical forms) that only manifest inflectional distinctions (for instance, *take, takes, took, has taken, will be taking*, etc.). Wordforms and phrases that express analytical forms are, of course, linguistic signs. Moreover, the main linguistic operation—linguistic union $\oplus$—is defined on the set of all signs of a given language: $s_1 \oplus s_2 = s_3$, as in **bush-** $\oplus$ **-es** = **bushes** or **sing-** $\oplus$ **A**$_{PAST}$ = **sang**. The operation $X \oplus Y$ means uniting the linguistic entities X and Y according to the rules of language **L** (taking into account the relevant properties of X and Y).

The notion of compositionality, so important for linguistics (especially, for the description of phraseology), is also formulated in terms of signs, as they are defined in the Meaning-Text approach.

Definition 4: Compositionality of a complex linguistic sign

> A complex sign s_1s_2 is called compositional if and only if s_1s_2 may be written as $s_1 \oplus s_2$; this means that the three components of the complex sign s_1s_2—its signified, signifier and syntactics—can be constructed, out of the corresponding components of the constituent signs s_1 and s_2, according to rules of **L**:
>
> 's_1s_2' = 's_1' $\oplus$ 's_2'; /s_1s_2/ = /s_1/ $\oplus$ /s_2/; and $\Sigma_{s1 \oplus s2} = \Sigma_{s1} \oplus \Sigma_{s2}$.

5.2.3 Word

The concept of word, in spite of its vagueness, is of vital importance for linguistics. However, as far as I know, there is still no rigorous and formal universally accepted definition of "word." One of the likely reasons for this is, quite probably, the same as in the case of *sign*—namely, the polysemy and vagueness of the word *word* in natural languages. Sharpening the concept of "word" is only possible within the framework of a sufficiently formalized notional apparatus. To illustrate my point, I will offer here the definitions not of "word," which, as I think, cannot be formally defined, but of notions that are invoked to replace it. These definitions are drastically simplified; for their full versions, see Mel'čuk 1993–2000: vol. 1, 167–252.

The first step is to draw a distinction, on the one hand, between a wordform and a lexeme (both entities are loosely called "words"), and, on the other hand, between a wordform of language and a wordform of speech.

Informally, a wordform is a word taken in one sense and in a particular grammatical form. Thus, for the verbs $PAINT_{(V)}1$ 'put paint on a

5.2 A LINGUISTIC CONCEPTUAL APPARATUS

surface ...' ~ PAINT$_{(V)}$2 'produce a painting ...', the corresponding signs **paint1, paints1, painted1, painting1** ~ **paint2, paints2, painted2, painting2**, etc. are different wordforms. Formally speaking, a wordform is a linguistic sign which is, in most cases, complex (except in isolating languages—that is, languages that have little or no morphology). A wordform is defined by two properties: autonomy and minimality. I will now introduce these two notions.

Definition 5: Autonomy of a linguistic sign

A linguistic sign s_1 is called autonomous iff:
- Either s_1 is strongly autonomous—that is, it can appear between two full pauses.
- Or s_1 is weakly autonomous—that is, it cannot appear between two full pauses, but
  1) s_1 can form, together with a strongly autonomous sign s_2, a strongly autonomous complex sign s_1s_2; and
  2) s_1 satisfies one of the three conditions of weak autonomy: it is separable, or unselective, or transmutable.

Otherwise, a linguistic sign is non-autonomous.

The three conditions of weak autonomy are hierarchically ordered: if the first one is met, this is sufficient to establish the weak autonomy of the sign; otherwise, the second condition has to be checked. If the second condition is met, the sign is also weakly autonomous; otherwise, recourse is had to the third condition. If it is met, the sign is still weakly autonomous. The sign is non-autonomous iff it fails the three conditions.

- **Separability.** A sign s_1 is separable from s_2 within the strongly autonomous complex sign s_1s_2 iff it can be linearly separated from s_2 by a strongly autonomous sign s_3 added to s_1s_2, so that we obtain $s_1s_3s_2$. For instance, in Russian, the preposition **v** 'into' [= s_1] normally cannot be uttered alone; but both **komnatu** 'room$_{ACC}$' [= s_2] and **v komnatu** 'into room$_{ACC}$' [= s_1s_2] are strongly autonomous, and in the phrase *v našu komnatu*, the possessive adjective **našu**

[= s_3] 'our' also is strongly autonomous; therefore, **v** is separable and, as a consequence, it is a weakly autonomous sign.

- **Unselectivity**. A sign s_1 is unselective iff its use is not limited to cooccurrence with s_2 (or with signs of s_2's type). For instance, again in Russian, the emphatic particle **že** ≈ 'as for' is not separable from the wordform on which it bears (it is a clitic,[27] more precisely—a postclitic), and it can attach to a wordform of any class and type: *Ty že utrom ne zvonil* lit. 'As for you, you did not call in the morning' ~ *Ty utrom že ne zvonil* lit. 'As for the morning, you did not call' ~ *Ty utrom ne zvonil že* lit. 'As for calling, in the morning you didn't call'; therefore, **že** is a weakly autonomous sign.

- **Transmutability**. A sign s_1 is transmutable iff, in different contexts, it is linearly positioned with respect to s_2 in different ways. A Spanish adverbal clitic s_1 is not separable from its governing verb s_2 and is highly selective (it only combines with finite verbs, infinitives or gerunds); yet it is weakly autonomous because it changes its position with respect to s_2:

(50) Spanish

a. *¡Tómalo!* 'Take it!' ~ *¡No lo tomes!* lit. 'Don't take it!'
[postposition with an affirmative imperative *vs.* anteposition with a negative imperative]

b. *Quisiera poder tomarlo*   '[I/He/She] would.like be.able take it'.
~
Lo quisiera poder tomar lit. '[I/He/She] it would.like be.able take'.

Definition 6: Minimality (of a linguistic sign)

> A linguistic sign **s**—autonomous or non-autonomous—is called minimal iff it cannot be represented in terms of two or more signs of the same type as itself.

The English simple signs **ballet** and **school** are autonomous and minimal, while the complex sign **ballet school** is autonomous, but, of course, not minimal: **ballet school** = **ballet** ⊕ **school**. Similarly, the suffixes **-er** (*eat+er*) and **-s** are non-autonomous minimal signs, while the complex sign **-ers** is non-autonomous, but not minimal: **-ers** = **-er** ⊕ **-s**.

Having introduced the auxiliary notions of autonomy and minimality of a linguistic sign, I am ready for the definition of wordform.

Definition 7: Wordform

> A segmental linguistic sign **s** is a **wordform** iff it is autonomous and minimal.

Autonomy separates wordforms from parts of wordforms—that is, from morphs (radicals and affixes); thus, **-er** and **-s** are not wordforms since, although they are minimal, they are not autonomous: they are suffixes. Minimality separates wordforms from configurations of wordforms—that is, from phrases. Thus, **ballet school** is not a wordform, since, although it is autonomous, it is not minimal: it is a phrase consisting of two autonomous minimal signs, wordforms.

Remember the following general methodological principle of linguistics:

> Any unit of language **L** shares the general properties of all units of the same type in **L**.

In particular, all **L**'s wordforms have, if not the same, at least similar semantic, syntactic, morphological and phonological properties. I will leave this fact aside in order not to encumber the presentation.[28]

Definitions 8/9: Wordform of language/of speech

> 1. A wordform is a **wordform of language** iff it can appear in any syntactically appropriate context or, at least, in most appropriate contexts.
>
> 2. A wordform is a **wordform of speech** iff it is possible only in some special contexts where it is created by syntactic rules—as a result of either splitting a wordform of language in two or merging two wordforms of language into one.

The opposition "wordform of language *vs.* wordform of speech" is of course based on the well-known Saussurian opposition "*langue* vs. *parole*," which is traditionally rendered in English as "language *vs.* speech." Language, as the reader understands, is the device that ensures the correspondence between Meanings and Texts; it is represented, in our approach, by the Meaning-Text model. Wordforms of language are elements of lexemes, the latter being stored in the lexicon—that is, in the language (= in the brains of the speakers). Wordforms of speech, on the other hand, are produced in the text—that is, in particular contexts— out of wordforms of the language, according to general rules of the language.

Let me now illustrate the notion of wordform. All signs mentioned in examples for Definition 5 are wordforms of language: they are autonomous (at least, weakly) and minimal. Here are some examples of wordforms of speech:

(51) a. German

    The verb ZU+MACHEN 'close':
    (i) *Er machte die Tür **zu*** 'He closed the door'. ~
    (ii) *Ich weiß, daß er die Tür **zu**machte* 'I know that he closed the door'.

The verbal derivational prefix **zu-** is automatically separated from its verb and placed at the end of a main clause. In this position, **zu-** has all the properties of a German wordform (German even has a preposition **zu** 'to', which is a wordform of language). We have to recognize this separated prefix **zu-** in (51a-i) as a wordform, but an "occasional" one—a wordform of speech.

    b. (i) French

      *à le Canada 'in the Canada' ⇒ ***au*** /o/ *Canada*

The preposition À 'in' preceding the article LE (definite, masculine singular) is "fused" with it, if LE itself precedes a consonant, thus producing a new sign, **au**. (If LE precedes a vowel, À and LE do not fuse and *le* is truncated to *l'*: *à l'Ontario* 'in the Ontario', **au Ontario*.) The sign **au** features all the properties of French wordforms and nothing prevents us from considering it a wordform of speech.

(ii) Polish
na niego 'at him' ⇒ **nań**   /naɲ/
dla niego 'for him' ⇒ **dlań**   /dlaɲ/
z niego 'from him' ⇒ **zeń**   /zeɲ/
do niego 'to him' ⇒ **doń**   /doɲ/

Several prepositions governing the accusative or the genitive can "fuse" with the following pronoun **niego** 'him', producing a complex wordform of speech (a slightly old-fashioned expression, typically found in literary texts).

The wordforms of language are united into lexemes. A wordform of speech does not, of course, belong to a lexeme.

Definition 10: Lexeme

> A **lexeme** is a set of all wordforms and phrases that express analytical forms whose distinctions are strictly inflectional.

The lexeme TAKE$_{(V)}$ 'X gets hold of Y in X's hands' (*Mary took a cup*) includes the following lexical items:

– wordforms: [*to*] *take*, [*I, you, ...*] *take, takes, took, taken, taking, ...*
– phrases: *will take, would take,* [*to*] *have taken,* [*I, you, ...*] *have taken, has taken, had taken, am taking, are taking, have been taken, ...*

A lexeme is a lexicographic unit: all its elements—that is, wordforms and phrases—have by definition the same lexicographic properties and can be described by the same lexical entry.

☞ The notions of inflectional category and its values (= grammemes) are defined prior to and independent of the notion of lexeme: see Mel'čuk 2006a: 21–23.

 Many lexemes in any language contain just one wordform: this is true of all so-called invariant words, such as prepositions and conjunctions, as well as adverbs, ideophones, interjections, some adjectives, etc.; for instance, ABOUT, FOR, WHEN, HERE, ACHOO!, THE, HAZEL [eyes]. In isolating languages (such as Chinese or Vietnamese) most lexemes consist of just one wordform. But as we know from mathematics, a set containing one element is not the same thing as the element itself: $\{\varepsilon\} \neq \varepsilon$.

5.2.4 Cases, ergative construction, voices

Finally, I would like to present an example of the potential of well-defined notions in a linguistic description and of the extent to which rigorous terminology is crucial. This example is technically complex, but I hope that the reader's tenacity will be fully rewarded. It concerns an African language—Maasai, one of the Eastern Nilotic languages of Kenya and Tanzania (along with Maasai, this linguistic group includes Turkana, Teso, Ngasa, Lango, and several smaller languages) and deals, first of all, with the notion of **case** (see the Glossary).

An Eastern Nilotic language typically has two cases, traditionally called nominative and accusative. For more than half a century, it has been said that these cases have amazing properties that oppose Eastern Nilotic languages—in particular, Maasai—to all other languages of the Earth. Let us open a complete grammar of Maasai, the only one available at present: Tucker & Mpaayei 1955 (= T&M; this is a perfect description of a language: precise, consistent and very clear). This is what it says about cases:

- The accusative is the basic (= lexicographic) form of the noun.
- The nominative is derived from the accusative (by means of a tonal apophony).
- The nominative, but not the accusative, is governed by prepositions.
- The accusative is used to mark:
- a Direct Object [= DirO];
- a fronted topic (= prolepsis);
- a noun used in direct address (if it is not introduced by a vocative particle, which governs the nominative);
- a copular attribute with the verb RÁ 'be';
- a Possessor: ɔlčɔré lɔ́ **layíònì**$_{ACC}$ 'friend that of.boy' = 'boy's friend' (lɔ́ is a linker).

5.2 A LINGUISTIC CONCEPTUAL APPARATUS

- The nominative marks:
- any syntactic subject except for the subject of a passive form (keep in mind that it will be shown that what T&M call the "subject" is in fact not the subject!);
- all oblique complements, including those which are governed by a preposition.

With the exception of the first property of the accusative, this characterization of both cases is extremely exotic: I do not know of a similar situation outside the domain of Eastern Nilotic. Moreover, this description of the nominative and the accusative leads to an even more bizarre treatment of the Maasai passive: the subject of a passive form is said to be in the accusative, while the agentive complement is in the nominative. For instance, T&M describe sentences such as those in (52) in the following way:

(52) Maasai (´ indicates the high tone, and ˆ, the rising-falling tone)

a. É   + rík + i   nkíshú   aainei   lmórrân
   3.PL$_{SUB}$.3.PL$_{OBJ}$ lead **PASS** cow-PL.ACC my young.warrior-PL.NOM
   'My cows are.lead by.young.warriors' (T&M: 81, §94).

☞ The Maasai transitive verb shows bi-personal agreement—as seen from (52a), the finite verb ('lead') agrees both with its syntactic subject and its direct object.

b. É   + ɪrɔrɔkɔ + kí   yíóók   ɪltʊŋaná
   3.PL$_{SUB}$.1.PL$_{OBJ}$ greet-PAST **PASS** we-ACC person-PL.NOM
   'We were.greeted by.people' (T&M: 132, §172).

According to T&M, in (52b), the Main Verb shows subject agreement (in 3PL) with the agentive complement 'persons' (the expression corresponding to the English *by*-phrase) rather than with 'we', which T&M call the subject of the passive. At the same time, the Main Verb shows object agreement (in 1PL) with the presumed subject. But, generally speaking, the Maasai finite verb shows subject agreement with the subject, and object agreement with the DirO. This is a major incongruity, which I propose to resolved below.

Based on this description, E. Keenan (1976: 326–328) developed a new theory of voice. However, the apparent outlandishness of the cases, voices, and agreement patterns in Maasai—as described by T&M—stems simply from a terminological confusion.

Cases. In their analysis of Eastern Nilotic languages, Africanists have called the nominative the noun form that appears in a sentence in the role of the syntactic subject, and the accusative is considered the form that plays the role of the DirO. In other words, they simply follow Latin grammar! However, it is logically incorrect to identify a grammatical case by the syntactic role it marks: in principle, a noun marked by a given case may appear in different syntactic roles, while a given syntactic role of a noun may be marked by different cases.* Otherwise, there would be no need to distinguish syntactic roles and the cases that mark them.

The nominative is to be defined (in any language with cases) as the case of naming, or nomination, which corresponds to its Latin etymology. By definition, this is the basic case, the case of the lexicographic form of a noun; thus, if a language has cases, it necessarily has the nominative. If we accept this definition and invert the current case names in Eastern Nilotic, a fairly familiar picture emerges: the basic case in Maasai is, of course, the nominative—wrongly called the accusative. The form of what I call the nominative serves as the base for the production, by means of tonal apophonies, of the form of the oblique

---

* Here are a couple of Russian examples.
 – The **accusative** can mark a direct object, a complement of a preposition and a durational circumstantial:
  (i) a. *Dajte–[nam ešče]*–**dir-obj**→*nedel+ju*$_{SG.ACC}$*!* 'Give us a week more!'
   b. *na*–**prepositional**→*nedel+ju*$_{SG.ACC}$ 'for a week'
   c. *Nedel+ju*$_{SG.ACC}$←**duration-circum**–*bolit golova* '[I] have had a headache for a week'.
 – A **complement of a preposition** can be marked by any case except the nominative:
  (ii) a. *na*—**prepositional**→*nedel+ju*$_{SG.ACC}$ 'for a week'
   b. *bez*–**prepositional**→*nedel+i*$_{SG.GEN}$ 'without a week'
   c. *k*—**prepositional**→*nedel+e*$_{SG.DAT}$ 'to a week'
   d. *s*—**prepositional**→*nedel+ej*$_{SG.INST}$ 'with a week'
   e. *o*—**prepositional**→*nedel+e*$_{SG.PREP}$ 'about a week'

case (which T&M call the nominative). The oblique can be governed by a preposition; it marks as well the agentive complement. All this is typologically quite common: Old French, Kurdish and the Pamir languages exhibit exactly the same distribution and use of their two cases, the nominative and the oblique. The nominative case marking the DirO and the oblique case as a marker of the syntactic subject should not cause surprise, either: this is a classic **ergative construction** (see Mel'čuk 1988: 153–263 and 1997).[29]

Ergative construction. The ergative construction in Maasai embraces all the verbs, including all intransitives. Such a phenomenon is also found in other languages, for instance, in Megrelian and Wappo.

(53) a. Megrelian

    (i) *K'oč+Ø+**k**   kumortu*
        man   SG ERG   came
    'The man came' (the nominative: *k'oč+**i***).

    (ii) *K'oč+Ø +**k**   gaagibu   c'q'ar+Ø +**i***
        man   SG ERG   heated   water   SG   NOM
    'The man heated water'.

    (iii) *Muš+ep+**k**   karxana+Ø+Ø   geiašenes*
        worker PL ERG   plant   SG NOM   built
    'Workers built the plant'. ~

    *Karxana+Ø +**k**   iišenu   muš +ep + iše*
    plant   SG ERG   was.built   worker PL   INSTR
    'The plant was built by workers'.

The ergative case in **-k** (different from the nominative in **-i/-Ø**) marks the syntactic subject with all verbs, but only in the aorist; the DirO of a transitive verb is in the nominative.

    b. Wappo (Thompson *et al.* 2006: 10–12; t̠ stands for an alveolar /t̠/, phonemically opposed to the dental /t/):

    (i) *K'ew+**i**   čica+Ø$_{NOM}$ t̠'ata?*   'The man killed the bear'.
        man   SUBJ bear   NOM   killed

    (ii) *K'ew*+Ø   *čic*+*i*   *t'ata?*   'The bear killed the man'.
         man   NOM bear SUBJ killed
    (iii) *Čic*+*i*   *t'olkhe?*   'The bear was caught'.
         bear   SUBJ was.caught
    (iv) *Čic*+*i*   *tuč'akhi*   'The bear is big'.
         bear   SUBJ be.big
    (v) *Čic*+*i* *olah t'a?*+Ø *nehkhi?* 'The bear has four paws'.
        bear SUBJ four paw   NOM have

The subjective case in **-i** (different from the nominative in **-Ø**) marks the syntactic subject with all verbs, including passives and qualificative verbs, and in all tenses. The DirO of a transitive verb is in the nominative, just like Megrelian.

Voices. Let us return to the Maasai sentences in (52) and repeat them here, this time with correct case labels:

(54) Maasai

    a. *É*   + *rík* + *í*   nkíshú   aainei   lmúrrân
       $3.\text{PL}_{\text{SUB}}\cdot 3.\text{PL}_{\text{OBJ}}$ lead **PASS** cow-PL.NOM my   young.warrior-PL.OBL
  'My cows are.lead by.young.warriors' (T&M: 81, §94).

    b. *É*   + *ɪrɔrɔkɔ* + *kí* yíóók   ɪltʊŋaná
       $3.\text{PL}_{\text{SUB}}\cdot 1.\text{PL}_{\text{OBJ}}$ greet-PAST **PASS** we-NOM person-PL.OBL
  'We were.greeted by.people' (T&M: 132, §172).

These sentences present not just a simple passive, but a different voice—a **partial demotional passive**. The wordforms *nkíshú* 'cows' and *yíóók* 'we' are both in the nominative; since they are elements of an ergative construction, they are DirOs rather than subjects (that is why the Main Verb agrees with them using the objectival agreement). A verb in this voice cannot have a free lexical subject, since it already has an indefinite-personal subject $\emptyset_{3\text{PL}}$ (roughly, '«they»'), semantically equivalent to *Fr.* ON and *Ger.* MAN. The diathesis of the partial demotional passive in Maasai, seen in (55)—that is, the correspondence between the semantic and deep-syntactic actants of the verb form—is as follows: X ⇔ **III** (X = 'young warriors'), Y ⇔ **II** (Y = 'cows'), see (55b). The basic diathesis of a transitive Maasai verb is, as is to be expected, X ⇔ **I**, Y ⇔ **II** (this is the active), see (55a):

(55) a. *Lmŭrrân   é   +rík +Ø   nkíshú   aainei*
young.warrior-PL.OBL 3.PL$_{SUB}$.3.PL$_{OBJ}$ lead ACT cow-PL.NOM my
'Young warriors are leading my cows'.

b. *Ø$_{3PL}$ é   +rík +i   nkíshú   aainei*
«they» 3.PL$_{SUB}$.3.PL$_{OBJ}$ lead PASS-DEM cow-PL.NOM my
lmŭrrân
young.warrior-PL.OBL
lit. '[«They»] are leading my cows by young warriors'.

The Maasai demotional passive is similar to the French partial demotional passive, shown in (56b):

(56) a. *Les survivants$_I$ ont raconté des histoires$_{II}$ horribles.* ⇒
'The survivors have told some horrible stories'.
b. *Il a été raconté des histoires$_{II}$ horribles par$_{III}$ les survivants*
lit. 'It has been told some horrible stories by the survivors'.

☞ There is a difference between the French and Maasai demotional passives: in French, the syntactic subject of the passive form is not an indefinite-personal pronoun as in Maasai, but a semantically empty—so-called impersonal—pronoun IL.

T&M explicitly state (p. 79) that "the [Maasai] Passive could be regarded as a specialized form of the 3rd person active, in that it takes a «contained object». (Compare French «On vous appelle» for: «You are called.»)." The authors sensed the truth, but were unable to properly express it, since they lacked the necessary notions and terms.[30]

It is easy to multiply the examples, but those I have advanced—based on the notions of case, ergative construction, and voice, as applied to Maasai and other East-Nilotic languages —should already make clear that linguistics badly needs a unified system of rigorous notions and standard terminology. Without such notions and terms, linguistic discussions often turn into a "dialogue of the deaf," making mutual understanding between linguists impossible. It is my hope that the Meaning-Text approach will add its modest conceptual and terminological offerings to the general-linguistics well.

5.3 Meaning-text linguistics and the description of linguistic meaning

I first read about the formal description of meaning more than half a century ago, in 1961. The description proposed was as formal as that of the structure of wordforms or sentences. The writers were Alexander Zholkovsky, Nina Leont´eva, and Jurij Martem´janov: Žolkovskij *et al.* 1961; and the technique developed for this description was demonstrated in Žolkovskij 1964a, b, c—papers that appeared in the quasi-periodical *Mašinnyj perevod i prikladnaja lingvistika* [= MPiPL; 'Machine Translation and Applied Linguistics'], volume 8, 1964, along with several other studies dedicated to the same topic. In my intellectual life, these papers were a sort of "Big Bang," because it was at this moment that I took the first steps towards Meaning-Text theory. Even today, I still keep an old copy of *MPiPL 8* at hand, in the way some people keep their family bible within arm's reach. Shortly thereafter, the club was joined by Jurij Apresjan (1969a, b, 1974) and Anna Wierzbicka (Wierzbicka 1969, 1972, 1980, 1996). The formal description of linguistic meanings has many aspects, but here, only one of these will be considered: semantic decompositions, introduced in Section *4.1*.

The decompositions of meanings, or semantic decompositions, are performed on semantemes and carried out in terms of semantemes—that is, meanings that are signifieds of lexical units of language **L**. This is done in accordance with the following four rules.

Sem-Decomposition Rule 1: Rigorous expansion of semantemes
> Every decomposable semanteme 'σ' must be represented in terms of semantemes 'σ_1' ⊕ 'σ_2' ⊕ ... ⊕ 'σ_n' such that 1) $n \geq 2$ and 2) every 'σ_i' is semantically simpler than 'σ'.

☞ The symbol ⊕, which we have encountered more than once, stands for the operation of linguistic union.

Under semantic decomposition, each meaning is represented using at least two simpler meanings. The term *simpler*, as applied to one of two compared semantemes 'σ$_1$' and 'σ$_2$', has to be construed as a technical term (without psychological connotations):

> The meaning 'σ$_2$' is simpler than the meaning 'σ$_1$' if and only if 'σ$_2$' participates in a decomposition of 'σ$_1$', but not vice versa:
> 'σ$_1$' = 'σ'...**σ$_2$**...σ''', but not *'σ$_2$' = 'σ'...**σ$_1$**...σ'''.

At the outset, before any semantic decompositions have been performed, it is by no means always clear which of the two compared semantemes (in a given lexicon) is the simpler. However, a sufficient number of subsequent decompositions, pushed deep enough, will always lead to the correct correlation. In the process, two simple and natural operations are used:

> 1. **Substituting** one of two equal meanings for the other:
>   **if** we have 'σ$_1$' = 'σ'...**σ$_2$**...σ''',
>   **then** instead of 'σ$_1$' ⊕ 'σ$_3$' we can write 'σ'...**σ$_2$**...σ''' ⊕ 'σ$_3$' (and, of course, vice versa).
> 2. **Canceling** superfluous meanings after substitution, if any.

The operation of substitution is crucial for semantic theory; see below, Sem-Decomposition Rule 3, p. 149. It should be stressed that substitution is done only *salva significatione*: the resulting text can be stylistically unacceptable, but it must leave the meaning intact.

Thus, take the semantemes 'astronomer' and 'astronomy'. Which one is simpler? The following two statements are both true:

Astronomy is a science done by astronomers.

and

An astronomer is a person who does astronomy.

Does this mean that we can define 'astronomy' by 'astronomer' as well as 'astronomer' by 'astronomy'? Absolutely not. Let's say, for argument's sake, that the meaning 'astronomer' is simpler. Then we have:

(i) 'astronomy' = 'the science done by astronomers'.

The next step is the decomposition of the semanteme 'astronomer':

(ii) 'astronomer' = 'person who does the science of celestial bodies'.

Now, let us substitute 'astronomer' in the definition (i) by its definition in (ii); the result is (iii):

(iii) 'astronomy' = 'the science done by people who do the science of celestial bodies'

From (iii) we deduce, by canceling the superfluous repetition of meanings, (iv):

(iv) 'astronomy' = 'the science of celestial bodies' (because 'the science done by people who do science of Y' = 'science of Y')

We thus conclude that 'astronomy' is simpler than 'astronomer':

(v) 'astronomer' = 'person who does astronomy'

The "inverse" definition is formally impossible!

A systematic application of Sem-Decomposition Rule 1 has at least two important consequences: no logical circles in the definitions and the isolation of semantic primitives.

No logical circles

Logical circles in the system of lexicographic definitions is one of the main scourges of existing dictionaries. Take, for instance, *Le Petit Robert de la langue française* 2009 (electronic version; circles are indicated by boldface); let's begin with the definition of one of the senses of the verb APPUYER.

> APPUYER I.3 'support' : 'fournir un **soutien**' 'provide backing' (*appuyer un candidat aux élections* 'provide backing to a candidate at the election')

This definition contains the noun SOUTIEN, which is defined—in the relevant sense—as follows:

> SOUTIEN 2 'backing' : 'action de **soutenir**' 'action of backing' (*soutien électoral* 'electoral backing')

The definition of SOUTIEN refers, in its turn, to the definition of the verb SOUTENIR:

> SOUTENIR B.2 'back$_{(V)}$' : '**appuyer** en défendant' 'provide backing by defending' (*soutenir un candidat* 'back a candidate')

5.3 THE DESCRIPTION OF LINGUISTIC MEANING

But SOUTENIR is defined in terms of APPUYER, sending us right back to where we started.

A logical circle leads to absurdity; I will show this by using substitutions and cancellations:

APPUYERI.3 'fournir un **soutien**' = 'fournir une action de **soutenir**'
= '**soutenir**';
SOUTENIRB.2 '**appuyer** en défendant' = '**soutenir** en défendant';
'soutenir' = 'soutenir en défendant'.

And this result is absurd: *A = A + B.

The same picture emerges if we consider the following words from an authoritative Russian dictionary (*Malyj Akademičeskij Slovar'*, 1981–1984):

SPOSOBSTVOVAT´ 'contribute' : 'okazyvat´ pomošč´´ 'give help', **sodejstvovat´**' 'assist'
SODEJSTVOVAT´ 'assist' : 'okazyvat´ sodejstvie 'give assistance', **sposobstvovat´**' 'contribute'
SODEJSTVIE 'assistance' : **pomošč´**' 'help$_{(N)}$', **podderžka**' 'support$_{(N)}$'
PODDERŽIVAT´ 'support$_{(V)}$' : 'okazyvat´ **pomošč´/sodejstvie**' 'give help/assistance'
POMOŠČ´ 'help$_{(N)}$' : '**sodejstvie** 'assistance', učastie 'participation'

Such examples can be multiplied *ad infinitum*, but this is not worth doing: lexicographic "definitions" with logical circles are not acceptable. To ensure the absence of logical circles we have to observe the rule of rigorous expansion of semantemes. For instance, here are the tentative sketches of the lexicographic definitions for the Russian verbs SPOSOBSTVOVAT´ 'contribute' and SODEJSTVOVAT´ ≈ 'assist', which are free of logical circles—thanks to the systematic decomposition of their meanings ('cause1' stands for involuntary causation, and 'cause2', for voluntary causation).

SPOSOBSTVOVAT′ ≈ 'contribute'

X sposobstvuet Y-u ≈ 'X contributes to Y': '|[process Y(α) taking place and X acting on α,]| X causes1 that Y(α) takes place in a better way'

Položitel′nye primery sposobstvujut razvitiju zdorovogo obščestva
'Positive examples contribute to.the.development of.a.healthy society'
[Positive examples acting on the members of the society cause1 that the development of this society takes place in a better way].

SODEJSTVOVAT′ ≈ 'assist'

X sodejstvuet Y-u in Z(Y) 'X assists Y in Z(Y)': '|[activity Z(Y) taking place and X acting on α related to Z,]| X causes2 that Z(Y) becomes easier or possible for Y'

Fon Bjulov sodejsyvoval mne v ustrojstve koncertov
'Von Bülow assisted me in organizing concerts'
[I was engaging in organizing concerts; von Bülow acting on entities related to organizing concerts was causing2 that this organization was becoming easier or possible for me].

Systematic decomposition of semantemes of **L** in terms of simpler semantemes of **L** inescapably leads, sooner or later, to some **indecomposable semantemes**—that is, to a set of semantemes such that **L** has no simpler semantemes. These are **semantic primitives**, or, as they are called now, **semantic primes**.[31] A serious quest for semantic primitives was initiated by Anna Wierzbicka and has been successfully carried out by her and her collaborators for about 50 years now (Wierzbicka 1969, 1972, 1980, 1987, 1991, 1996, 2006, Goddard & Wierzbicka (eds.) 2002). For the time being, 65 semantic primitives have been isolated (Goddard & Wierzbicka 2014: 12). However, there is an important difference between Wierzbicka's approach (known as *Natural Semantic Metalanguage*, or NSM) and the treatment of semantic primitives in the Meaning-Text approach:

– Wierzbicka's goal is to isolate **linguistically universal** semantic primitives, which are found in all languages and thus constitute a universal lexicon of human thought.

5.3 THE DESCRIPTION OF LINGUISTIC MEANING

– Meaning-Text linguistics aims at discovering **language-specific** semantic primitives—that is, semantemes that will remain as an irreducible residue after a sufficient number of consecutive decompositions of **L**'s semantemes.

It is quite possible that national semantic primitives in different languages will be in (almost?) one-to-one correspondence with each other, and thus they will more or less coincide with Wierzbicka's primitives... *Qui vivra verra!* (See Mel'čuk 1989.) As of yet, Meaning-Text linguistics cannot propose a list of semantic primitives even for one language; however, here are a few good candidates for this role in English:

1) 'speak'   2) 'this.speech.act'

3) 'entity'   4) 'fact'   5) 'space1' [boundless extent]

6) 'time1' [experience of duration]

7) 'set$_{(N)}$1' [mathematical sense]

8) 'actII.1' [act upon something]   9) 'actII.2' [do something]

10) 'more.than'   11) 'not'   12) 'entail'

13) 'and' [logical conjunction]   14) 'or' [logical disjunction]

Interestingly, these semantic elements are not genuine, "all-natural" English words. Rather, they are results of a sophisticated semantic analysis.

For the time being, Meaning-Text linguistics focuses on semantic decomposition within the lexicons of particular languages.

Sem-Decomposition Rule 2: Standardization of semantemes

To ensure the possibility of formal manipulations with semantic decompositions, these have to be written in a highly standardized semantic metalanguage. This means the observance of the following requirements:

1. All semantemes used in a decomposition should be well defined: no ambiguity in semantemes.
2. All intuitively identical meanings should be expressed by identical semantemes: no synonymy of semantemes.

To satisfy the first requirement, it is necessary to strictly distinguish all separate senses of any polysemous word of **L** and supply all the lexemes thus obtained with lexicographic numbers, which will serve as semanteme distinguishers. This is no easy task, but lexicographers are well acquainted with it: it has been their lot for centuries, and will continue to be.

 In our examples lexicographic numbers are not systematically used—for ease of perusal. At the same time, examples are chosen in such a way that the ambiguity of some elements in the lexicographic definition does not interfere with understanding.

It is incomparably more difficult to satisfy the second requirement. Consider, for instance, current definitions of some common artifacts—devices, tools and instruments (from *LDOCE Online*, slightly simplified; synonymous expressions indicating the intended use of the artifact in question are underscored):

CATCH 'hook or something similar <u>for</u> fastening a door'
BOLT 'metal bar that <u>you</u> slide across a door or window <u>to</u> fasten it'
SPOON 'object that <u>one uses for</u> eating'
HAMMER 'tool <u>used for</u> hitting nails into wood'
KNIFE 'metal blade fixed into a handle, <u>used for</u> cutting'
CLOCK 'instrument that <u>shows</u> what time it is'

Without entering into the question of the adequacy of these definitions (numerous objections could be raised against them), note that the underscored semantemes are semantically equivalent in the context of these definitions:

'α for Y-ing' ≡ 'α you Z to Y' ≡ 'α one uses for Y-ing' ≡
'α used for Y-ing' ≡ 'α that Zs to Y'

Therefore, one formulation is needed that could replace them all. Such a formulation could be 'α designed for X to Y':

CATCH 'device designed for X to fasten a door with—a hook or ...'

BOLT 'device designed for X to fasten a door with—metal bar that X slides ...'
SPOON 'utensil designed for X to carry liquid food to the mouth ...'
HAMMER 'tool designed for X to hit Y with ...'
KNIFE 'tool designed for X to cut Y with ...'
CLOCK 'instrument designed for X to determine time ...'

Sem-Decomposition Rule 3: Adequacy of decompositions

The decomposition of the semanteme 'σ' into the semantemes '$σ_1$' ⊕ '$σ_2$' ⊕ ... ⊕ '$σ_n$' must, of course, correspond to the researcher's intuition. But this is not sufficient: a formal principle is needed to buttress the intuition. Such a principle is the requirement for 'σ' and '$σ_1$' ⊕ '$σ_2$' ⊕ ... ⊕ '$σ_n$' to be mutually substitutable in any context:

> The decomposition '$σ_1$' ⊕ '$σ_2$' ⊕ ... ⊕ '$σ_n$' of the semanteme 'σ' and the semanteme 'σ' are mutually substitutable in any context *salva significatione*.

This means, in particular, that every element of the decomposition of 'σ' is **necessary** and all of them, taken together, are **sufficient** to specify 'σ' and only 'σ'.

Sem-Decomposition Rule 4: Using only maximal semantic blocks in decompositions

> If the decomposition of the semanteme 'σ' of **L** contains a configuration of semantemes '$σ_1$' ⊕ '$σ_2$' ⊕ ... ⊕ '$σ_n$' that it is equal to the semanteme 'σ″' ('$σ_1$' ⊕ '$σ_2$' ⊕ ... ⊕ '$σ_n$' = 'σ″'), then the configuration '$σ_1$' ⊕ '$σ_2$' ⊕ ... ⊕ '$σ_n$' must be replaced by 'σ″'.

The semanteme 'σ″' is called a maximal block with respect to the configuration '$σ_1$' ⊕ '$σ_2$' ⊕ ... ⊕ '$σ_n$'.

Sem-Decomposition Rule 4 (formulated in Apresjan 1969a: 14 and 1969b: 421; see also Apresjan 1974: 95) guarantees a "stepwise" semantic decomposition such that on each single step the decomposition is minimal (= the shallowest possible).

Maximal decomposition—that is, up to semantic primitives—makes the definition unreadable, whereas the intuition of speakers is the main instrument for evaluating definitions. Thus, take the tentative definition of CLOCK given above:

(57) a. CLOCK$_{(N)}$1: 'instrument designed for X to determine time2 …'.

Its semantic components can themselves be decomposed as follows (the definitions are borrowed, with minor modifications, from *LDOCE Online*):

    INSTRUMENT3 : 'piece of equipment designed for X to measure magnitude Y and showing its value …'
    DESIGN$_{(V)}$2 : 'plan or develop Y for a specific purpose …'
    DETERMINE1 : 'find_out the facts about Y …'
    TIME2 : 'particular point in time1'

Making the necessary substitutions and cancellations, we obtain (57b):

    b. CLOCK$_{(N)}$1 : 'piece of equipment developed for measuring time1 for X to find_out particular point in time1 …'.

(57b) is already more difficult to grasp than (57a), but we are as yet far from semantic primitives, with the exception of 'time1'. Let us take a further step:

    PIECE3 : 'single thing of a particular type …'
    EQUIPMENT1 : 'things that X needs to do a particular job or activity …'
    DEVELOP$_{(V)}$1 : 'bring Y into being by work …'
    MEASURE$_{(V)}$1 : 'find numerical value of Y …'

This gives us (57c):

    c. CLOCK$_{(N)}$1 : 'single thing of things that X needs to do a particular job or activity brought into being by work for finding numerical value of time1 for X to find_out particular point in time1 …'.

I dare the reader to understand this definition on the first (or even the second) attempt! And there still are quite a few components to be decomposed ('need', particular', 'job', 'activity', etc.). Conclusion: the **maximal depth** of semantic decomposition leads to definitions that are too unwieldy to be useful.

The **arbitrary depth** of semantic decomposition makes the definition—well, arbitrary.

Therefore, the **minimal depth** of decomposition is accepted, which means decomposing a meaning into maximal blocks. Maximal blocks make a semantic decomposition more surveyable and explicitly demonstrate the links between related meanings.

However, unlike Rules 1–3, Rule 4 is not logically necessary: a decomposition of a semanteme that observes Rule 4 is fully equivalent to a decomposition of the same semanteme that does not observe this rule. But Rule 4 is very important methodologically.

The observance of Rules 1–4 ensures the unicity of semantic decompositions (up to semantic equivalence, of course). In other words, following Rules 1–4, different researchers obtain the same decompositions for any given meaning.

5.4 Meaning-Text linguistics and the lexicon: the Explanatory Combinatorial Dictionary [= ECD]

5.4.1 Introductory remarks

> The Meaning-Text approach gives pride of place to the lexicon, which is the solid base of a language; the grammar is considered to be a "derived" language component—a system of rules embodying useful generalizations over observed lexicographic properties of lexical units.

Such a view of the lexicon presupposes a special type of lexicon; what is meant here is *Explanatory Combinatorial Dictionary*, or ECD. A preliminary specimen of such a dictionary for Russian (283 vocables) was published in 1984 (Mel'čuk & Zholkovsky 1984).

Work on a Russian ECD was launched in 1965, by Alexander Zholkovsky and myself. We saw the future dictionary as the main part of any linguistic model, which was for us the same as a scientific description of a language—in this case, Russian. This dictionary was designed to be a repository of all relevant information about individual words, presented in a completely formal and systematic way. Later on, our approach came to be known as a *theory of linguistic models of the Meaning-Text type*, or, for short, Meaning-Text theory [= MTT] (Mel'čuk 1974). Soon, several colleagues joined us, first of all—Jurij Apresjan, whose participation turned out to be the most valuable. The first ECD was the goal of a team of about 20 people over 10 years—all of them volunteers, supplying different degrees of collaboration: our ECD was not a working project of any official institution. The first ECD was created by a group of enthusiasts in our free time.

In the process, many papers were published, so that slowly but steadily the ECD became known outside our narrow circle. Some colleagues experimented with other languages: English, Polish, Tatar, Japanese, German, French. The ECD was highly appreciated by specialists in the domain of lexicography and linguists, but the prospects of publishing it in the USSR were not good: the political question marks hanging over the authors caused the only prospective publisher—"Soviet Encyclopedia"—to shirk away from the ECD. In spite of the fact that we had a signed contract with this publisher, the ECD was never printed in the USSR. In 1976, I was fired from my job at the Institute of Linguistics of the Academy of Sciences, the victim of political accusations—after I published a letter of support for Andrey Sakharov and Sergey Kovalyov in the "New York Times".[32] As a result, I became a "social parasite" and, faced with harassment from the police, I had to emigrate. Zholkovsky was to follow me, very shortly afterwards. Automatically, we became non-persons, and the last hopes for the publication of the ECD in the USSR died.

But "manuscripts do not burn" (M. Bulgakov). The manuscript of the ECD made a spectacular escape from its Soviet prison, with the help of two American colleagues. The Canada Research Council generously agreed to finance the production, and finally, thanks to the Wiener

Slawistischer Almanach Publishing House and its Editor-in-Chief, Tilmann Reuther, the Russian ECD saw the light of day.

Today, besides the Russian ECD, we have an important fragment of a French ECD: Mel'čuk *et al.* 1984–1999 (511 vocables); there is also a pedagogical dictionary of French derivations and collocations developed along ECD lines, but drastically simplified for the general public: Mel'čuk & Polguère 2007 (386 vocables). In what follows I will, however, use examples from the Russian ECD—not only because I do not have a representative fragment of an English ECD, but also because I think that an English reader can better appreciate a dictionary supplying information about the lexical stock of a foreign language.

5.4.2 The three main properties of an ECD

An ECD is a monolingual (= English-English, French-French, etc.) dictionary; it is in the same class as well-known existing monolingual dictionaries. However, three key properties differentiate an ECD from those other dictionaries: its theoretical orientation, its consistently active character and its formalization.

Theoretical orientation

The ECD is directly linked to a linguistic theory—namely, the Meaning-Text theory; it incorporates the results from the most recent research in modern semantics and syntax and, at the same time, it allows the researcher to experimentally verify his hypotheses. In this sense, it is a scientific lexicon, free from pedagogical and/or commercial constraints.

Active character

Most of conventional monolingual dictionaries are **passive**, or **analytic**, dictionaries: they are directed at an Addressee (a listener or reader) and designed to aid the reader to understand the text. In sharp contrast, an ECD is an **active**, or **synthetic**, **dictionary**: it is aimed at the needs of a Speaker (or a writer), and it is designed to help produce a text. Consequences of this distinction are twofold:

- An ECD allows the user to find all available means for the expression of a meaning that he wants to express and to select among them those that best fit the speech situation and the linguistic context; this is the **paradigmatic aspect** of text production.
- An ECD allows the user to find all the correct ways to combine the linguistic means selected in a sentence; this is the **syntagmatic aspect** of text production.

An ECD can, of course, be "inverted" and used in the opposite direction—that is, from text to meaning. Nevertheless, its philosophy and central organizing principle is the synthetic orientation, in accordance with the Meaning-Text approach.

Formalization

An ECD by principle excludes any reliance on the user's intuition, on his ability to reason by analogy, or guess something from examples. All the linguistic information supplied in an ECD is presented in an explicit way and specified strictly in terms of previously defined means—that is, in a formalized metalanguage. A Russian ECD can in principle be used by somebody who does not know a word of Russian or by a computer (provided, of course, that the lexicographic metalanguage is adapted to the user's abilities). However, an ECD is in no way intended for use by computers. Its goal is to present, explicitly and exhaustively, all the information that an average speaker of Russian is supposed to have about each individual Russian word. To put it differently, the ECD lays claim to a scientific description of the Russian lexicon, without concessions to pedagogical, typographic, or commercial considerations. As a result, the ECD is not easy to use: to exploit it successfully, to the full extent, the user has first to master the descriptive formalism, which can require several days. However, is this too high a price to pay for a scientific description? Even high school manuals of mathematics and physics can daunt a reader. There is no reason to believe that a scientific description of a language's lexicon should be any more straightforward.

The latter two properties of ECDs—their active character and advanced formalization—underlie the choice of the unit of lexicographic description and that of the format of this description, or the structure of a lexical entry.

The **unit of description** in an ECD is not a polysemous word, as it is in modern monolingual dictionaries.

- On the one hand, it is a lexical unit [= LU]—that is, a word or an idiom (a multiword non-compositional set expression). Idioms, such as ⌜CALL IT A DAY⌝, ⌜FALL FROM GRACE⌝, ⌜KEEP AN EYE OUT⌝, ⌜PULL Y's LEG⌝, etc. are a legitimate part of the lexicon and are each afforded a complete lexical entry, as if they were words.

- On the other hand, it is a monosemous unit: a lexeme (= a word taken in one well-defined sense) or one sense of a polysemous idiom; an LU is by definition monosemous. Each LU is entitled to a lexical entry, and each lexical entry describes an LU:

$$\boxed{\text{an LU = a lexical entry.}}$$

All LUs that have identical signifiers and semantically related signifieds are united in super-entries, called **vocables**; a vocable corresponds to a polysemous word or a polysemous idiom of a traditional dictionary.

The standard **formal structure of a lexical entry** will be presented now.

5.4.3 A lexical entry in an ECD: three major zones

I will describe an ECD lexical entry, concentrating on three of its major zones: the semantic zone (*5.4.3.1*), the syntactic combinatorial zone (= the zone of syntactic cooccurrence, *5.4.3.2*) and the lexical combinatorial zone (= the zone of semantic derivation and restricted lexical cooccurrence, *5.4.3.3*).

5.4.3.1 The semantic zone in an ECD lexical entry

The semantic zone of a dictionary article for a headword LU L contains the lexicographic definition of L and L's connotations.

The definition of L. Compared to current dictionaries, the definitions in an ECD have the following characteristics.

- If L has a predicative meaning, L's definition involves as the definiendum (the lexeme or the idiom to be defined) not simply L but the so-called **propositional** form of L. L's propositional form is an expression consisting of L and the variables that represent L's semantic actants. Thus, what is defined is not the verb DEPEND, but the expression 'X depends on Y'; not simply the noun AUTHORITY4, but 'X, an authority among Ys on Z'; not the adjective SUFFICIENT, but '[X,] sufficient for Z to do Y'.

- An ECD definition of L is L's strict **semantic decomposition**, which allows this dictionary to avoid logical circles in the system of definitions.*

Semantic decompositions have been discussed and illustrated in Subsections *4.1* and *5.3*. The systematic decomposition of lexical meanings of language **L** in an ECD leads, in due course, to semantic atoms—elementary meanings whose further decomposition in terms of lexical meanings (= semantemes) of **L** is not possible; they have to be specified by a list. These meanings are also known as **semantic primitives**, see *5.3*, p. 146.

- An ECD definition of L describes the meaning of L in all its uses without exception; in existing dictionaries, this is very often not the case. Thus, Ožegov's Russian dictionary defines the noun STYD 'shame$_{(N)}$' as 'feeling of strong confusion caused1 by being aware of one's reprehensible act', and the verb STYDIT´SJA 'be ashamed' as 'experience shame because of somebody/something'—that is, 'experience feeling of strong confusion caused1 by being aware of one's reprehensible act because of somebody/something'. This definition, even once its poor formulation is corrected, does not cover the uses of the verb STYDIT´SJA in such sentences as *On styditsja svoej bednosti* ⟨*svoego nizkogo proisxoždenija, svoix negramotnyx roditelej*⟩ 'He is ashamed of his poverty ⟨of his low origins, of his

---

* Logical circles are the bane of many existing dictionaries, see *5.3*, p. 144*ff*.

5.4 THE EXPLANATORY COMBINATORIAL DICTIONARY

illiterate parents⟩', where no 'reprehensible acts' are mentioned. Such examples abound in monolingual dictionaries.[33] However, an ECD—by virtue of observing the formal rules for semantic decompositions—offers adequate definitions, at any rate, in principle. In practice, of course, an ECD's definitions can often be inadequate: its authors are only human, and people make mistakes; but the strictly formal and standardized structure of its definitions crucially facilitates the discovery of mistakes.

As a result, an ECD's definitions are not easy for a human user to grasp: this is the price to be paid for adequacy and exactness. For instance, the lexemes STYD and STYDIT′SJA are defined in a Russian ECD as follows.

STYD 'shame$_N$', noun, masculine

'styd X-a za Y pered Z-om' lit. 'X's shame for Y before Z' = 'X's shame about Y in front of Z' =
'X's passive negative feeling caused1 by the fact that:
  X believes that Y^1—an act or property of X or of entity Y^2 that belongs to X's personal sphere—is very bad;
  X feels unpleasant about X-self because of Y;
  X believes that person Z, having perceived Y^1, will believe that Y^1 is bad and will feel unpleasant about X because of Y^1;
  X would like to do something in order to hide Y from Z;
this feeling is of the kind that people usually have in these situations'.

STYDIT′SJA 'be ashamed', verb, reflexive

'X styditsja za Y pered Z-om' lit. 'X is ashamed for Y before Z' =
'X experiences shame about Y in front of Z'.

 Remember that although the definitions are written in English, what is defined are Russian lexemes, not their English near-equivalents.

The lexical connotations of L. A lexical connotation of the head word L is a meaning that is associated with the referent of L by language **L**, but is not part of L's definition. Thus, ASS [animal] connotes «silliness» (*John behaved like an ass*), and MULE, «stubbornness»

(*John is stubborn as a mule*); however, a particular ass can be (and often is) quite intelligent, and a mule is not necessarily stubborn, so that the indicated characteristics should not be included in the definitions of the names of these animals. Rather, they must appear in a different part of the lexical entry. Likewise, the noun WIND connotes «speed» (*The horse ran like the wind*) and «freedom» (*as free as the wind*), while AIR, «emptiness» (*airheaded*, *hot air*), etc. (Iordanskaja & Mel'čuk 2009).

5.4.3.2 The syntactic cooccurrence zone in an ECD lexical entry

The syntactic cooccurrence zone contains the **government pattern** [= GP] of L—a table that specifies for each semantic actant of L all possible means for its expression (the GP was mentioned above, 3.3.3, p. 80). Thus, the GP of the Russian verb VOSXIŠČAT′SJA 'admire' (*X vosxiščaetsja Y-om* 'X admires Y') is as follows:

X ⇔ I	Y ⇔ II
1. N_{NOM}	1. N_{INSTR}
	2. *tem, čto* CLAUSE
	3. *tem,* WH-word CLAUSE
	desirable

This GP tells us that the Sem-actant X of *vosxiščat′sja* is expressed by its DSynt-actant **I**, which is implemented by a noun in the nominative. Analogously, Y is expressed by DSynt-actant **II**, implemented in one of three ways:

– either by a noun in the instrumental (*Ivan*$_{X\text{-}NOM}$ *vosxiščalsja Mariej*$_{Y\text{-}INSTR}$ lit. 'Ivan was.admiring with.Maria');

– or by a subordinate clause of the type *tem, čto* CLAUSE lit. 'with.this that CLAUSE' (... *tem, čto ona tak masterski lžët* lit. 'with.this that she so masterfully was.lying');

– or else by a subordinate clause of the type *tem,* WH-word CLAUSE (... *tem, kuda on zabralsja* lit. 'with.this where he could.get' = '[was admiring] the fact that he could get there').

5.4 THE EXPLANATORY COMBINATORIAL DICTIONARY

The noun VOSXIŠČENIE 'admiration' (*vosxiščenie X-a Y-om* 'X's admiration for Y') has, along with these same three possible expressions of the Sem-actant Y (*vosxiščenie sposobnostjami rebënka* lit. 'admiration with the child's talents' or *vosxiščenie tem, čto/naskol´ko rebënok sposobnyj* lit. 'admiration with the fact that the child is so talented'), a fourth possibility: preposition PERED 'before' + N_{INSTR} (*vosxiščenie pered sposobnostjami rebënka* lit. 'admiration before [= for] the child's talents'); the verb VOSXIŠČAT´SJA does not have this means for expressing DSynt-actant II: **vosxiščat´sja pered sposobnostjami rebënka* lit. 'admire before the child's talents'.

The GP of an LU L is supplied with the necessary constraints concerning the cooccurrence of L's syntactic actants or the cooccurrence of the surface means for their implementation. For instance, the verb STYDIT´SJA 'be ashamed' allows either [STYDIT´SJA] *svoej bednosti*$_{Y\Leftrightarrow II}$ 'of.one's poverty', or [STYDIT´SJA] *sosedej*$_{Z\Leftrightarrow III}$ lit. 'of.neighbors' = 'in front of the neighbors', but not both objects in the given forms together: **stydit´sja sosedej svoej bednosti* lit. 'be ashamed of the neighbors of one's poverty'; the correct expression is *stydit´sja svoej bednosti* **pered** *sosedjami* lit. 'be ashamed of [= about] one's poverty before [= in front of] neighbors'. This fact is specified by a special rule (= a GP constraint), which accompanies the GP; in our case, it is Rule 3).

STYDIT´SJA 'be ashamed' (*X styditsja Y-a pered Z-om* 'X is ashamed about Y in front of Z')

Government Pattern

| X ⇔ I | Y ⇔ II | Z ⇔ III |
[who is ashamed]	[of what he is ashamed]	[before whom he is ashamed]
1. N_{NOM}	1. N_{GEN}	1. N_{GEN}
	2. *togo, čto* CLAUSE	2. *pered* 'before' N_{INSTR}
	3. *togo,* WH-word CLAUSE	
	4. *za* 'because of' N_{ACC}	
	5. V_{INF}	

1) $C_{II.4}$: N denotes a human or a human act
2) $C_{II.5}$: $D_I(D_{II}(S.)) = D_I(S.)$

3) **Impossible**: $C_{II} + C_{III.1}$

☞ The expression of the form $C_{M.N}$ specifies the concrete linguistic means that implements the DSynt-actant M: C stands for 'column', M gives the number of the column (i.e., the number of the DSynt-actant), and N, the number of the line. Thus, $C_{III.2}$ means 'DSynt-actant III is implemented by the linguistic means in column III and line 2'.

In this way, the GP of the head word L specifies all possible combinations of the syntactic actants of L, taking into consideration their surface form.

5.4.3.3 The semantic derivation and lexical cooccurrence zone in an ECD lexical entry

The semantic derivation and lexical cooccurrence zone in an ECD article embodies the most important feature that the ECD offers in comparison with other dictionaries—a **lexical function zone**. Lexical functions were introduced and discussed in *4.2, p. 90ff*; here, I will demonstrate their use in a dictionary.

A **lexical function** [= LF] is, roughly speaking, a very general—that is, sufficiently abstract—meaning 'f', which is implemented by a lexeme L' whose choice depends on the lexeme L for which the meaning 'f' is expressed: $f(L) = L'$. Thus, if L = CRIME and 'f_i' = 'one who does ...', then f_i(CRIME) = L' = CRIMINAL; if L = LECTURE, then f_i(LECTURE) = LECTURER. This f_i is the LF S_1 (*nomen agentis*): a paradigmatic LF. But if 'f_j' = 'do', then f_j(CRIME) = COMMIT (*commit a crime*); with L = LECTURE and the same 'f_j', L' = DELIVER (*deliver a lecture*). In this case, f_j is the LF Oper_1 (a semantically empty support verb): a syntagmatic LF.

In the lexical entry for L, paradigmatic LFs specify all L'_i that can be used in text instead of L: L's synonyms, antonyms, conversives, structural derivatives (nominalizations, verbalizations, adjectivalizations, adverbializations), *nomina agentis/patientis/loci*, etc. For instance, if L = PIG and 'f_k' = 'place where ...', then L' = PIGSTY; with L

= PISTOL and the same 'f_k', L' = HOLSTER; f_k(CRIME) = CRIME SCENE. In this case, f_k is the LF S_{loc}.

Syntagmatic LFs describe restricted lexical cooccurrence. But what is this? In all standard cases, cooccurrence of lexemes is determined by their meaning. *Please choose a stick of black color/a purse of black color* are quite normal, trivial expressions, while #*Please choose a sigh of black color* sounds weird; however, in order to be aware of that, one does not need to be a good English speaker, since the reason is purely semantic: you cannot understand how a sigh —an immaterial act—can be of any color. The expression #*a sigh of black color* does not violate any rule of English, so that this incompatibility should not be specifically indicated in a grammar or a lexicon of English: the incompatibility of the noun *sigh* with the expression *of black color* follows from the incompatibility of their meanings. It is clear *a priori* that lexemes meaning 'sigh' and 'of black color' will not be compatible in any language.

Now, take such expressions as *make a lecture, *make a crime or *make a favor: here we have another story. Semantically, everything is in order, and the meaning of these phrases is clear. However, they are ungrammatical, since they violate purely linguistic norms of lexical cooccurrence. Instead of *make*, English prescribes the use of three different verbs: *deliver a lecture*, *commit a crime* and *do a favor*. A different language might require different verbs. In French, you *make* lectures and favors and *commit* crimes, in Russian you *read* lectures, *perform* crimes and *make* favors, etc. This is what we call **restricted lexical cooccurrence** and what is formally described in terms of syntagmatic lexical functions.

The whole of semantic derivatives and restricted lexical cooccurrence in a language can be described by means of between 50 and 60 simple standard LFs and their combinations. An ECD lexical entry for an LU L specifies the values of all LFs applicable to L; in this way, the semantic derivatives and restricted lexical cooccurrence of L are covered fully and systematically. Let me illustrate with two Russian nouns— the lexemes OŠIBKA1 'spelling mistake' and OŠIBKA2 'erroneous act'— and five syntagmatic LFs: 'do' [= $\mathtt{Oper}_1$], 'begin' [= $\mathtt{Incep}$], 'take place' [= `Func`$_0$], 'liquidate' = 'do so that Y does not take place anymore' [= `Liqu`] and 'very'/'intense' [= `Magn`].

OŠIB|KA1 'spelling, calculation, etc. mistake'

    `Oper`$_1$: *dopustit´* 'accept', *sdelat´* 'do' [~*ku v* 'in' N$_Y$]
    [`Magn`^{quant} + A$_2$] : *polnyj* 'full' [~*ok*]
    `IncepFunc`$_2$: *vkralas´* 'crept into' [*v* 'into' N$_Y$]
    `LiquFunc`$_2$: *ispravit´* 'correct', *ustranit´* 'remove' [~*ku v* 'in' N$_Y$]
    `Magn` : *grubaja* 'rude'

OŠIB|KA2 'erroneous act'

    `Oper`$_1$: *dopustit´* 'accept', *sdelat´* 'do', *soveršit´* 'accomplish' [~*ku*]
    `IncepFunc`$_0$: *proizošla* 'happened', *slučilas´* 'occurred', **coll.** *vyšla* 'resulted'
    `LiquFunc`$_0$: *ispravit´* 'correct' [~*ku*]; *iskupit´* 'expiate' [~*ku*]
    `Magn` : *grubaja* 'rude'; *ser´ëznaja* 'serious' < *nepopravimaja* 'irreparable', *tragičeskaja* 'tragic'

Different lexical units that compose the value **f**(L) of an LF **f** applied to an LU L need not to be completely synonymous. Thus, *ser´ëznaja ošibka* 'serious mistake' ≠ *nepopravimaja ošibka* 'irreparable mistake'. In such cases, the semantic difference is marked in the lexical entry for L in various ways. In the lexical entry for OŠIBKA2, the symbol " < " shows that an irreparable mistake is "more" than a grave mistake. But the semantic difference between the elements of the value of an LF applied to a LU L can be other than those of degree. For instance, 'tragic mistake' implies consequences of a moral nature (human sufferings or death), which are absent from even 'the most serious mistake' and 'irreparable mistake'. To account for these differences, the lexicographer can distinguish semantic subtypes of lexical functions, attach semantic distinguishers to the elements of the value of the given LF, etc.; however, I cannot go into such details here.

 Note that differences in the values of LFs applied to a lexical item can force the splitting of this item into two lexemes. In other words, LFs are instrumental for sense discrimination.

5.4 THE EXPLANATORY COMBINATORIAL DICTIONARY 163

Each element of the value **f**(L) carries, when needed, its own government pattern and all other constraints necessary for its correct use in text.

In the next section I will present two lexical entries from the Russian ECD (Mel'čuk & Zholkovsky 1984), which should give the reader a fairly good idea of how this dictionary is constructed. This published fragment of a Russian ECD includes 750 lexemes, united in 283 vocables. Russian has probably 500,000 lexemes (a rough estimate); it follows that the published Russian ECD covers only a minuscule part of the Russian lexicon—namely, 0.15%. However, the first and most difficult step has been taken, and the ECD cause is alive and well. A lexicographic group in Moscow, headed by Ju. Apresjan, is actively developing a Russian dictionary based on similar ideas: Apresjan *et al*. 2004 and Apresjan (ed.) 2010, 2014.

The ECD presents a finely detailed model for the elaboration of other dictionaries, both monolingual and bilingual; see, for instance, Mel'čuk *et al*. 1984–1999 and Mel'čuk & Polguère 2007 for French (*5.4.1*, p. 153), Alonso Ramos 2005, 2006 and Vincze *et al*. 2011 for Spanish, and Mackenzie 2015 for Eastern Penan. There are also possibilities opening up for new applications: an ECD can be used as, or in conjunction with, a manual for language learners, as a reference book for translators, editors or journalists, as a lexical database for automatic text processing, etc. At first sight, an ECD with its many formalisms, can look quite forbidding. However, as previously noted, it does not take too long to grasp the most essential of these. Furthermore, one can use an ECD while ignoring many of its formalisms—for example, the names of the lexical functions (`Oper`, `Labor`, `PredAble`, ...). If the user has mastered the language in question sufficiently, he can simply read the lists of phrases (i.e., the values of the LFs), without understanding the formal expressions in the left-hand column. He will be able to deduce the meanings, and he will see how the phrases should be used. Thus, an ECD is by no means restricted to specialists or people with a taste for formalisms; most of the information it contains is available to everybody.

5.4.4 Two sample lexical entries of a Russian ECD

Two full lexical entries from the published Russian ECD will serve as an illustration: the verb VOSXIŠČAT´SJA 'admire' and the noun VOSXIŠČENIE 'admiration' (some corrections have been introduced that seem necessary now, more than 30 years later). To make it easy for the reader, all lexicographic information is given directly in English. The English glosses of Russian expressions are as literal as possible.

VOSXIŠČÉNI|E ⟨VOSXIŠČÉN´|E⟩, ~ja, **no** plural; noun, neuter

Definition

> *vosxiščenie X-a Y-om* 'X's admiration for Y':
> 'X's intense positive feeling caused1 by the fact that X, perceiving Y, considers Y to be very good, this feeling being of the kind of that a person usually has in these situations' [= $S_0(vosxiščat´sja)$].

> Cf. LJUBOVANIE ≈ 'watching with pleasure'

Government Pattern

X ⇔ I	Y ⇔ II
[whose admiration]	[admiration for what]
1. N_{GEN}	1. N_{INSTR}
2. $A_{(poss)}(N)$	2. *pered* 'before' N_{INSTR}
	3. (*pered*) *tem, čto* lit. 'before/for this that' CLAUSE
	4. (*pered*) *tem* lit. 'before/for this', WH-word CLAUSE

> *vosxiščenie Peti ⟨publiki⟩* 'Pete's ⟨public's⟩ admiration'
> *moë ⟨Petino⟩ vosxiščenie* 'my ⟨Pete's⟩ admiration'
> *vosxiščenie mamy učenikom ⟨ego sposobnostjami⟩* 'Mom's admiration for this pupil ⟨for his talents⟩'
> *vosxiščenie publiki (pered) krasotoj vida* 'the public's admiration for the beauty of the view' ⟨*pered osoboj korolja* 'before the King's personality'⟩
> *moë vosxiščenie (pered) tem, čto u nix stol´ko xorošix knig* 'my admiration before/for the.fact that they have so many good books'

5.4 THE EXPLANATORY COMBINATORIAL DICTIONARY

moë vosxiščenie (pered) tem, skol´ko u nix xorošix knig 'my admiration before/for the.fact that they have so many good books'

Lexical Functions

Syn_n	: *vostorg*1 'delight', *èntuziazm* 'enthusiasm'
Anti_n	: *otvraščenie* 'disgust'
Gener	: *čuvstvo***I.1a** [~*ja*] 'feeling'; *èmocija* 'emotion'
V_0	: *vosxiščat´sja* 'admire'
usual.S_1	: *poklonnik* 'admirer'
S_2	: **literary** *ob"ekt* 'object¹2', *predmet* 'object¹1' [~*ja*]
A_1	: *ispolnennyj* 'filled', *polnyj* 'full' [~*ja*] //*vosxiščënnyj*1 'admiring'
[Magn + A_1]	: *preispolnennyj* 'overfilled' [~*ja* ⟨~*em*⟩]
Able_2	: *dostojnyj (vsjačeskogo)* 'worth of (all) admiration' [~*ja*] //*vosxititel´nyj* 'admirable'
PredAble_2	: *zasluživat´ (vsjačeskogo)* [~*ja*] 'deserve (all) admiration'
Magn	: *glubokoe* 'deep' | G(V.) ≠ IncepOper_1 < *neopisuemoe* 'undescribable', *polnoe* 'full', *soveršennoe* 'perfect'
NonMagn	: *umerennoe* 'moderate' < *slaboe* 'weak'
$\text{Magn}_1^{\text{quant}}$	: *vseobščee* 'universal' | D_I(V.) = Λ
Ver_1	: *iskrennee* 'sincere', *nepoddel´noe* 'unfeigned'
AntiVer_1	: *delannoe* 'feigned', *preuveličennoe* 'exaggerated', *pritvornoe* 'simulated'
Adv_1	: *v* 'in' [~*i*] | D_I(V.) = Λ [*On zastyl v vosxiščenii* lit. 'He froze in admiration'. = 'He was stock-still with admiration'.]; *s* 'with' [~*em*] | G = Y‚$_{\text{psych}}$‚, D_{II}(V.) = Λ, **not** V.→Magn [*On pročël èto s* (*polnym) *vosxiščeniem* 'He read this with (*full) admiration'.]
Adv_2	: *k* 'to' [~*ju*] | **if not** V.→Magn_1, **then** D_I(B.) ≠ Λ [*K neopisuemomu vosxiščeniju rebënka, Maša snova zavizžala* lit. 'To the child's undescribable admiration Masha squealed again'.]
Oper_1	: *ispytyvat´* 'experience' [*pered* 'before' N ~*e*], *byt´* 'be' [*ot* 'from' N_Y *v* 'in' ~*i*]

IncepOper$_1$: *prijti* 'come' [*ot* 'from' N$_Y$ *v* 'into' ~*e*] [*Ja prišël v vosxiščenie ot eë zamečanija* lit. 'I came into admiration from her remark'.]

CausOper$_1$: *privesti*II.2 'bring' [N$_{X\text{-ACC}}$ *v* 'into' ~*e*] [*Svoim zamečaniem ona privela menja v vosxiščenie* lit. 'By her remark, she brought me into admiration' = '... she made me admire her'.]

Oper$_2$: *vnušat'* 'instill' [N$_{X\text{-DAT}}$ ~*e*] | **no** perf. aspect; *vyzyvat'* 'provoke' [(*u* 'at' N) ~*e*]

FinFunc$_0$: *projti* 'pass'

Labor$_{12}$: *otnosit'sja* 'have an attitude' [*k* 'towards' N$_Y$ *s* 'with' ~*em*]

IncepLabor$_{21}$
 : *privesti*II.1 'bring' [N$_{X\text{-ACC}}$ *v* 'in' ~*e*] [*Eë zamečanie privelo menja v vosxiščenie* lit. 'Her remark brought me into admiration'.]

Conv$_{21}$Manif→Z
 : [N$_{Z\text{-NOM}}$] *dyšat'* 'breathe' [~*em*] | D$_{II}$(V.) = Λ, Z is a communication from X [*Ego pis'mo dyšalo vosxiščeniem* lit. 'His letter breathed with admiration'. = '... exuded admiration'.]

A$_2$Manif : *ispolenneyj* 'filled', *polnyj* 'full' [~*ja*] | G = *look, smile, gesture, letter, ...*; D$_{II}$(V.) = Λ //*vosxiščënnyj*2 'rapt' [*rëv* 'roar', *vzdox* 'gasp', ...]

SingS$_0$NonMagnManif
 : *notka* 'trace, suggestion' [~*ja*]

Adv$_1$Caus$_1$Manif
 : *s* 'with' [~*em*] | D$_{II}$(V.) = Λ //*vosxiščënno* 'admiringly'

Perm$_1$Manif
 : *ne skryvat'* 'not conceal' [(*svoego* 'one's') ~*ja*]

A$_2$Perm$_1$Manif
 : *neskryvaemoe* 'unconcealed'

NonPermManifNonAble$_1$
 : *ne v silax skryt'* [*svoë* 'one's' ~*e*] 'unable to conceal'

5.4 THE EXPLANATORY COMBINATORIAL DICTIONARY

```
Degrad^motor (body)—Sympt_23
```
: *zameret'* 'freeze, become stock-still' [*ot* 'from' ~*ja* ⟨*v* 'in' ~*i*⟩] | $D_{II}(V.) = \Lambda$

```
Excess^fulg (eyes)—Sympt_123
```
: [*u* 'at' N (*ot* 'from' ~*ja*)] *svetit'sja* 'glow', *sijat'* 'shine' | $D_I(V.)$ = person, $D_{II}(V.) = \Lambda$ [**U tolpy glaza sijali ot vosxiščenija* lit. 'By the crowd, the eyes shone with admiration' = 'The eyes of the crowd...'.]

```
exclaim—Sympt_23
```
: *axnut'* ≈ 'gasp' [*ot* 'from' ~*ja* ⟨*v* 'in' ~*i*⟩]

Notations

1. ⟨ ⟩ : the angular brackets, as everywhere in *LMT*, enclose variants.
2. $\cap$: 'with intersection' (an approximate `Syn` or `Anti`).
3. G(X) : G is the syntactic governor of X; if X is not specified, G is the Synt-governor of the expression whose conditions of use include the symbol G.
4. $D_i(X)$: X's deep-syntactic actant *i*.
5. $D_i(X) = \Lambda$: X's deep-syntactic actant *i* is empty—that is, it cannot be expressed. Thus, D_I(VOSXIŠČENIE) cannot be expressed if VOSXIŠČENIE is modified by the adjective VSEOBŠČIJ 'universal': *ko vseobščemu vosxiščeniju *detej* 'to the universal admiration *of the kids'. The reason is obvious: in this context, VSEOBŠČIJ expresses D_I (≈ **'all** admire').
6. G = Y means that DSynt-governor [= G] of the collocation *s vosxiščeniem* 'with admiration' denotes Y, the source and the object of admiration: the sentence *Ivan s vosxiščeniem uznal, čto dom prodan* 'Ivan learned with admiration that the house had been sold' implies that Ivan's admiration was caused by the fact "Ivan learned that the house had been sold." $Y_{\cdot psych\cdot}$ means that the collocation *s vosxiščeniem* combines mainly with verbs denoting information processing in the human psyche (SLUŠAT' 'listen', DUMAT' 'believe', VSPOMINAT' 'remember', RASSKAZYVAT' 'tell', etc.).

Examples

Ix vosxiščenie dlilos´ nedolgo 'Their admiration did not last long'. | *Vaš postupok zaslužiwaet vsjačeskogo vosxiščenija* 'Your act deserves all admiration'. | *Vdoxnovennaja igra pianista privela v vosxiščenie ves´ zal* 'The pianist's inspired performance brought the entire audience into admiration'. | *Pis´mo ego dyšalo glubokom vosxiščeniem i ljubov´ju* 'His letter exuded deep admiration and love'. | *On s neskryvaemym vosxiščeniem* ⟨= Adv$_1$Caus$_1$Manif = *vosxiščënno*⟩ *smotrel na učitelja* 'He looked at his teacher with unconcealed admiration'. | *Deti s vosxiščeniem* ⟨= Adv$_1$ ≠ *vosxiščënno*⟩ *uznali o priezde cirka* 'The children learned with admiration about the arrival of the circus'. | *Krome ruž´ja, ja dal emu nož, ot kotorogo on prišël v polnoe vosxiščenie* 'In addition to the gun, I gave him a knife, from which he came into full admiration'. | *Tščatel´nost´ ego analiza ne možet ne vyzvat´ vosxiščenija* 'The accuracy of his analysis cannot fail to provoke admiration'. | *Uvidev ëlku, devočka zamerla v glubokom vosxiščenii; glazki u neë zasijali* 'Seeing the Christmas tree, the little girl stood stock-still with deep admiration; her eyes shone'.

VOSXIŠČÁ|T´SJA, ~jus´, ~etsja; imperfective aspect

Definition

X vosxiščaetsja Y-om 'X admires Y':

'[α] |[perceiving Y,]| X has admiration [*vosxiščenie*] for Y, or [β] X produces utterances that express X's admiration for Y'.

☞ The symbols «|[ ]|» indicate the presupposition part of the definition: see Note 19, p. 209.

The symbols [α] and [β] are used to identify the two respective parts of the definition—for the ease of reference (see Constraints to the Government Pattern below).

Cf. LJUBOVAT´SJA 'watch with pleasure'.

Government Pattern

X ⇔ I [who admires]	Y ⇔ II [admires what]
1. N$_{NOM}$	1. N$_{INSTR}$ 2. *tem, čto* lit. 'by.the.fact that' CLAUSE 3. *tem* lit. 'by.the.fact', WH-word CLAUSE 4. "CLAUSE"

5.4 THE EXPLANATORY COMBINATORIAL DICTIONARY   169

1) $C_{II.4}$: $V_{\cdot[\alpha] + [\beta]}$
2) If $V_{\cdot[\alpha]}$, then Y = Λ **is undesirable**

☞ These two constraints are linked to the fact that the definition of VOSXIŠČAT′SJA is disjunctive: it includes the marker of disjunction OR, because this verb can mean either 'have admiration', or 'have admiration and express it in words'. VOSXIŠČAT′SJA can govern a clause (= Direct Speech, $C_{II.4}$) only when used for the second meaning.

My vse vosxiščaemsja vašej knigoj 'We all admire your book'. | *Maša gromko vosxiščalas′ tem, čto rebënok uže govoril* ⟨*tem, kakoj rebënok soobrazitel′nyj*⟩ lit. 'Masha loudly was.admiring the.fact that the. toddler already could.talk ⟨the.fact how the.toddler was.smart⟩'. | *«Potrjasajušče!» – vosxitilas′ Maša* lit. '«Brilliant!»—admired [= 'said admiringly'] Masha'.

Undesirable: ?*Maša vosxiščalas* 'Masha was.admiring'.

Lexical Functions

```
Conv₂₁       : vosxiščat′ 'cause admiration'
S₀⊂          : vosxiščenie 'admiration' | for V·[α]
usual.S₁     : poklonnik 'admirer'
Sing         : //vosxitit′sja 'have had admiration (and have produced
               utterances expressing it)'
MagnAble₁    : vostoržennyj 'prone to admire anything'
Pred.too.Able₁
             : po 'for' i-omu (j-omu) povodu 'pretext' | i = 'any', j =
               melkij 'tiny', ničtožnyj 'insignificant' [Maša vosxišča-
               etsja po vsjakomu melkomu povodu lit. 'Masha
               admires [= feels admiration] for any tiny pretext'.]
Able₂        : vosxititel′nyj 'admirable'
PredS₁Able₂
             : byt′ prelest′ 'be a charm' [On prosto prelest′! 'He
               simply is a charm!'], coll. byt′ vostorg₃ 'be delight' [On
               prosto vostorg′! 'He simply is a delight!']
Magn         : //vostorgat′sja 'be delighted' < ⌐byt′ bez pamjati⌐ lit.
               'be without memory'
```

```
NonMagn     : umerenno 'moderately'
Ver₁        : iskrenne 'sincerely'
[AntiVer + too.Magn]
            : neumerenno 'excessively'
Speaker signals that he V.
            : //Ax! 'Ah!', Ox! 'Oh!', Ogogo! ≈ 'Wow!', Ux ty!
              'Wow!', coll. (Kak) zdorovo! '(How) gorgeous!', coll.
              Vot èto da! ≈ 'This is something!'
Speaker signals that he V. people Y
            : //low-register Vo ⟨Nu⟩ daët ⟨dajut⟩! ≈ lit. 'He/They really
              give/s something!'
```

☞ The symbol // indicates so-called **fusion** (an element of an LF value is fused with this LF's keyword): the result is the expression of the meaning of the phrase "LF + its keyword" that does not contain the keyword.

Examples

Gosti počitali objazannost'ju vosxiščat'sja psarnej Kirila Petroviča – odin Dubrovskij molčal i xmurilsja [A.S. Puškin] 'The guests believed it to be their obligation to admire Kiril Petrovich's kennel; Dubrovsky was alone to keep silent and frown'. | *Ja iskrenne vosxiščalsja ego talantom* 'I was sincerely admiring his talent'. | *Rita gromko vosxiščalas' kartinoj* lit. 'Rita was loudly admiring the painting'. | *«Kakie u vas vsë imena udivitel'nye», – vosxitilsja Avrosimov, gotovyj vosxiščat'sja vsem* [B. Okudžava] '«What amazing names you all have!»—said Avrosimov admiringly; he was ready to admire anything'. | *Nam ne predpisyvalos' vosxiščat'sja v iskusstve tem ili drugim; my sami delali svoj vybor* 'Nobody was requiring us to admire this or that in art; we were making our choices ourselves'.

5.5 Meaning-Text linguistics and dependencies in natural language

The main formalism used in the Meaning-Text approach for semantic and syntactic representations is that of **dependency relations**.

A dependency is a binary relation that is anti-reflexive, anti-symmetric and non-transitive.[34] Dependency is designated by **D** and shown

5.5 MEANING-TEXT LINGUISTICS AND DEPENDENCIES

by an arrow: X→Y means 'Y depends on X'; X is the **governor** of Y, while Y is a **dependent** of X. Linguistic dependencies link different linguistic units (semantemes, lexical units, and grammemes) in the corresponding structures.

5.5.1 Three types of linguistic dependency

Natural languages distinguish at least three types of syntagmatic dependency between elements in texts—semantic, syntactic, and morphological dependencies. (I will not consider here other syntagmatic relations between linguistic units, such as communicative dependency and anaphoric links.)

Semantic dependency [= Sem-**D**] holds between semantemes— that is, between the signifieds of lexical units. 'L_1'–sem→'L_2' means that semanteme 'L_2' is an argument of the predicative semanteme 'L_1': 'L_1'('L_2'). However, it is convenient to use a simplified representation of 'L_1'–sem→'L_2', writing L_1–sem→L_2. For instance, take sentence (58):

(58) *Then he struggled with the heart* [Yeats];

in it, we have

THEN–sem→STRUGGLE, HE←sem–STRUGGLE–sem→HEART,
and HEART–sem→HE.

Syntactic dependency [= Synt-**D**] holds between lexemes. L_1–synt→L_2 means that L_1 determines the distribution of the phrase L_1–synt→L_2 in the syntactic structures of language **L**—that is, L_1 determines the **passive syntactic valence** of this phrase. The linear position of L_2 in a clause is, in most cases, determined with respect to L_1: L_2 either precedes L_1, or follows it, or else can precede or follow L_1 depending on the context. In (58), lexemes are syntactically linked as follows:

STRUGGLE$_{IND, PAST}$–synt→THEN, STRUGGLE$_{IND, PAST}$–synt→HE,
STRUGGLE$_{IND, PAST}$–synt→WITH, WITH–synt→HEART$_{SG}$,
HEART$_{SG}$–synt→THE

Note that, in the pair of lexemes THEN and STRUGGLE in sentence (58), the Sem-**D** and the Synt-**D** are mutually inverse:

THEN–**sem**→STRUGGLE, but THEN←**synt**–STRUGGLE

 This is so because the Sem-**D** ("what is the argument of what?") and the Synt- **D** ("what controls the syntactic distribution of what?") are of a radically different nature, and there is no reason for them to be "in agreement." This fact is discussed in some detail below.

Morphological dependency, or Morph-**D**, holds between grammemes and/or syntactic features of LUs.[35] L_1–**morph**→L_2 means that a grammeme or a syntactic feature of L_1 determines some grammemes of L_2. In the phrase HE$_{SG}$–**morph**→BE$_{IND, PRES, 3, SG}$ (*he is* [*struggling*]) the grammeme SG of the pronoun HE imposes the grammeme SG on the verb, and the pronoun's syntactic feature «3rd person» imposes the grammeme 3 on it, resulting in [*he*] *is*. In the French phrase LE$_{FEM, SG}$←**morph**–PROVINCE$_{(fem)SG}$–**morph**→BEAU$_{FEM, SG}$ (*la belle province* 'the beautiful province') the grammeme SG of the noun PROVINCE and its syntactic feature «fem» impose the grammemes SG and FEM on the article LE 'the' (⇒ *la*) and the adjective BEAU 'beautiful' (⇒ *belle*).

Sem-**D**s and Synt-**D**s exist in all languages and they appear in all sentences of a language. In a sentence, they form connected structures: all LUs of a sentence are interconnected by Sem-**D**s and Synt-**D**s. For this reason, both types of dependency are explicitly reflected in formal representations of sentences—by means of semantic networks and syntactic trees. Morph-**D**s do not exist in many languages and they do not necessarily appear in any sentence of a language that has them; they may not form connected structures even in sentences where they appear.[36] Therefore, Morph-**D**s do not have an explicit reflection in formal linguistic representations of utterances: they are, of course, formally accounted for, but in a different way: they are used by syntactic rules, which compute, when need be, the Morph-**D**s necessary to produce correct morphologization of a syntactic structure.

The mutual autonomy of these three types of dependency is manifested in the fact that they combine in all logically possible ways—

5.5 MEANING-TEXT LINGUISTICS AND DEPENDENCIES

lexemes L_1 and L_2 in one clause can be related by any one of 14 logically possible combinations of dependencies of the three types. A full list of all possible combinations of dependency types is given in Appendix III; here I will give three examples from this list:

2. L_1–sem→L_2: *Mary*$_{L_2}$ and *kiss*$_{L_1}$ in *Mary wants to kiss John*; there is no direct syntactic or morphological dependency between *Mary* and *kiss*.

9. $L_1\overset{\text{—synt→}}{\text{—morph→}}L_2$: wordforms *in*$_{L_1}$ and *res*$_{L_2}$ in the Latin phrase *in medias res* lit. 'into middle things' = 'into the midst of things'. Here the preposition IN 'into' syntactically and morphologically dominates the noun RES$_{PL}$ 'things', imposing the accusative on it; L_1 and L_2 are not linked semantically. (The preposition 'into' semantically dominates 'medium' = 'the midst', which is implemented by the adjective MEDIUS 'middle': 'into–sem→medium'; *medias* is the feminine form of the adjective MEDIUS in the accusative of the plural—it agrees with the accusative of the plural of the feminine noun RES.)

13. $L_1\overset{\underset{\text{←morph—}}{\text{—synt→}}}{\text{←sem—}}L_2$: wordforms *mirov+ê*$_{L_1}$ and *nû*$_{L_2}$ in the Kurmandji phrase *mirovê nû* lit. 'man new' = 'new man'; the adjective, syntactically dependent on the noun, is its semantic governor, just as with any adjective in any language. However, in this case, the adjective does more: it is the noun's morphological controller, since it imposes on the noun a special grammeme expressed by **-ê** (a suffix called "izafet," a marker of the fact that this noun has a postposed dependent).

5.5.2 Criteria for syntactic dependency

Sem-Ds are perceived through meaning, and Morph-Ds (agreement, including congruence, and government) are observable through form; but the Synt-Ds that mediate between these are purely abstract entities that cannot be grasped mentally or sensorily. Therefore, establishing Synt-Ds in language **L** requires **formal criteria**. More precisely, in order to elaborate the set of surface-syntactic relations [= SSyntRels] for language **L**, three types of criteria have to be involved:

A : Criterion for establishing the presence of a syntactic relation between L_1 and L_2 in a given utterance, or for syntactic connectedness: L_1–**synt**–L_2 or L_1–s̸y̸n̸t̸–L_2?

B1–3: Criteria for establishing the direction of the syntactic relation between L_1 and L_2, or for syntactic dominance: L_1–**synt**→L_2 or L_1←**synt**–L_2?

C1–3: Criteria for establishing the type of the syntactic relation holding between L_1 and L_2: what is the SSyntRel **r** in L_1–**r**→L_2?

In what follows these criteria are described rather loosely, as I am trying to convey a general idea, while leaving aside several important details; for a complete presentation, see Mel'čuk 2009 and 2015: 412–434.

Criterion A : The presence of a syntactic link between L_1 and L_2, or "Are L_1 and L_2 syntactically connected in this utterance?"

The presence of a syntactic link between two given lexemes in a given utterance is established based on prosody and linear order.

> Two lexemes L_1 and L_2 in an utterance **U** are directly linked by a syntactic relation (= L_1–**synt**–L_2) if and only if the following two conditions are simultaneously met:
> 1. L_1 and L_2 are able to form a prosodic unity (= a phrase) in **L**.
> 2. The linear position of one of the lexemes L_1 and L_2 in **U** is determined by the other.

Criteria B1–3 : The direction of the syntactic link between L_1 and L_2, or "In L_1—L_2, which is the head?"

Criterion B1 (syntactic): the passive valence of the phrase L_1–**synt**–L_2.

> In the phrase L_1–**synt**–L_2, the lexeme L_1 is the syntactic governor of L_2 (= the head of the phrase), if the passive valence of the whole phrase is determined by the passive valence of L_1 to a greater extent than by the passive valence of L_2.

The **passive valence** of the phrase *with Mary* is fully determined by the preposition WITH; therefore, WITH–**synt**→MARY.

5.5 MEANING-TEXT LINGUISTICS AND DEPENDENCIES

If L_1 and L_2 have identical passive valence, Criterion B1 cannot identify the governor; Criterion B2 is to be invoked.

Criterion B2 (morphological): morphological links between the phrase L_1–**synt**–L_2 and its external context.

> In the phrase L_1–**synt**–L_2, the lexeme L_1 is the syntactic governor of L_2 (= the head of the phrase), if L_1 determines some grammemes of certain lexemes external to the phrase or if certain external lexemes determine some grammemes of L_1.

L_1 is the morphological contact point of the phrase L_1–**synt**→L_2.

In the Russian phrase *štat*$_{(masc)}$ *Nebrask+a*$_{(fem)}$ lit. 'State [of] Nebraska' Criterion B1 gives no answer (both components are nouns that have the same passive valence); but Criterion B2 identifies the noun ŠTAT$_{(masc)}$ as the governor:

1) In *so štat+om*$_{INSTR}$ *Nebrask+a*$_{NOM}$ 'with [the] state [of] Nebraska' only ŠTAT receives the grammeme of the governed instrumental case from the "outside"—namely, from the preposition SO 'with' (NEBRASKA remaining in the nominative).

2) An adjective and the finite verb agree with ŠTAT$_{(masc)}$ rather than with NEBRASKA$_{(fem)}$: *Amerikansk+ij*$_{MASC, SG, NOM}$ *štat*$_{SG, NOM}$ *Nebrask+a*$_{SG, NOM}$ *byl+Ø*$_{MASC, SG}$ ... '[The] American state [of] Nebraska was ...', *amerikansk+omu*$_{MASC, SG, DAT}$ *štat+u*$_{SG, DAT}$ *Nebrask+a*$_{SG, NOM}$ '[to.the] American state [of] Nebraska', etc.

Criterion B2 is, of course, only applicable in a language that has inflectional morphology.

If Criterion B2 does not work (either because **L** has no agreement and no government or because L_1 and L_2 have identical morphological properties), Criterion B3 must be applied.

Criterion B3 (semantic): the denotation of the phrase.

> In the phrase L_1–**synt**–L_2, the lexeme L_1 is the syntactic governor of L_2 (= the head of the phrase), if the denotation of the phrase is a subset of the denotation of L_1 rather than a subset of the denotation of L_2.

L_1 determines the kind of the denotation of the phrase. In the phrase *noun suffix* the syntactic governor is SUFFIX, because the phrase *noun suffix* denotes a type of suffix, not a type of noun.

Criteria C1–3: The type of the syntactic link between L_1 and L_2, or "In L_1–r→L_2, what is the surface-syntactic relation **r**?"

For a configuration L_1–**r[?]**→L_2, one has to establish the type of SSyntRel **r[?]**. If at least one of the requirements stated in Criteria C1–3 is not satisfied, the hypothetical SSyntRel **r[?]** must be split into two (or more) SSyntRels.

Criterion C1 (minimal pairs): semantic contrast.

The hypothetical SSyntRel **r[?]** can be accepted as a SSyntRel of **L** iff it does not give rise to a semantic contrast.

> The configuration L_1–**r[?]**→L_2 cannot be implemented by two actual phrases that
> 1) contrast semantically, but
> 2) are formally distinguished only by syntactic expressive means— that is, by word order, syntactic prosody, or syntactic grammemes.

The Russian configuration DESJAT´←**r[?]**–KILO 'ten←**r[?]**–kilos' has two surface realizations having different meanings: *desjat´ kilo* 'ten kilos' vs. *kilo desjat´* 'maybe ten kilos'. The formal difference between the phrases *desjat´ kilo* and *kilo desjat´* is purely syntactic: word order. Therefore, the hypothetical SSyntRel **r[?]** must be split into two SSyntRels:

DESJAT´←**quantificative**–KILO ⇔ *desjat´ kilo*

and

DESJAT´←**approximate-quantificative**–KILO ⇔ *kilo desjat´*

Criterion C1 does not allow one to unite under the same SSyntRel two sets of semantically contrasting constructions. This is a particular case of the application of the more general minimal pair criterion.

5.5 MEANING-TEXT LINGUISTICS AND DEPENDENCIES

Criterion C2 (substitutability): substitutability in syntactic structures.

☞ $\Delta_{(X)}$ stands for 'SSynt-tree Δ whose top node is a lexeme of the syntactic class X'.

The hypothetical SSyntRel **r[?]** can be accepted as a SSyntRel of language **L** iff it has the following property (= Quasi-Kunze Property):

> **L** has a syntactic class X other than substitute pronouns and such that in any SSynt-structure $\overline{S}$ a phrase L–r[?]→$\Delta_{(Y)}$ can be replaced with L–r[?]→$\Delta_{(X)}$ (but not necessarily vice versa) without affecting the well-formedness of $\overline{S}$.

To put it differently, each SSyntRel of **L** must have a prototypical dependent that is acceptable with any governor. Thus, consider the phrases

    HAVE–r1[?]→SLEEP$_{PAST.PART}$ (*have slept*)

and

    BE–r2[?]→ SLEEP$_{PRES.PART}$ (*be sleeping*)

In these, the hypothetical SSyntRel **r[?]** does not possess the Quasi-Kunze property:

    *have–r$_2$[?]→sleeping and **be–r$_1$[?]→slept*;

English has no potential dependent that would work in both cases. Therefore, the hypothetical SSyntRel **r[?]** must be split into two SSyntRels:

    HAVE–**perfect-analytical**→SLEEP$_{PAST.PART}$ ⇔   *have slept*

and

    BE–**progressive-analytical**→ SLEEP$_{PRES.PART}$ ⇔   *be sleeping*

Criterion C2 precludes the unity of a particular **r[?]** where it does not possess the Quasi-Kunze property.

The things are different with the pair of phrases of the following form:

    SLEEP–r1[?]→JOHN (*John sleeps.*)

and

    BE–r$_2$[?]→ SMOKE$_{INF}$ (*To smoke is [harmful.]*)

An infinitive cannot depend on the verb SLEEP as its subject: *To smoke sleeps*, and that is true of most English verbs. But a noun works in all cases—that is, with any verb: *John is harmful*. A noun is the syntactic class X required by C2 Criterion for a prototypical dependent. As a result, $r_1[?]$ and $r_2[?]$ can be united into one SSyntRel **r** = **subjectival**:

SLEEP$_{PRES}$–subjectival→JOHN ⇔ *John sleeps.*
and
BE$_{PRES}$–subjectival→SMOKE ⇔ *To smoke is [harmful.]*

Criterion C3 (repeatabilty): repeatability with the same governor.

The hypothetical SSyntRel **r[?]** can be accepted as a SSyntRel of **L** iff it is either non-repeatable or unlimitedly repeatable.

> A SSyntRel **r** is non-repeatable iff only one arc labeled **r** can start from a given node; it is unlimitedly repeatable iff any number of arcs arc labeled **r** can start from a given node.

What is forbidden is limited repeatability—say, just two or three arcs labeled **r**.

To understand the necessity of Criterion C3, consider example (59). Persian abounds in expressions of the following form:

(59) *Män name+ha+ra   post   kärd+äm*
    I   letter PL DirO sending$_N$ did 1.SG
    lit. 'I letters sending did'. = 'I sent letters'.

We see here a verb–noun collocation *post kärd+än* 'sending do' = 'send' [**-än** being the marker of the infinitive] of a type that is widespread in Persian: *därs dädän* 'lesson give' = 'teach', *däst zädän* 'hand hit' = 'touch', *täbrik goftän* 'congratulation say' = 'congratulate', etc. The noun component POST (DÄRS, DÄST, TÄBRIK) looks like a DirO. However, a transitive verb with this object remains transitive and controls a "genuine" DirO—in (59), NAMEHA 'letters'—which can have the suffix **-ra**, marker of the DirO. A hypothetical SSyntRel **r[?]** (= hypothetical **direct-objectival** SSyntRel) could appear in such expressions only twice, so that this SSyntRel would be limitedly repeatable, which is forbidden by Criterion C3. Therefore, for the expressions of the type illustrated in (59), the SSyntRel **r[?]** must be split in two: NAMEHA←**dir-obj(ectival)**–KÄRD–**quasi-dir-obj**→POST; the noun component of such collocations (= the base) is a quasi-direct object (different from the pseudo-direct object, mentioned in Appendix II, p. 186, No. 4). To consider the DirO and the Quasi-DirO as the same clause element would create unnecessary problems, since there are significant differences in their syntactic behavior.

An apparent exception to Criterion C3 is found in so-called resumptive clitics in Balkan languages [37], as well as in Spanish:

(60) a. Albanian (*th* = /θ/, *ë* = /ə/, *j* =/j/)

   (i) *Barin   e   thanë   në furrë*
       grass-ACC **it-ACC** dried-3.PL in oven
       'The grass was dried in the oven'. =
       lit. 'Grass it «they».dried in oven'.

   (ii) *Mos i   thuaj njeriu!*
        not **he-DAT** tell nobody-DAT
        'Don't tell anybody!' = lit. 'Not him tell nobody!'

b. Spanish (*z* = /θ/, *j* = /χ/)

   *Al azúcar Julio **le** tiene una viva aversión*
   lit. 'To.the sugar Julio **to.it** has a strong aversion'.

In the case of a resumptive clitic the corresponding SSyntRel is repeated just twice, which looks like a violation of Criterion C3. However, there is in fact no violation: the resumptive clitic does not express a separate actant, but simply duplicates the expression of the same actant.

Using the criteria formulated above (and, in many cases, analogy as well), a researcher can establish, for language **L**, a list of **L**'s SSyntRels, just in the same way he would establish the inventory of cases or phonemes. A tentative list of English SSyntRels is proposed in Appendix II, p. 184*ff.*

Summing Up

The moment has come for me to take leave of my readers and wish them good luck in their future encounters with languages and linguistics. Some Arctic people have a nice custom: when a guest is preparing to travel home or simply leave to go somewhere else, the host offers him something useful or pleasant for the trip; in the first place, some food, but other things are acceptable, too—like adornments or pieces of clothing.* What can I offer the reader who is leaving this book?

I can summarize the contents of the *LMT* by outlining the six most important ideas put forward in the book. A linguistic description must:

- Be a description of **meaning-text correspondences**, implemented in the direction from meaning to text. I hope that my examples have shown the fruitfulness of a synthetic orientation for linguistic research and description. Language is spoken, and the Speaker is the leading figure. People speak in order to express some meanings, so the elaboration of semantic metalanguage is a prime task for linguists.
- Be a **functional model** of a particular language or of one of its fragments. Formal modeling of linguistic phenomena is in fact the only efficient methodology for studying and describing languages.
- Include, as its vital component, an **explanatory combinatorial dictionary**, which supplies all the linguistic information needed for the correct use of each lexical unit.
- Be based on **powerful paraphrasing**, on the semantic as well as deep-syntactic level.

---

* Alutor even has a special verb that denotes this action: TƏQAVIVƏK 'X offers a gift to Y who has been X's guest and is leaving X's house'.

- Be based on a **rigorous notional apparatus**. Well-defined notions and the corresponding terminology are vital for linguistics—especially, as stated at the beginning of the book, because linguists are forced to use a natural language when talking about languages.
- Be based on **dependencies between linguistic elements**. The words of any text are arranged in a linear order, but this arrangement, as well as groupings of words (≈ phrases) observed on the surface are merely the means a language uses to express the links—that is, dependencies—between elements in multidimensional thoughts.

And now, dear reader, be well, do good job and stay in touch!

Appendices

Appendix I : Phonetic Table

C'	palatalized consonant C
C'	glottalized (= laryngealized) consonant C
C^h	aspirated consonant C
C^w	rounded (= labialized) consonant C
Ç	pharyngealized (= emphatic) consonant C
V̄	long vowel V
Ṽ	nasal vowel V
ʌ	back middle open unrounded vowel [d*u*ck]
æ	front low unrounded vowel [b*a*ck]
β	voiced bilabial fricative consonant [*Sp.* lo*b*o 'wolf']
c	voiceless alveolar affricate consonant [= t͡s]
č	voiceless palato-alveolar affricate consonant [*ch*in]
ć	voiceless alveo-palatal affricate consonant
ð	voiced interdental fricative consonant [*th*e]
e	front middle closed unrounded vowel [*Fr.* *é*]
ɛ	front middle open unrounded vowel [*Fr.* *è*]
ə	central middle unrounded vowel [so-called "shwa"]
ġ	voiced uvular fricative consonant
γ	voiced velar fricative consonant
h	voiceless laryngeal fricative consonant [*h*and]
ħ	voiceless pharyngeal fricative consonant
ɨ	high central unrounded vowel

j	voiced palatal fricative consonant [*yoke*]/
	in Spanish: palatal glide [*Sp. pie* 'foot']
ɟ	voiced palatal stop consonant [as in *Would͡ you*...]
λ	voiced palatal lateral liquid [*Sp. ll, It. gl*]
ŋ	voiced velar nasal consonant [*ng*]
ɲ	voiced palatal nasal consonant [*Fr., It. gn; Sp. ñ*]
o	back middle closed rounded vowel [*Fr. eau*]
ɔ	back middle open rounded vowel [*Fr. comme*]
q	voiceless uvular stop consonant
r̄	voiced strong alveolar vibrant consonant [*r* with several thrills: *Sp. perro* 'dog']
š	voiceless postalveolar fricative consonant [*sh*]
θ	voiceless interdental fricative consonant [*think*]
u	back high rounded tense vowel [*fool*]
ʊ	back high rounded lax vowel [*full*]
w	voiced bilabial fricative consonant [*win*]/
	in Spanish : labiovelar glide [*Sp. puerta*]
x	voiceless velar fricative consonant [*Ger. ch*]
χ	voiceless uvular fricative consonant [*Sp. j*]
ž	voiced post-alveolar fricative consonant [*Fr. jour*]
ǯ	voiced palato-alveolar affricate consonant [*John*]
ʔ	voiceless laryngeal [= glottal] stop consonant [= glottal stop]
ʕ	voiced pharyngeal stop consonant [Arabic *'ayn*]
´	rising/high tone
`	falling/low tone
ˆ	rising-falling tone
ˇ	falling-rising tone
¯	level tone

Appendix II: Surface-Syntactic Relations of English

The proposed list of surface-syntactic relations of English has been compiled based on Mel'čuk & Pertsov 1987, with several corrections and additions (taking into account Iomdin 2010). It is, however, incomplete and, in many respects, controversial. Establishing the inventory of SSyntRels of a language is a challenging task, which by far surpasses the capacities of a single researcher (especially if he is not an English speaker and not even an expert on English syntax). Therefore, dear reader, please bear with me: what you see is no more than an extensive illustration..

The SSyntRels in this list are classified according to the following three major parameters:

Subordinate SSyntRels ~ Coordinate SSyntRels

A subordinate SSyntRel r_i in the phrase L_1–synt-r_i→L_2 is characterized by different syntactic behavior of L_1 and L_2, while a coordinate SSyntRel r_j in the phrase L_1–synt-r_j→L_2 implies potentially similar syntactic behavior of L_1 and L_2.

Clause-Level SSyntRels ~ Phrase-Level SSyntRels

A clause-level SSyntRel r_i links the syntactic heads of phrases within a clause, while a phrase-level SSyntRel r_j links the elements within a phrase.

Valence-Controlled SSyntRels ~ Non-Valence-Controlled SSyntRels

A valence-controlled SSyntRel **r** in the phrase L_1–synt-r→L_2 is specified in the government pattern of L_1; it corresponds to L's active syntactic valence.

Within the groups of SSyntRels thus obtained more specific divisions are drawn: the type of the phrase (nominal, prepositional, …) , the type of the SSyntRel (actantial, copredicative, …), etc.

First, here is a synopsis of the list of the SSynt-relations of English.

I Subordinate Surface-Syntactic Relations: 1–54
    I.1 Clause-Level SSyntRels: 1–20
        I.1.1 Valence-Controlled = Actantial SSyntRels
        I.1.2 Non-Valence-Controlled SSyntRels
            I.1.2.1 Copredicative SSyntRels

APPENDICES

    I.1.2.2 Circumstantial SSyntRels
    I.1.2.3 Extra-structural SSyntRels
I.2 Phrase-Level SSyntRels: 21–54
    I.2.1 Any Type of Phrase SSyntRels, Non-Valence-Controlled
    I.2.2 Nominal Phrase SSyntRels
        I.2.2.1 Valence-Controlled
        I.2.2.2 Valence-Controlled and Non-Valence-Controlled
        I.2.2.3 Non-Valence-Controlled
    I.2.3 Prepositional Phrase SSyntRels, Valence-Controlled
    I.2.4 Verbal Phrase (= Analytical Form) SSyntRels, Non-Valence-Controlled
    I.2.5 Conjunctional Phrase SSyntRels, Valence-Controlled
    I.2.6 Word-Like Phrase SSyntRels, Non-Valence-Controlled
II Coordinate Surface-Syntactic Relations: 55–58

And now, the list itself.

I Subordinate Surface-Syntactic Relations: 1–54

I.1 Clause-Level (= Clausal) SSyntRels: 1–20

    I.1.1 Valence-Controlled (= Actantial) SSyntRels: 1–12

1. Subjectival

[*As the*] ***reader***←subj–*will* [*have seen…*] | ***I***←subj–*am* [*fine.*]
That←subj–[*John left*]–*amazed* [*us.*] | ***It***←subj–*amazed*–[*us that John left.*]
It←subj–*was* [*dawning.*] | [*There*] *exist*–[*three*]–subj→*conditions.*
To←subj–[*read*]–*is* [*to empower,*] ***to***←subj–[*empower*]–*is* [*to write,*]
    to←subj–[*write*]–*is* [*to influence.*]
Enough←subj–*has* [*been said on this topic.*]
[*Which way*] ***to***←subj–[*choose*]–*must* [*be decided later.*]
[*The*] ***easiest***←subj–[*of these solutions*]–*turned* [*out to be the last one.*]

2. Pseudo-subjectival

[*It*] *amazed*–[*us*]–pseudo-subj→***that*** [*John left.*]
[*There*]–pseudo-subj→*exist* [*three* ***conditions***].

3. Direct-objectival

see–dir-obj→***John***; [*He*] *knew*–dir-obj→***this***.
[*He*] *knew*–dir-obj→***that*** [*Mary was in town.*]
worth–[*a*]–dir-obj→***trip***; [*It is quite*] *like*–dir-obj→***John***.

[*Which* **way**←dir-obj–[*to*]–*choose* [*must be decided later.*]]
make–[*possible*]–dir-obj→*neutralizing* [*the consequences*]
make–dir-obj→***it*** [*possible to neutralize the consequences*]
want–dir-obj→***to*** [*know*]
[*I*] *need*–dir-obj→***to*** *know*–[*what*]–dir-obj→***to*** [*expect.*]

4. Pseudo-direct-objectival

make–[*it possible*]–pseudo-dir-obj→***to*** [*neutralize the consequences*]
make–[*it clear*]–pseudo-dir-obj→***that*** [*we want to neutralize the consequences*]
[*The rumor*] *has*–[*it*]–pseudo-dir-obj→***that*** [*you are looking for a job.*]

5. Indirect-objectival

give–indir-obj→***John*** ⟨*him*⟩ [*some money*]
give–[*some money*]–indir-obj→***to*** [*John, who needs it*]
[*France*] *offers*–[*Iraq*]–indir-obj→***Christians*** [*asylum after Mosul threat.*]

6. Oblique-objectival

[*with no*] *objections*–obl-obj→***from*** [*the Minister*]
☞ The synonymous phrases *the Minister's objections* and *objections by the Minister* have different SSyntSs: *the Minister's*←possessive–*objections* and *objections*–agentive→***by*** [*the Minister*]
agreement–obl-obj→***between*** [*Stalin and Hitler*]
so–[*tired*]–obl-obj→***that*** [*she could not eat*]; *too*–[*tired*]–obl-obj→***to*** [*go out*]
too–[*sweet*]–obl-obj→***to*** [*my taste*]
Down–obl-obj→***with*** [*the Mullahs!*]
help–[*her*]–obl-obj→***move*** [*to London*]
identify–[*this element*]–obl-obj→***as*** [*a suffix*]

7. Infinitival-objectival

can–inf-obj→***read***; *should*–inf-obj→***read***

8. Copular

be–copul→***easy***; *become*–copul→***easy***; *be*–[*a*]–copul→***teacher***
become–[*a*]–copul→***teacher***
be–copul→***without*** [*a hat*]; *be*–copul→***of*** [*small comfort*]
turned–[*out*]–copul→***to*** [*have departed*]
[*To read*] *is*–copul→***to*** [*empower.*]

9. **Subject-attributive-objectival** (the complement semantically bears on the subject)

[*This task*] *seems*–subj-attr-obj→***easy***.
[*This task was*] *found*–subj-attr-obj→***easy***.

10. **Object-attributive-objectival** (the complement semantically bears on the object)

find–[*this task*]–obj-attr-obj→***easy***
consider–[*him*]–obj-attr-obj→***happy***
consider–[*him*]–obj-attr-obj→***to*** [*be happy*]
believe–[*him*]–obj-attr-obj→***to*** [*be dumb*]
make–[*it*]–obj-attr-obj→***possible*** [*to neutralize the consequences*]
judge–[*him*]–obj-attr-obj→***guilty***

11. **Agentive**

written–agent→***by*** [*McGuire*]; *arrival*–agent→***of*** [*McGuire*]
[*a*] *translation*–agent→***by*** [*McGuire*]; *baffled*–agent→***by*** [*quantifiers*]
shooting–agent→***of*** [*the hunters*: 'the hunters shoot']
[*She was*] *sent*–[*a letter*]–agent→***by*** [*McGuire.*]
[*His thumb is too sore*] ***for***←agent–[*him to*]–*play* [*next week.*]

12. **Comparative**

more–[*important*]–compar→***than*** [*Peter*]; *older*–compar→***than*** [*Peter*]
as–[*important*]–compar→***as*** [*Peter*]
[*John loves Mary*] *more*–compar→***than*** [*Peter.*]

I.1.2 Non-Valence-Controlled SSyntRels: 13–21

I.1.2.1 Circumstantial SSyntRels: 13–18

13. **Subjective-copredicative**

[*John*] *returned*–subj-copred→***rich***.
[*These fighting*] *continued*–subj-copred→***unabated***.

14. **Objective-copredicative**

[*They*] *sent*–[*John home*]–obj-copred→***rich***.

I.1.1.2 Circumstantial SSyntRels: 15–18

15. Circumstantial

walk–circum→***fast***; *delve*–circum→***deeply***
[*He*] *works*–circum→***there*** ⟨*in* [*this office*]⟩. | [*He*] *works*–circum→***abroad***.
[*He will*] *write*–[*next*]–circum→***week*** ⟨*tomorrow*⟩.
[*A new store*] *opened*–[*three*]–circum→***miles***–circum→***West*** [*from here.*]
[*He*] *went*–[*out, his*]–circum→***gun*** [*in his left hand.*]
With←circum–[*her paper finished, Helen*]–*can* [*afford this trip.*]
Having←circum–[*rushed off, he*]–*forgot* [*his umbrella.*]
To←circum–[*simplify the procedure, Dr. Copulati*]–*has* [*recourse to the following technique.*]
When←circum–[*summer approaches,*]–*start* [*preparing your car.*]
Holidays←circum–[*or no holidays, I*]–*have* [*to finish my paper.*]

16. Modificative-circumstantial[38]

[*As always*] ***elegant***,←mod-circum–[*John*]–*walked* [*away.*]

17. Appositive-circumstantial

[*An old*] ***man***,←appos-circum–[*John*]–*works* [*less.*]

18. Attributive-circumstantial

Abroad,←attr-circum–[*Alan*]–*works* [*less.*]
While←attr-circum–[*in France, Alan*]–*works* [*less.*]

I.1.2.3 Extra-structural SSyntRels: 19–20

19. Parenthetical

Oddly,←parenth–[*Alan*]–*works* [*less.*]
[*Alan,*] ***naturally***,←parenth–*accepted* [*the offer.*]
As←parenth–[*we have known for some time, Alan*]–*works* [*less.*]
To←parenth–[*give an example, I*]–*will* [*consider nominal suffixes.*]
[*It*] *was,*–[*Alan*]–parenth→***said***, [*a very hot day.*]
[*It*] *was,*–parenth→***as*** [*Alan said, a very hot day.*]

20. Adjunctive

OK,←adjunct–[*I*]–*agree*. | ***Mary***,←adjunct–[*where*]–*are* [*you?*]

I.2 Phrase-Level SSyntRels: 21–54

I.2.1 Any Type of Phrase SSyntRels, Non-Valence-Controlled: 21

21. Restrictive

still←restr–*taller*; is–restr→***still*** [*here*]; ***most***←restr–*frequent*
not←restr–*here*; ***not***←restr–*me*
so←restr–*rich*; ***too***←restr–*tired*; ***that***←restr–*far*; *boys*–restr→***only***
[*Alan*] ***just***←restr–*arrived*.

I.2.2 Nominal Phrase SSyntRels: 22–40

I.2.2.1 Valence-Controlled SSyntRels: 22

22. Elective

[*the*] *poorest*–elect→***among*** [*peasants*];
[*the*] *best*–elect→***of*** ⟨***from***⟩ [*these boys*]
[*the*] *most*–[*intelligent*]–elect→***of*** ⟨***from***⟩ [*these boys*]
five–elect→***of*** [*these books*]

I.2.2.2 Valence-Controlled and Non-Valence-Controlled SSyntRels: 23–28

23. Possessive

Alan's←poss–*arrival*; ***Alan's***←poss–*bed*
Last ***year's***←poss–*wishes are this* ***year's***←poss–*apologies*.

24. Compositive

man←compos–[-*machine*]–*interaction*;
car←compos–*repair*; ***noun***←compos–*phrase*
fax←compos–*transmission*←compos–*network*←compos–*access*←compos–
  cost←compos–*optimization*←compos–*proposal*
color←compos–*blind*
road←compos–*test* [*a car*]; ***guest***←compos–*conduct* [*an orchestra*].

25. Modificative

comfortable←modif–*beds*; ***visible***←modif–*stars*; ***French***←modif–*production*

26. Absolute-modificative

[*His first*] *attempt*–[*a*]–abs-modif→***failure***, [*John ...*]
[*He went out, his*] *anger*–abs-modif→***gone***.
[*He went out, (with) his*] *gun*–abs-modif→***in*** [*his left hand.*]
[*With the Central*] *Bank*–abs-modif→***refusing*** [*to budge, there were no ruble buyers.*]

27. Attributive

learners–attr→***with*** [*different backgrounds*]
dress–attr→***of*** [*a beautiful color*]
years–attr→***of*** [*war*]; [*the*] *bed*–attr→***of*** [*Alan*]
[*a*] *man*–[*the same*]–attr→***age***
[*the*] *most*–[*expensive car*]–attr→***in*** [*France*]
☞ But: [*the*] *most*–[*expensive*]–elect→***of*** [*French cars*]
man–attr→***of*** [*courage*]; *life*–attr→***abroad***; *hundreds*–attr→***of*** [*books*]
tons–attr→***of*** [*debris*]

28. Descriptive-attributive

[*Professor*] *Wanner,*–descr-attr→***from*** [*Stuttgart, was also present.*]

I.2.2.3 Non-Valence-Controlled SSyntRels: 29–40

29. Determinative

a←determ–*bed*; ***those***←determ–*beds*; ***my***←determ–*bed*

30. Quantitative

three←quant–*beds*; [*three*←num-junct–]***thousand***←quant–*people*
  NB: But *thousands*–attr→*of*–[*people*], where THOUSAND is not a NUM, but an N.

31. Descriptive-modificative

[*these*] *beds,*–descr-modif→***comfortable*** [*and not expensive*], ...

32. Relative

[*the*] *paper*–[*that I*]–relat→***read*** [*yesterday*]
[*the*] *paper*–[*I*]–relat→***read*** [*yesterday*]; *the girl*–[*who*]–relat→***came*** [*first*]

33. Descriptive-relative

[*this*] *paper*–[*which I*]–descr-relat→***read*** [*yesterday*]
Alan,–[*who*]–descr-relat→***loves*** [*her so much, should return.*]

34. WH-relative

[*He disappeared God*] ***knows***←WH-rel–*where.*
[*He does you*] ***will***←WH-rel–[*never guess*]–*what.*

35. Qualifying-appositive

Alan–[*the*]–qual-appos→***Powerful***

36. Naming-appositive

[*the*] ***Gobi***←name-appos–*desert*; [*the*] ***Volga***←name-appos–*river*
[*the heavy*] *cruiser*–name-appos→***"Saratoga"***; *Lake*–name-appos→*Erie*
[*the*] *town*–name-appos→*of Mount-Royal*

37. Identifying-appositive

[*the*] *term*–ident-appos→***"suffix"***; *equation*–ident-appos→***(23)***
Section–ident-appos→***B***

38. Descriptive-appositive

[*This*] *term*–descr-appos→***("suffix")*** [*will be considered later.*]
John,–[*a professional*]–descr-appos→***vet***, [*came over.*]
[*You forget about*] *me,*–[*your*]–descr-appos→***mother***.
[*The sales totaled*] *$10, 000,*–descr-appos→***down*** [*from June.*]

39. Sequential

man–sequent→***machine*** [*interaction*]; [*flights*] *Paris*–sequent→***London***
English–sequent→***German*** [*dictionary*]
English–sequent→***to*** [*German translation*]

40. Patientive

translation–patient→***of*** [*this text*]
shooting–patient→***of*** [*the hunters*: 'the hunters are shot']

I.2.3 Adpositional Phrase SSyntRels, Valence-controlled: 41–42

41. Prepositional

in–prepos→***bed***; *without*–[*three hundred*]–prepos→***dollars***
[*The iota operator is different*] *in*–prepos→***that*** [*its interpretation depends on the context.*]
to–prepos→***go*** [*to bed*]
[*Do you ever do anything*] *besides*–prepos→***offer*** [*your apologies?*]

42. Postpositional

[*ten*] ***centuries***←postpos–*ago*; [*a few*] ***years***←postpos–*back*
[*the whole*] ***month***←postpos–*through*
[*The motion passed, our*] ***objection***←postpos–*notwithstanding*.

I.2.4 Verbal Phrase (= Analytical Form) SSyntRels, Non-Valence-Controlled: 43–46

43. Perfect-analytical

has–perf-analyt→***written***; *has*–perf-analyt→***been*** [*beaten*]

44. Progressive-analytical

was–progr-analyt→***writing***; [*has*] *been*–progr-analyt→***writing***

45. Passive-analytical

was–pass-analyt→***written***; [*was*] *being*–pass-analyt→***written***

46. DO-analytical

does–do-analyt→***write***; *does*–[*not*]–do-analyt→***write***

I.2.5 Conjunctional Phrase SSyntRels, Valence-controlled: 47–50

47. Subordinate-conjunctional

[*Suppose*] *that*–[*Alan*]–subord-conj→***comes***.
[*so*] *as*–[*not*]–subord-conj→***to*** [*irritate Leo*]

48. Coordinate-conjunctional

[*Alan*] *and*–coord-conj→***Helen***; [*Alan,*] *but*–[*not*]–coord-conj→***Helen***
[*Do you have a place for us*] *or*–[*we*]–coord-conj→***must*** [*leave now?*]

49. Comparative-conjunctional

than–compar-conj→***Helen***; *as*–compar-conj→***always***

50. Absolute-conjunctional

If–[*a*]–abs-conj→***pronoun***, [*the grammatical subject may* ...]
while–abs-conj→***in*** [*bed*]; *once*–abs-conj→***here***

I.2.6 Word-Like Phrase SSyntRels, Non-Valence-controlled: 51–54

51. Verbal-junctive

give–verb-junct→***up***; *bring*–verb-junct→***down***; *feel*–verb-junct→***about***

52. Numeral-junctive

fifty←num-junct–*three*; *fifty*←num-junct–*third*

53. Binary-junctive

if–[...]–bin-junct→***then*** ...; *the*←bin-junct–[*more* ...]–*the* [*more* ...]
either←bin-junct–[...]–*or* [...]

54. Colligative

[*is*] *dealt*–collig→***with*** [stranded prepositions]

II Coordinate Surface-Syntactic Relations: 55–58

55. Coordinative

John,–coord→***Mary,***–coord→***Pete***; *fast,*–coord→***gently,***–coord→***skillfully***
John,–coord→***and***[–coord-conj→*Mary*]; *fast,*–coord→***but*** [*gently*]
John was–[*reading,*]–coord→***and***–[[*Mary patiently*]–coord-conj→*waited.*]

56. Elliptical-coordinative

[*He*] *works*–[*a lot,*]–ellipt-coord→***but*** [*only at night.*]
[*He eats*] *vegetables,*–[*however, not*]–ellipt-coord→***boiled***.

57. Pseudo-coordinative

in–[*Siberia*]–pseudo-coord→***on***–[*the Ob shore, not*]–pseudo-coord→***far*** *from Novosibirsk*
[*six*] *dollars*–pseudo-coord→***and*** [*80 cents*]
[*six*] *dollars*–[*80*]–pseudo-coord→***cents***]

[*Such are all voiced*] *consonants,*–[*in particular,*]–pseudo-coord→/***b***/ [*and* /g/.]
tomorrow–pseudo-coord→***night***; *Monday*–[*next*]–pseudo-coord→***week***
Saturday–pseudo-coord→***night***, [–pseudo-coord→***at*** *a quarter to eleven*]

58. Explanatory-coordinative

[*Mary*] *gave*–[*me a smile, which*]–explan-coord→***was*** [*nice.*]
[*Smoking*] *is*–[*harmful, which*]–explan-coord→***is*** [*well known.*]

APPENDICES 195

Appendix III: Possible Combinations of the Three Types of Linguistic Dependency between Two Lexemes in a Clause

Remember, any two lexemes L_1 and L_2 in an utterance can, generally speaking, be linked (or not linked) by anyone of the three major types of dependencies: semantic, syntactic and morphological. The combination of those produces 14 cases, all of which are represented in natural languages.

1. $L_1 \quad\quad L_2$:	L_1 and L_2 are not linked by any dependency in the given clause; for instance, JOHN$_{L_2}$ and AFTER$_{L_1}$ in *John began to weaken after 8 miles*.
2. L_1 –sem→ L_2 :	L_1 and L_2 are linked only semantically; for instance, JOHN$_{L_2}$ and WEAKEN$_{L_1}$ in *John began to weaken*. Cf. combination 10.
3. L_1 –synt→ L_2 :	L_1 and L_2 are linked only syntactically; for instance, TAKUSAN$_{L_2}$ 'many' and YOMU$_{L_1}$ 'read' in Jap. *Yoko+wa hon+o takusan yom+u* lit. 'Yoko$_{THEME}$ book$_{ACC}$ many read$_{PRES}$' = 'Yoko reads many books'; semantically, 'takusan' bears on 'hon', morphologically, TAKUSAN is an invariant adverb.
4. L_1 –morph→ L_2 :	L_1 and L_2 are linked only morphologically; for instance, IČ$_{L_1}$ 'our' and HEBGNU-(*jič*)$_{L_2}$ 'fled.our' in Tabassaran *Ič mudur uc^{wh}u+na hebgnu+jič* lit. 'Our goat.kid to.you fled.our' = 'Our goat kid fled to you', where the verb *hebgnu* morphologically depends on the pronominal adjective *ič* 'our' (the verb agrees with *ič*), there being no Sem-D or Synt-D between them.
5. L_1 $\genfrac{}{}{0pt}{}{-\text{sem}\rightarrow}{-\text{synt}\rightarrow}$ L_2 :	L_1 and L_2 are linked by identically directed Sem-D and Synt-D, without Morph-D; for instance, READ$_{L_1}$ and NEWSPAPER$_{L_2}$ in *John is reading a newspaper*.

6. $L_1 \xrightarrow{\text{—sem}\rightarrow}_{\leftarrow\text{synt}-} L_2$:	L_1 and L_2 are linked by opposite-directed Sem-D and Synt-D, without Morph-D; for instance, INTERESTING$_{L_1}$ and NEWSPAPER$_{L_2}$ in *an interesting newspaper*, where the noun NEWSPAPER is the Sem-argument of the predicate 'interesting' (= semantically depends on the adjective INTERESTING), while being its syntactic governor.
7. $L_1 \xrightarrow{\text{—sem}\rightarrow}_{-\text{morph}\rightarrow} L_2$:	L_1 and L_2 are linked by identically directed Sem-D and Morph-D, without Synt-D; for instance, the clitic LE$_{\text{DAT-}L_2}$ 'to.him/to.her' in *Sp. Juan le quiere dar un libro* 'Juan to.him wants to.give a book' = 'Juan wants to give him a book' semantically depends on the verb DAR$_{L_1}$, as well as morphologically (DAR prescribes the dative form of the clitic), but has no syntactic link with it. (Syntactically, the clitic *le* depends on the Main Verb QUERER 'want', forming with it a prosodic phrase and having its linear position in the clause also determined by it.)
8. $L_1 \xrightarrow{\text{—sem}\rightarrow}_{\leftarrow\text{morph}-} L_2$:	L1 and L2 are linked by opposite-directed Sem-D and Morph-D, without Synt-D; for instance, in *Fr. Marie est devenue belle* 'Marie has become beautiful', the noun MARIE$_{L_2}$ semantically depends on the adjective BEAU$_{L_1}$ 'beautiful' ('Marie' is the argument of the predicate 'beautiful'); the adjective BEAU$_{L_1}$ morphologically depends on MARIE—agrees with it in gender and number.
9. $L_1 \xrightarrow{\text{—synt}\rightarrow}_{-\text{morph}\rightarrow} L_2$:	L_1 and L_2 are linked by identically directed Synt-D and Morph-D, without Sem-D; for instance, the preposition AB$_{L_1}$ 'from' and URBS$_{L_2}$ 'city' in *Lat. ab urb+e condita* lit. 'from city founded' = 'from the foundation of the city [= of Rome]', where the preposition governs the ablative of the noun.

10. $L_1 \overset{\text{—synt}\rightarrow}{\underset{\leftarrow\text{morph—}}{}} L_2$:	L_1 and L_2 are linked by opposite-directed Synt-D and Morph-D, without Sem-D; for instance, JOHN$_{L_2}$ and BEGIN$_{L_1}$ in *John begins to weaken*, where syntactically, JOHN depends on BEGIN, and morphologically, the other way around (*begins* agrees with *John* is person and number); semantically, they are not linked; JOHN semantically depends on WEAKEN: 'begin–1→weaken–1→John'. Cf. combination 2.
11. $L_1 \overset{\text{—sem}\rightarrow}{\underset{\text{—morph}\rightarrow}{\text{—synt}\rightarrow}} L_2$:	L_1 and L_2 are linked by identically directed Sem-D, Synt-D and Morph-D; for instance, *see*$_{L_1}$ *her*$_{L_2}$, where SHE$_{L_2}$ depends on SEE$_{L_1}$ semantically, syntactically, and morphologically.
12. $L_1 \overset{\text{—sem}\rightarrow}{\underset{\leftarrow\text{morph—}}{\text{—synt}\rightarrow}} L_2$:	L_1 and L_2 are linked by identically directed Sem-D and Synt-D, while Morph-D between them goes in the opposite direction; e.g., polypersonal agreement of the Main Verb in a caseless language. E.g., in Abkhaz *Nadš'a*$_{L_{2-1}}$ *sara*$_{L_{2-2}}$ *i+s+əl+teit'ašʷqʷ'ə*$_{L_{2-3}}$ lit. 'Nadsha [a woman] to.me gave a.book', where the verb form *isəlteit'*$_{L_1}$ manifests agreement with its three caseless actants—in person, number and gender (**i-** is the prefix of an inanimate singular DirO, **s-** marks the 1st person singular IndirO, and (**ə**)**l-** is the exponent of the 3rd person singular feminine subject). Semantically and syntactically, the actants depend on the verb, while morphologically, it depends on the actants.

13. $L_1 \begin{smallmatrix}\text{—sem→}\\\leftarrow\text{synt—}\\\text{—morph→}\end{smallmatrix} L_2$:	L_1 and L_2 are linked by identically directed Sem-D and Morph-D, while Synt-D between them goes in the opposite direction; e.g., in the Persian modificative construction *ketab+e nav* 'book-IZAFET new', where KETAB$_{L_2}$ 'book' semantically and morphologically depends on the adjective NAV 'new': 'ketab' is the argument of 'nav', and KETAB receives from NAV the marker **-e** ("izafet", which signals the presence of a postposed dependent); at the same time, the noun KETAB is the syntactic governor of the adjective NAV.
14. $L_1 \begin{smallmatrix}\leftarrow\text{sem—}\\\text{—synt→}\\\text{—morph→}\end{smallmatrix} L_2$:	L_1 and L_2 are linked by identically directed Synt-D and Morph-D, while the Sem-D between them goes in the opposite direction; e.g., a modifying adjective LONG$_{L_2}$ in Fr. *longues préparations* 'long preparations' depends on PRÉPARATION$_{L_1}$ syntactically and morphologically, while being semantically its governor ('long–1→preparations').

Notes

[1] (Foreword, p. x) **Dead languages.** Not all dead languages are dead in the same sense. There are two types of dead languages: Type I, which are like Latin, and Type II, which are like Etruscan. A Type I dead language is not spoken anymore, but it has not disappeared—it has morphed into some "younger" languages that are alive and well today. Thus, Latin was transformed into numerous Romance languages (French, Spanish, Italian, Portuguese, etc.), and Old Church Slavonic (a.k.a. Old Bulgarian) became Modern Bulgarian. Type II dead languages disappeared completely, without leaving a surviving descendent—like Etruscan or Sumerian.

[2] (1.1, p. 3) **Correspondence.** A correspondence (in the mathematical sense) is a set of rules that relate two sets A and B in such a way that each element of A is linked to several elements of B, and vice versa. In our case, A is the set of meanings and B, the set of texts of a language; linguistic correspondence associates an element $a \in A$ (i.e., a meaning) with several elements $b_i \in B$ (i.e., with all the texts that carry this meaning), and an element $b \in B$ (i.e., a text) with several elements $a_j \in A$ (i.e., with all the meanings this text can carry).

Correspondences fall into three major types:

- One-to-one correspondences, where an element $a \in A$ can be associated with one and only one element $b \in B$, and vice versa.
- One-to-many correspondences, where an element $a \in A$ can be associated with several elements $b_i \in B$, but not vice versa.
- Many-to-many correspondences, where an element $a \in A$ can be associated with several elements $b_i \in B$, and vice versa.

Meaning-Text correspondence—that is, natural language—is many-to-many: one meaning can have many expressions (this is synonymy), while one text can express many meanings (ambiguity).

[3] (*1.1*, p. 5) **The number of lexical units in a language.** Since the discussion of lexical units and their meanings occupies such an important place in the Meaning-Text approach, I have to justify my rough estimate.

Take, for instance, German. The figure for the number of entries in major German dictionaries oscillates between 85 000 and 170 000, the average being ≈ 130 000 entries. These, however, are headwords only. If we assume an average of 5 different senses per headword we obtain the approximate figure of ≈ 650 000 entries. Adding idioms to this, we come close to a million lexicographic senses—that is, lexical units: ≈ 10^5 ~ 10^6. *The New English-Russian Dictionary* (Apresyan, Yu. & Mednikova, È., 2002, Moscow, Russkij Jazyk Publishers) contains 250 000 entries; with the same average number of senses per headword we even go over a million LUs. A Spanish dictionary commonly has fewer entries: thus, *Diccionario de la Real Academia Española*, 2014, edición 23ª (http://buscon.rae.es/drae) contains about 100 000 headwords; but then in Spanish the polysemy is more frequent than in German or English—say, 8 senses per headword. Taking idioms into account, we arrive again at approximately the same number: ≈ 1 000 000 LUs. Finally, the French *Le Petit Robert* (2009) contains 60 000 entries and 300 000 senses; by sharpening sense discrimination and including idioms, we find ourselves again in the vicinity of half a million plus LUs.

Of course special studies are needed to establish the number of LUs in a given language in a more precise way, but it is safe to believe that, on the average, a major written language has about one million LUs. (This is, of course, an upper estimate. In practice, a language can have far fewer LUs—maybe half of this number. However, this estimate gives us an order of magnitude.)

[4] (*1.2*, p. 13) **The procedural component of the Meaning-Text model.** The MTM does not, of course, preclude a procedural submodel that performs the transition from text to meaning (and vice versa). But the elaboration of corresponding procedures is not within a linguist's domain, and I am not competent to undertake such a task. Therefore, strictly for those tactical reasons, procedural issues are not addressed in this book.

[5] (*2.1*, p. 19) **Formal grammar.** In linguistics, the term *formal grammar* is commonly used to denote a logical device that generates (= specifies) a set of expressions called *formal language*. Here is a very simple example of formal grammar,

where S stands for 'sentence', NP, for 'noun phrase', VP, for 'verb phrase', N is a noun, and V is a verb:

S ⇒ NP + VP
NP ⇒ NP + *of* + NP
NP ⇒ N
VP ⇒ V + NP

This grammar specifies the following infinite set of strings (= the formal language)

N + V, N + V + N, N + *of* + N + V, N + V + N + *of* + N,
N + *of* + N + V + N + *of* +N, ...

However, the terms *formal grammar* and *formal language* as applied to natural language are quite inconvenient. First, by *language* linguistics understands not the set of linguistic expressions, but the device that produces them —that is, what is called above *formal grammar*. Second, the formal grammar of language **L** includes its lexicon and its GRAMMAR, but in quite a different sense. This terminological mess forces me to prefer the term model.

[6] (2.2, p. 20) **Enantiosemy.** These two "inverse" senses of the noun MODEL present an example of enantiosemy. Enantiosemy is a property of a polysemous word that has a sense denoting a relation **R** and another sense that denotes the inverse relation R^{-1}. In our case, one sense of the noun MODEL is 'model Y is the source of the representation X' (as in *She was his model for this picture*), and another—the inverse relation 'model X is a representation of source Y' (as in *a model of a train*).

Enantiosemy is not that infrequent in natural language. Thus, the verb [to] RENT means both 'let have temporarily for money' [X rents Y to Z] and 'begin to have temporarily for money' [Z rents Y from X]. The French HÔTE means 'host' and 'guest', the Hindi adverb KAL—'yesterday' and 'tomorrow'. The Russian noun GOST′ 'guest' and *Lat.* HOSTIS are of the same origin: they come from the Indo-European stem **ghosti*- 'foreign, stranger', but HOSTIS means 'enemy', cf. HOSTILE. (By the way, the English GUEST also has the same origin as *Lat.* HOSTIS and *Rus.* GOST′; *Lat.* HOSTIS underlies *Fr.* OTAGE, as well as *Eng.* HOSTAGE and HOST—via the meaning 'group of enemies', 'army'.) *Rus.* ZAPOMNIT′ 'memorize' corresponds etymologically to *Pol.* ZAPOMNIEĆ, which means 'forget'. The adjective DUBIOUS means both 'one who doubts Y' (*I am dubious about wine competitions*), and 'Y such that people doubt it' (*This wine competition seems dubious to me*).

Enantiosemy appears when a word with a very general and vague meaning 'σ' diachronically develops—within one language or in two related languages—into two words, each having a more specific meaning, '$σ_1$' and '$σ_2$', both being "fragments" of the meaning 'σ'.

Enantiosemy is a special type of antonymy.

[7] (*2.3.2*, p. 27) Let us compare CHINK with POETASTER. POETASTER means, roughly, 'bad poet, I despising **bad** poets' (not just all poets!); it expresses the Speaker's feelings about a particular poet whom he considers bad—that is, POETASTER does not carry an offensive generalization and thus is not a propaganda word. (Of course it is derogatory for the person whom you call POETASTER, but this is because of the opinion expressed, not because of the word itself.)

[8] (*2.3.2*, p. 27) **Positive propaganda words.** Normally, language also has propaganda words expressing the Speaker's **positive** attitude towards Xs. The number of these is, however, significantly lower than that of negative evaluatives. This is a curious fact about natural languages in general: a language nuances the negative to finer degree and expresses it in more detail than is the case with the positive. Thus, slurs and offensive terms are more numerous than terms of endearment. Interestingly, it seems to me that English has far fewer propaganda words than, for instance, French or Russian.

[9] (*2.3.2*, p. 29) The Japanese example requires the following two grammatical comments.

- The form *watasi*+**wa** is the communicative Theme (= topic) of the clause; the suffix **-wa**, obligatory marker of the Theme, means something like ≈ 'as for …'. From a syntactic viewpoint, *watasiwa* is neither the subject nor an oblique object, but a so-called prolepsis: an element of the clause positioned at its beginning and structurally linked to the rest of it in a very loose way (a prolepsis can always be omitted without affecting the grammaticality of the clause). The meaning 'My father is a doctor' is verbalized in Japanese as follows: '$\mathbf{I}_{\text{prolepsis}}$ father doctor is'.

- The forms *kowa+i*, *samu+i* and *hosi+i* are conjugated adjectives in the present, something like 'afraid.is', 'cold.is', 'needing.is'. The Japanese adjective has also a past form: *kowa+katta*, *samu+katta* and *hosi+katta*.

[10] (2.3.1, p. 42) **Phonic *vs.* phonetic *vs.* phonemic.** The term *phonic* is used to refer to any linguistic phenomenon related to sound (= articulatory and/or acoustic), be it phonetic or phonemic. The notions of 'phonetic' *vs.* 'phonemic' correspond to a vital distinction drawn in linguistics.

A phone, or a linguistic sound, of **L** is a class of concrete articulated sounds that the speakers of **L** produce and recognize as sounds of **L**; phones are studied and described by phonetics. The notation of a text in terms of phones is its phonetic transcription, shown by square brackets: [tʰéⁱk] *take*, [stéⁱk] *steak*, [kʰít] *kit* or [lítl̩] *little*. Phones are distinguished by phonetic features. Thus, in English, [tʰ] and [t] are opposed by the phonetic feature "aspiration."

A phoneme of **L** is a set of phones such that no pair of its phones can be used to distinguish two words of **L**. To put it differently, the phones of the same phoneme never distinguish the signifiers of two linguistic signs—that is, they cannot make a meaning-bearing distinction; they are distributed according to phonetic context, and their distribution is perfectly predictable. Thus, the English phones [tʰ] and [t], seen in *take* vs. *steak* never distinguish English words; both belong to the phoneme /t/ and are distributed according to the following rule: [tʰ] appears before a stressed vowel as long as another consonant does not precede it, while [t] appears elsewhere. Phonemes are studied and described by phonemics. The notation of a text in terms of phonemes is its phonemic transcription, shown by slashes: /téⁱk/ *take*, /stéⁱk/ *steak*, /kít/ *kit* or /lítl/ *little*. Phonemes are defined and opposed by phonemic features. Thus, in English, /t/ is a PLOSIVE dental consonant, and /s/ a FRICATIVE dental consonant: they are opposed by the phonemic feature "plosive ~ fricative."

A phonetic feature of **L** may or may not be a phonemic feature of **L**—this depends on the language. In English, the phonetic feature of aspiration, as we just saw, is not a phonemic feature, but in Korean it is: *tap* 'answer' ~ *tʰap* 'tower', *ki* 'flag' ~ *kʰi* 'be tall'. In Russian, the length of vowels is not phonemic—that is, the opposition "V : V̄" (short vowel *vs.* long vowel) never distinguishes the meanings of words; therefore, the two possible vocative forms [mám] *Mam!* 'Mommy!' ~ [mā́m] *Ma-am!* must be phonemically written as /mám/. But in German the vowel length distinguishes words: [kám] *Kamm* 'comb' ~ [kǎm] *kam* '[he/she] came', [ófen] *offen* 'open' ~ [ōfen] *Ofen* 'oven, stove', [íren] *irren* 'be mistaken' ~ [ĭren] *Iren* 'Irishmen', etc. Therefore in German such pairs must be phonemically transcribed in different ways: /kám/ ~ /kǎm/, etc.

[11] (*3.2.2*, p. 49) **A set of paraphrases.** It seems worthwhile to show, using the example in (19), how such a huge number of paraphrases can be obtained.

The meaning of the sentence under consideration is divided into chunks such that a chunk is implemented by a lexical expression of the language found in the sentence. Sentence (19) has seven such chunks; in Figure 10 below, each chunk is represented by one column, which contains several variant ways of expressing the given chunk of meaning (the number under the column indicates the number of variants in it). These lexical variants can then be combined in all possible ways to form full sentences. For instance, taking the boldfaced elements, one obtains the following paraphrase:

(i) *As Orwell is convinced, his political engagement causes an improvement of the quality of his works.*

The total number of potential paraphrases is obtained by multiplying the numbers of variants in each column; in this case, we have: $1 \times 9 \times 4 \times 3 \times 32 \times 9 = = 31\,104$.

①	②	③	④
Orwell	sure certain convinced conviction **as ... is convinced** does not doubt has no doubts believes without a shadow of a doubt there are no doubts	active activity activism **engagement**	politics **political** politically
1	9	4	3

⑤	⑥	⑦
thanks to due to **cause** make ensure as a result	become better get better improve **improvement**	work works writings creation (literary) production quality of his works **quality of his works** quality of his writings quality of his (literary) production
positive impact beneficial impact positive influence beneficial influence to impact positively to influence positively to have a positive impact to have a positive influence		
32		9

Figure 10: A Sample of Lexical Variations Possible for an English Sentence

Not all combinations are grammatical, but then the lists of variants are far from complete. The paraphrases are not always strictly synonymous—yet we accept quasi-synonymous paraphrases, mutually substitutable *salva significatione* at least in some contexts.

[12] (*3.2.3*, p. 54)

Semantic derivatives. A Sem-derivative of a lexical unit L is another lexical unit L' whose meaning includes the meaning of L, the semantic difference 'δ' = 'L'' – 'L' being regular in the language—that is, in some cases, 'δ' is expressed by an affix. Thus, THIEF is a semantic derivative of STEAL, since the semantic difference between the two—'person who…'—is regular in English: cf. MURDER ~ MURDER+ER and thousands of similar derivations. As a rule, a Sem-derivative is described by means of a paradigmatic lexical function, see *4.2*, p. *97ff*.

Collocations. A collocation is a binary compositional phraseme one element of which—the base—is freely selected by the Speaker for its meaning and syntactic properties, while the second element—the collocate—is selected as a function of the base: for instance, *sleep* [base] *like a log* [collocate] or *fight* [base] *tooth and* *nail* [collocate]. As a rule, a collocation is described by means of a syntagmatic lexical function, see *4.2*, p. 65*ff*.

[13] (*3.2.5*, p. 55) **Fictitious lexemes.** Here is a good example of a Russian fictitious lexeme whose meaning does not coincide with that of any Russian genuine lexeme: «PRIMERNO» NUM lit. 'approximately NUM' ≈ 'the Speaker is not sure whether the number NUM is correct'. (The Russian adverb *primerno* means 'approximately'.) «PRIMERNO» represents the approximate-quantitative construction, which is implemented on the surface by having the noun precede the numeral that quantifies it. In a normal quantitative construction a numeral precedes the noun just as in English:

DESJAT′←ATTR–STUDENT$_{PL}$ ⇔ *desjat′ studentov*
'ten students'

vs.

«PRIMERNO»←ATTR–DESJAT′←ATTR–STUDENT$_{PL}$ ⇔ *studentov desjat′*
'maybe ten students'

But «PRIMERNO» ≢ PRIMERNO! Thus, somebody invited to John's birthday party can answer the question about John's age "I don't know, *let sorok*" 'I don't know, maybe forty years', but not *"I don't know, *primerno sorok let*" 'I don't know, approximately forty years'. Cf. also *raza dva* lit. 'times two' = 'maybe two times' vs. **primerno dva raza* 'approximately two times'. This construction expresses more the doubts of the Speaker about the number than the number's approximate character.

[14] (*3.2.6*, p. 65) **Discrepancies between the DMorphS and the SMorphS of a wordform.** The morphology of English is quite impoverished; therefore, my examples come from other languages. Here are three typical cases of "grammemes *vs.* morphemes" discrepancies, shown by boxing.

- Cumulative expression of grammemes in the SMorphS (cf. Note 18): two or more grammemes are expressed by a single morpheme.

Russian DOM$_{\boxed{PL, GEN}}$ 'of houses' ⇔ {DOM-} ⊕ $\boxed{\{PL.GEN\}}$ ⇔ **dom+**$\boxed{ov}$

vs.

Turkish EV$_{PL, GEN}$ 'of houses' ⇔ {EV-} ⊕ {PL} ⊕ {GEN} ⇔ **ev+ler+in**

In Russian, several grammemes can be expressed by one morpheme (and, consequently, by one morph).

- The presence in the SMorphS of empty morphemes, which do not convey any meaning and do not correspond to any grammemes—for instance, so-called thematic elements [= THEM.EL]:

Russian ČITAT'$_{\text{IMPERF, IND, PAST, SG, FEM}}$ 'read' ⇔
⇔ {ČIT-} ⊕ {IMPERF} ⊕ {THEM.EL} ⊕ {PAST} ⊕ {SG.FEM} ⇔ **čit+aj+l+a** ⇔
⇔ *čitala* 'She was reading'

Spanish CANTAR$_{\text{IND, IMPF, 3, SG}}$ 'sing' ⇔
⇔ {CANT-} ⊕ {THEM.EL} ⊕ {IND.IMPF} ⊕ {3.SG}
⇔ **cant+a+ba+Ø** ⇔ *cantaba* 'He/She was singing'

☞ 1. In Russian:
— IMPERF stands for the imperfective aspect.
— In the verb ČITAT' the imperfective aspect is expressed cumulatively by the stem—together with the lexical meaning, by the megamorph **čit-**.
— /j/ of the THEM.EL is truncated before a consonant by a morphonological rule.
— The indicative mood is expressed by the absence of the particle **by** [= бы], which marks the subjunctive: another grammeme/morpheme discrepancy.
— The grammemes SG and FEM are expressed cumulatively (one more discrepancy).

2. In Spanish:
— IMPF is *imperfecto*, a verbal past tense expressing duration or repetition.
— The grammemes IND and IMPF, on the one hand, and 3 and SG, on the other, are expressed cumulatively, creating an additional discrepancy.

- Multiple expression of a grammeme in the SMorphS:

Hebrew LEJLA$_{\text{PL, 1, SG}}$ 'my nights' ⇔ {LEJLA} ⊕ {PL} ⊕ {PL} ⊕ {1.SG} ⇔
⇔ **lejl+ot+a+j**

Non-segmental morphological signs—apophonies, reduplications and conversions—further complicate the correspondences between the DMorphS (a grammemic structure) and the SMorphS (a morphemic structure).

[15] (*3.3*, p. 73) Numerous rules of this type should, of course, be generalized and presented in a more abstract form as **schemata** of sets of rules—for instance, as follows:

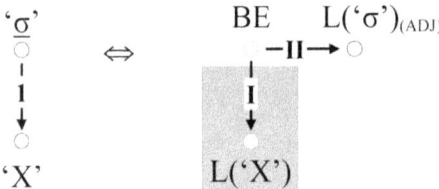

I have not done so here for simplicity's sake.

[16] (*3.3*, p. 73) A semantically loaded syntactic construction carries a meaning of lexical type. Thus, Russian construction N_{NOM} + KAK + N_{NOM} 'N as N' means 'a most ordinary N' (*stol kak stol* 'a most ordinary table'), etc. Another Russian construction—N + NUM, with the numeral in postposition—expresses the meaning ≈ 'maybe' (*kilo dvadcat'* 'maybe 20 kilos'). Such a construction is presented in the DSyntS of the sentence by a fictitious lexeme, see *3.2.3*, p. 54, and Mel'čuk 2013: 37*ff*.

[17] (*3.3*, p. 84) **Other types of DMorph-rules** (for a curious reader).

"Grammeme ~ reduplicationeme" rules

The Latin perfect
PERF ⇔ {**Red**$_{PERF}$}   [PRES *cad+o* 'I fall'   ~ PERF *ce-cid+ī*;
                             PRES *mord+e+o* 'I bite' ~ PERF *mo-mord+ī*]

"Grammeme ~ aphophoneme" rules

The English past
PAST ⇔ {**A**$_{PAST}$}   [PRES *sing* ~ PAST *sang*; PRES *lead* ~ PAST *led*]

"Grammeme ~ converseme" rules

The Swahili nominal plural
PL ⇔ {**Conv**$_{PL}$}
    [SG *m+tu* '[a] human' ~ PL *wa+tu*; SG *ji+cho* 'eye' ~ PL *ma+cho*;
     SG *ki+faru* 'rhino' ~ PL *vi+faru*]

Just as in other Bantu languages, Swahili nouns are divided into noun classes, similar to genders in such languages as Latin or Russian; each noun class controls the agreement of adjectives and verbs and is marked itself by a prefix on the noun. The plural of a noun in Swahili is formed by transferring the noun in a different noun class.

[18] (*3.3*, p. 84) **Cumulative expression**. By cumulative expression of grammemes we understand a simultaneous expression of several grammemes by one morph. Compare the Russian and Georgian wordforms of the nouns GORA/MTA 'mountain':

gor+*á*	~ *mta*+*∅* + *∅*	*gor*+*é*	~ *mta*+*∅* + *s*
SG.NOM	SG NOM	SG.DAT	SG DAT
gór+*y*	~ *mt* +*eb*+ *i*	*gor*+*ám*	~ *mt*+*eb*+*s*
PL.NOM	PL NOM	PL.DAT	PL DAT

Russian expresses the nominal number and case cumulatively (= by a single morph): these grammemes are never expressed separately, by different morphs. Georgian expresses the same grammemes agglutinatively: a number grammeme is expressed by its own morph, and a case grammeme is expressed by a different morph.

[19] (*4.1*, p. 89) **Presupposition**. A presupposition in the meaning 'σ' of a statement is the part 'σ″' of 'σ' that remains affirmed when the whole statement 'σ' is negated. In other words, a presupposition is not affected by a general negation. For instance (presupposition is shown by the special brackets "|[...]|"):

(i) a. *This film,* |[*shot by Zefirelli,*]| *plays tomorrow*. ~
   It is not true that *this film,* |[*shot by Zefirelli,*]| *plays tomorrow*.

What is negated in the second sentence of (i-a) is the meaning 'this film plays tomorrow'; but the sentence continues to communicate that this film was shot by Zefirelli.

   b. *This film,* |[*which plays tomorrow,*]| *was shot by Zefirelli*. ~
   It is not true that *this film,* |[*which plays tomorrow,*]| *was shot by Zefirelli*.

In the second sentence of (i-b) only the affirmation 'this film was shot by Zefirelli' undergoes negation; that it is playing tomorrow is maintained.

These examples show a presupposition in the meaning of a sentence. But presuppositions can also be found in the meaning of lexemes denoting semantic predicates; thus:

(ii) 'X helps Y to do Z with X's W' = '|[Y doing Z,]| X adds X's resources W to Y's efforts with the goal to facilitate Z for Y'

[20] (*4.1*, p. 89) Sentence (27d-ii) contains a phraseologized negation. A free negation does not affect presuppositions (see Note 19), while in DO NOT DOUBT the presupposition of DOUBT$_{(V)}$—'not believing that P' is in the scope of negation: 'not not believing that P' ⇒ 'believing that P'. To put it differently, the phrase DO NOT

DOUBT is a phraseme—more specifically, a non-standard collocation of DOUBT$_{(V)}$. This property of negation (see Iordanskaja 1986: 355–356) must be explicitly specified in the lexical entry for DOUBT$_{(V)}$.

[21] *(4.2, p. 102)* **Lexical Functions.** Lexical functions were discovered in the early summer of 1961, when I was working on a geological expedition in the semi-desert and mountains of South Kazakhstan. My job entailed long periods of stillness holding the measuring rod upright or treading slowly, the rod in my hand, to the point indicated to me by the geologist. During this time, I used to ponder on several problems of machine translation, which was then the focus of my linguistic research activities. In particular, I was looking for an efficient technique that would allow the computer to avoid checking the linguistic context many thousands of times in order to find a Russian translation equivalent of a polysemous English lexeme. Thus, HEAVY is translated as:

SIL′NYJ 'strong', if it modifies RAIN (*heavy rain* ≡ *sil′nyj dožd′*);

TJAŽËLYJ 'heavy', if it modifies LOSSES [military] (*heavy losses* ≡ *tjažëlye poteri*);

ZNAČITEL′NYJ 'significant', if it modifies LOSSES [financial] (*heavy losses* ≡ *značitel′nye poteri*);

DLITEL′NYJ 'long', if it modifies PRISON TERM (*heavy prison terms* ≡ *dlitel′nye sroki tjuremnogo zaključenija*);

VYSOKIJ 'high', if it modifies PRICE [figurative] (*heavy price* ≡ *vysokaja cena*);

BOGATYJ 'rich' or XOROŠIJ 'good', if it modifies CROP (*heavy crop* ≡ *bogatyj/ xorošij urožaj*); etc.

Such lexemes abound in languages: EXTENSIVE, HIGH, IMPORTANT, …, and also DO, MAKE, GIVE, GET, HAVE, … And each of them necessitates hundreds or even thousands of checks in a translation computer program. But at this juncture, a simple idea struck me: in all cases, for instance, with HEAVY, the adjective plays the role of an intensifier (in the very broad sense of the word); therefore, why not indicate for each Russian noun the adjectives that can express intensity with it? To do this in one language is much simpler, much quicker and much more interesting than to select equivalents for different languages. In this way, the first two LFs were born: `Magn` and `Oper`$_1$. Back in Moscow, I showed my sketches to A. Žolkovskij, who not only immediately grasped the potential of a such a methodology, but also drew fine semantic distinctions between different LFs. That is how a fruitful collaboration that lasted over ten years began: Žolkovskij & Mel′čuk 1965, 1966, 1967.

[22] (*5.2.2*, p. 125) **Radical.** By *radical* is understood a strictly synchronic—that is, modern—radical, as opposed to a historical *root*. A radical **R** is a morph whose syntactics mostly carries the information about the **inter**lexemic cooccurrence of a wordform that contains **R** with other wordforms in the sentence. Radicals are opposed to affixes; the syntactics of an affix mostly carries the information about the **intra**lexemic cooccurrence of this affix with other morphs in a wordform. Thus, the radical **talk-** of the wordform **talked** has, in its syntactics, the information about this verb's actants (*talk* to/with whom, *talk* about what) and about its lexical functions: *talk face to face* 'talk being close and looking at each other', *talk blue streak* 'talk rapidly and excitedly', *talk (cold) turkey* 'talk speaking very bluntly', etc. The syntactics of the suffix **-ed**, on the other hand, contains only one piece of combinatorial information—about the type of verbal radicals to which this suffix can attach.

[23] (*5.2.2*, p. 125) **Clausative** is the part of speech of a linguistic expression syntactically equivalent to an independent clause (hence the term): YES, NO; WOW!, YUCK!; HO!, GIDDY UP!; SEE YOU LATER; etc.

[24] (*5.2.2*, p. 125) **Possible links between the syntactics and the signified/signifier of a sign.** Strictly speaking, the syntactics of a sign can be linked to its signified and/or its signifier.

On the one hand, the cooccurrence of a sign is quite often conditioned, at least to some extent, by its signified and/or signifier. Thus, in German, all the names of strong alcoholic beverages are masculine: [*der*] SLIWOWITZ$_{(masc)}$, [*der*] WODKA$_{(masc)}$, [*der*] TEQUILA$_{(masc)}$, etc. In French, the noun whose signifier begins with a vowel requires the form **l'** of the definite article in the singular: *la eau /o/ 'water' ⇒ *l'eau*, *le arc 'arc' ⇒ *l'arc*. However, such conditioning is sporadic; even in these cases, there are exceptions: in German, [*die*] SPIRITUOSE$_{(fem)}$ 'strong spirit' is feminine; in French, many "vocalic" nouns require the full form of the article: *la hauteur* /laotœr/ 'height', but *l'auteur* /lotœr/ 'author'.

On the other hand, such conditioning can be more or less systematic: for instance, the syntactic features «human», «modal», «countable»/«uncountable» and the like can be deduced from the lexicographic definition of the corresponding lexeme. But insofar as such features characterize the syntactic behavior of lexemes (≈ their ability to participate in such and such syntactic constructions), it is convenient to allow for certain duplication of semantic information.

[25] (5.2.2, p. 127) **Iconicity.** These three forms of the demonstrative radical provide a nice example of the iconicity of linguistic signs—that is, they demonstrate the presence of a logical link between a signified and its signifier: the greater the distance between the Speaker and the object whose name is modified by the demonstrative adjective, the longer is the signifier of this adjective. Another example of iconicity is reduplication expressing the meaning 'too much' in Dyirbal, 5.2.2, (42), p. 122. On iconicity of linguistic signs, see Jakobson 1965 [1971: 350*ff*] and Haiman 1980.

[26] (5.2.2, p. 128) **Pro-Drop Languages.** A Pro-Drop [= Pronoun Dropping] language tends to omit, from actual sentences, a personal pronoun—especially, in the role of syntactic subject—if it does not carry a special communicative emphasis. Compare the Polish sentence (i-a) and its Russian equivalent (i-b), both meaning 'I always thought that writing was my vocation':

(i) a. *Zawsze myślałem, że pisanie jest moim powołaniem*
    lit. 'Always I.thought that writing is my vocation'.
 b. ***Ja*** *vsegda dumal, čto pisat'—èto moë prizvanie*
    lit. 'I always thought that write—this [is] my vocation'.

(i-a) does not need *ja* 'I': Polish is Pro-Drop; on the other hand, (i-b) sounds bizarre without *ja*: Russian is not Pro-Drop. In a story by F. Dostoevsky, "The Crocodile," the narrator says: "More than anything, I was angered by his feeling of self-importance—it was so inflated that he stopped using personal pronouns" (translation mine—IM). In Polish, the situation is just the opposite: to use *ja* too often is perceived as showing off.

[27] (5.2.3, p. 132) **Clitics.** A clitic is a wordform (that is, it belongs to a lexeme) deprived of the prosody characteristic of wordforms in the given language: stress or tone. Being "prosody-less," a clitic is almost non-autonomous and has to lean phonologically on a full-fledged wordform, which is called its host. English has, among others, a few clitics representing a truncated form of an auxiliary verb: *I'm*, *I've*, *I'd*, *I'll*. Clitics are typical of Romance and Balkanic languages: Fr. ***Je te l'envoie*** lit. 'I you it send' or Serb. *Jovan* ***ga je*** *video* lit. 'John him is having.seen' = 'John saw him'.

NOTES

[28] (*5.2.3*, p. 133) **Incongruous "wordforms."** It might be useful to give examples of incongruous "wordforms" that turn out to be not wordforms, but either affixes or phrases.

- The English possessive suffix **-'s** satisfies all three conditions of weak autonomy: it is separable, unselective and transmutable, cf. *the guy I am working with's bookcase.* Nevertheless, it is not a wordform of English, but a suffix, because 1) no language wordform of English consists of one consonant and 2) no language wordform of English has variants (similar to) /z/, /s/, /ɪz/. (Note that a speech wordform of English can consist of one consonant: for instance, the boldfaced wordforms in *He's, I'm, you'd* and *you've*. These, however, are produced by special truncation rules out of *is, am, had* and *have*. The possessive **-'s** has no corresponding full form.)

- A Spanish sign of the type **Escríbemelo** lit. 'Write me it' is not a wordform, but a phrase, since it is stressed on the fourth syllable from the end, while no Spanish wordform allows for the stress on a syllable further from the end than the antepenultimate one. Such nouns as RÉGIMEN and ESPÉCIMEN, which could have a "hyperdactilic" stress in the plural—**régimenes, *espécimenes*—move the stress to the right, producing the correct forms **regímenes, especímenes**. This fact is crucial in establishing the wordform status of the clitics **me** and **lo**.

[29] (*5.3.3*, p. 139) **Ergative construction.** In a language that has cases, the predicative construction "Synt-Subject←Main_Verb" is called ergative if and only if the Synt-Subject is marked by a case other than the nominative. (The predicative construction in which the Synt-Subject is marked by the nominative—as, for instance, in Germanic, Slavic, Romance, etc. languages—is called the nominative construction.)

[30] (*5.3.3*, p. 141) **The Maasai Passive Saga.** Several more recent descriptions of Maasai (in the late 20th century) indicate that the use of the agentive complement with the passive has become impossible. As a result, this form lost its status as a passive. At present, the diathesis of the Maasai verbal form in **-i** looks as follows:

X	Y
—	II

This is a typical subjectless suppressive, similar to what we find in Polish:

(i) *Nie przeczytano twoją książkę*$_{ACC}$
    lit. 'Not read /red/ your book$_{ACC}$'. = 'Your book was not read'.

The Polish suppressive is invariant—no moods, no tenses, no persons, no numbers; it does not allow even for a dummy subject.

For more on cases and voices, see Mel'čuk 2006a: 110–286.

[31] (*5.3*, p. 146) **Indecomposability of semantic primitives.** A semantic primitive is not necessarily absolutely indecomposable in any sense: it cannot be decomposed into semantemes of **L**, but in principle it can be rigorously defined by means of some extralinguistic notions—logical, mathematical, physical, etc. Thus, the semanteme 'no/not' (= negation) is a semantic primitive of English: the lexemes NO and NOT cannot be defined by means of semantically simpler English lexemes. However, in logic the negation "¬" (= 'no') is readily defined:

> negation ¬: operation such that if A is a true proposition,
> then ¬A is a false proposition, and vice versa.

This is a 100% correct definition, but by no means a lexicographic one: it defines the operation of negation rather than the corresponding word. Here are three more correct definitions that are, nevertheless, unacceptable to a lexicographer: WATER ≡ H_2O; LIGHT ≡ electromagnetic waves of frequency ϕ; CAT ≡ *Felis felis*. These definitions do not define the meaning of the corresponding words, but the underlying scientific notion. Lexical meanings—i.e., semantemes—'water', 'light' and 'cat'—are not semantic primitives: in a language dictionary of ECD type they can and must be decomposed.

[32] (*5.4.1*, p. 152) **Andréy Sákharov and Sergéy Kovalyóv.** Let me add here, for the benefit of younger readers who did not live through our turbulent times, that these two extraordinary human beings, both physicists by profession, were among the first Soviet dissidents and human right activists and contributed much to the fall of the Communist regime in the USSR.

[33] (*5.4.2.1*, p. 157) Even *LDOCE Online* is guilty on this respect. Thus, ASHAMED is defined as 'feeling embarrassed and guilty because of something you have done', which is, of course, false: one can feel ashamed because of one's ugly face, etc. Moreover, 'ashamed' is defined without reference to 'shame'!

[34] (*5.5*, p. 170) **Logical types of binary relations.**

- A relation **R** is reflexive iff $x\mathbf{R}x$—that is, if any element stands in this relation to itself; **R** is anti-reflexive iff this is never the case.

- A relation **R** is symmetrical iff from *x***R***y* it follows that *y***R***x*; **R** is anti-symmetrical iff this is never the case.

- A relation **R** is transitive iff from *x***R***y* and *y***R***z* it follows that *x***R***z*; **R** is anti-transitive iff this is never the case, but non-transitive iff this is sometimes the case, and sometimes not.

For instance, **R** = 'be in the same room as' is reflexive, symmetrical and transitive.

[35] (*5.5.1*, p. 172) **Syntactic features**. A syntactic feature of a lexeme L represents one of the particular characteristics that indicates the capacity of L to be used in a specific syntactic construction. For instance:

«adadj» : indicates an adverb that can depend on an adjective, a participle or another adverb (VERY [*broad*], RATHER [*distinguished*], QUITE [*rapidly*])

«attr!» : indicates an adjective that can be used only attributively—that is, only as a nominal modifier (FORMER, PREVIOUS, SUBSEQUENT, UPPER, etc.)

«rel» : indicates a pronominal word that can introduce a relative clause while being its element (WHICH, WHO, THAT4, WHERE, WHEN [*the day when I met her*], etc.)

[36] (*5.5.2*, p. 172) **Morph-Ds in an utterance**. Morph-Ds do not necessarily form a connected structure. Even in highly inflectional language, such as Russian, many sentences do not manifest a connected morphological structure. Here is a typical example (the arrows show Morph-Ds, the double-headed arrows show mutual Morph-Ds, and the symbol **I** indicates a breach in the Morph-structure):

(i) *Ja↔lovlju* **I** *v dalëkom←otgoloske* 'I am trying to catch in a far-away echo'

I *Čto↔slučitsja* **I** *na moëm←veku* 'What will.happen during my lifetime'

[B. Pasternak].

As one can see from this example, prepositions (and other invariant words) do not morphologically depend on anything; the same is true of subordinate clauses (in Indo-European languages).

[37] (*5.5.2*, p. 179) **Balkan languages**. Balkan languages include several Indo-European languages from different branches of the family that are spoken on and around the Balkans: a Romance language (Romanian), Slavic languages (Bulgarian, Macedonian and, to a lesser extent, Serbian, Croatian and Bosnian), Modern Greek and

Albanian. These languages have several common structural properties due to their long-standing contacts—postposed articles, absence or limited use of the infinitive, extensive use of clitics, etc. Balkan languages form a Sprachbund 'language union'.

[38] (Appendix II, No. 16, p. 188) The SSyntRels 16–18 are all circumstantial, since in their case the governor is necessarily a verb. Their triple distinction is parallel to the distinction between the three adnominal SSyntRels: **modificative** (*elegantly solve* ~ *an **elegant**←modif–solution*), **appositive** (***An old man**, the officer told us* ... ~ *The officer,–[an old]–*appos→***man**, told us*...) and **attributive** (***Abroad**, an American is always preoccupied* ... ~ *An American–*attrib→***abroad** is always preoccupied* ...).

References

Ahlsén, E. (2006). *Introduction to Neurolinguistics*. John Benjamins: Amsterdam/Philadelphia.

Alonso Ramos, M. 2004. Elaboración del Diccionario de colocaciones del español y sus aplicaciones. In: P. Bataner & J. de Cesaris (eds.), *De Lexicografía. Actes del I Simposium internacional de Lexicografía*, Barcelona: IULA y Edicions Petició, 149–162.

Alonso Ramos, M. 2005. Semantic Description of Collocations in a Lexical Database. In: Kiefer, F. *et al.* (eds.), *Papers in Computational Lexicography COMPLEX 2005*, Budapest: Linguistics Institute and Hungarian Academy of Sciences, 17–27.

Apresjan, Ju. D. 1969a. Tolkovanie leksičeskix značenij kak problema teoretičeskoj semantiki [Defining Lexical Meanings as a Problem of Theoretical Semantics]. *Izvestija AN SSSR, Serija literatury i jazyka*, 28: 1, 11–23.

Apresjan, Ju. D. 1969b. O jazyke dlja opisanija značenij slov [On a Language for the Description of Lexical Meanings]. *Izvestija AN SSSR, Serija literatury i jazyka*, 28: 5, 415–428.

Apresjan, Ju. D. 1974. *Leksičeskaja semantika. Sinonimičeskie sredstva jazyka [Lexical Semantics. Synonymical Means of the Language]*. Moskva: Nauka.

Apresjan, Ju. D. 1980. *Tipy informacii dlja poverxnostno-sintaksičeskogo komponenta modeli "Smysl ⇔ Tekst" [Types of Information Needed for the Surface-Syntax Component of the Meaning-Text Model]*. Wien: Wiener Slawistischer Almanach. [Reprinted in: Apresjan 1995: 8–101.]

Apresjan, Ju. D. 1995. *Izbrannye trudy. Tom II. Integral'noe opisanie jazyka i sistemnaja leksikografija [Selected Writings. Vol. II. An Integral Description of Language and Systematic Lexicography]*. Moskva: Jazyki russkoj kul'tury.

5. REFERENCES

Apresjan, Ju. D. 2010. Trëxurovnevaja teorija upravlenija: leksikografičeskij aspekt [A Three-Level Government Theory: Its Lexicographic Aspect]. In: Apresjan *et al.* 2010: 281–377.

Apresjan, Ju. D., Boguslavskij, I. M., Iomdin, L. L. & Sannikov, V. Z. 2010. *Teoretičeskie problemy russkogo sintaksisa. Vzaimodejstvie grammatiki i slovarja [Theoretical Problems of Russian Syntax. Interaction of Grammar and Lexicon]*. Moskva: Jazyki slavjanskix kul´tur.

Apresjan, Ju. D., Žolkovskij, A. K., Mel´čuk, I. A. 1968. O sisteme semantičeskogo sinteza. III. Obrazcy slovarnyx statej [On a System for Semantic Synthesis. III. Samples of Dictionary Entries]. *Naučno-texničeskaja informacija*, Serija 2, No. 11, 8–21.

Apresjan, Ju. D. *et al.* 2004. *Novyj ob´´jasnitel´nyj slovar´ sinonimov russkogo jazyka [New Explanatory Dictionary of Russian Synonyms]*. 2nd edition, corrected and enlarged. Moskva/Wien: Jazyki slavjanskoj kul´tury/Wiener Slawistischer Almanach.

Apresjan, Ju. D., ed. 2010. *Prospekt aktivnogo slovarja russkogo jazyka [A Project: An Active Dictionary of Russian Language]*. Moskva: Jazyki slavjanskix kul´tur.

Apresjan, Ju. D., ed. 2014. *Aktivnyj slovar´ russkogo jazyka [Active Dictionary of Russian Language]*. Vols 1–2 (A–B, V–G). Moskva: Jazyki slavjanskoj kul´tury.

Apresyan, Ju., Mel'čuk, I. & Žolkovsky, A. 1969. Semantics and Lexicography: Towards a New Type of Unilingual Dictionary. In: F. Kiefer (ed.), *Studies in Syntax and Semantics*, Dordrecht: Reidel, 1–33.

Auger, P. 1965. Les modèles dans la science. *Diogène*, No. 52, 3–15.

Bierwisch, M. 2011. Semantic Features and Primes. In: C. Maienborn, K. von Heusinger & P. Portner (eds.), *Semantics. An International Handbook of Natural Language Meaning*, Vol. 1, Berlin: de Gruyter/Mouton, 322–357.

Chao, Y.-R. 1962. Models in Linguistics and Models in General. In: Nagel *et al.* (eds.) 1962: 558–566.

Frege, G. 1892. Sinn und Bedeutung [Meaning and Denotation]. In: G. Frege, *Funktion, Begriff, Bedeutung*, 1962, Göttingen: Vandenhoeck & Ruprecht, 38–63.

Goddard, C. & Wierzbicka, A. 2014. *Words and Meanings*. Oxford: Oxford University Press.

Goddard, C. & Wierzbicka, A. (eds.) 2002. *Meaning and Universal Grammar. Theory and Empirical Findings*. Vols I–II. Amsterdam/Philadelphia: John Benjamins.

Haiman, J. 1980. The Iconicity of Grammar: Isomorphism and Motivation. *Language*, 56: 4, 515–540.

Halmos, P. 1957. Nicolas Bourbaki. *Scientific American*, 196: 5, 88–99.

Iomdin, L. 2010. O modeli russkogo sintaksisa [On a Model of Russian Syntax]. In: Apresjan *et al.* 2010: 21–43.

Iordanskaja, L. 1986. Propriétés sémantiques des verbes promoteurs de la négation en français. *Lingvisticæ Investigationes*, 10: 2, 345–380.

Iordanskaja, L. 2007. Lexicographic Definition and Lexical Cooccurrence: Presuppositions as a 'No-go' Zone for the Meaning of Modifiers. In: K. Gerdes, T. Reuther & L. Wanner (eds.), *Proceedings of the Third International Conference on Meaning-Text Theory* [MTT'07]. München/Wien: WSA [Sonderband 69], 209–218. See also: http://meaningtext.net/mtt2007/proceedings/19IordanskajaFinal.pdf.

Iordanskaja, L. & Mel'čuk, I. 1997. Le corps humain en russe et en français : Vers un Dictionnaire explicatif et combinatoire bilingue. In: *Hommage à Yves Gentilhomme* [= *Cahiers de lexicologie*, 70: 1], 103–135.

Iordanskaja, L. & Mel'čuk, I. 2009. Connotation (in Linguistic Semantics). In: S. Kempgen, P. Kosta, T. Berger & K. Gutschmidt (eds.), *The Slavic Languages. An International Handbook of their Structure, their History and their Investigation*, Berlin/New York: Mouton de Gruyter, 875–882.

Iordanskaja, L. & Paperno, S. 1996. *A Russian-English Collocational Dictionary of the Human Body*. Columbus, OH: Slavica Publishers.

Jakobson, R. 1965. Quest for the Essence of Language. In: R. Jakobson, *Selected Writings*, Vol. II, 1971, The Hague/Paris: Mouton, 345–359.

5. REFERENCES

Keenan, E. 1976. Towards a Universal Definition of Subject. In: Ch. Li (ed.), *Subject and Topic*, New York, etc.: Academic Press, 303–333.

Krifka, M. 2011. Varieties of Semantic Evidence. In: C. Maienborn, K. von Heusinger & P. Portner (eds.), *Semantics. An International Handbook of Natural Language Meaning*, Vol. 1, Berlin: de Gruyter/Mouton, 242–268.

Lux-Pogodalla, V. & Polguère, A. 2011. Construction of a French Lexical Network: Methodological Issues. In: *Proceedings of the First International Workshop on Lexical Resources, WoLeR 2011*. An ESSLLI 2011 Workshop, Ljubljana, Slovenia, 54–61.

Mackenzie, I. 2015. *Dictionary of Eastern Penan (incorporating principles of a lexicographic model known as the Explanatory Combinatorial Dictionary and including a grammar and an English-Penan index)*. Available on the WWW.

Mel'čuk, I. 1973. Towards a Linguistic «Meaning ⇔ Text» Model. In: F. Kiefer (ed.), *Trends in Soviet Theoretical Linguistics*, Dordrecht: Reidel, 33–57.

Mel'čuk, I. A. 1974. *Opyt teorii lingvističeskix modelej "Smysl ⇔ Tekst". Semantika, sintaksis [An Outline of a Theory of Meaning-Text Linguistic Models. Semantics and Syntax]*. Moskva: Nauka.

Mel'čuk, I. A. 1975. Opyt razrabotki fragmenta sistemy ponjatij i terminov dlja morfologii (k formalizacii jazyka lingvistiki) [Towards Elaboration of a Fragment of a System of Notions and Terms for Morphology (Formalization of the Language of Linguistics]. *Semiotika i informatika*, 6 (= *Semantičeskie i grammatičeskie problemy*), 6–50.

Mel'čuk, I. 1976. *Das Wort. Zwischen Ausdruck und Bedeutung*. München: Wilhelm Fink.

Mel'čuk, I. A. 1978. Formalizacija jazyka lingvistiki (k postanovke voprosa) [Formalization of the Language of Linguistics (The Problem Stated)]. *International Review of Slavic Linguistics*, 3: 3, 313–331.

Mel'čuk, I. 1981. Meaning-Text Models: A Recent Trend in Soviet Linguistics. *Annual Review of Anthropology*, 10, 27–62.

Mel'čuk, I. 1982. *Towards the Language of Linguistics*. München: Wilhelm Fink.

Mel'čuk, I. 1988. *Dependency Syntax: Theory and Practice*. Albany (NY): The SUNY Press.

Mel'čuk, I. 1989. Semantic Primitives from the Viewpoint of the Meaning-Text Linguistic Theory. *Cuaderni di semantica*, 10: 65–102.

Mel'čuk, I. 1992. Towards a Logical Analysis of the Notion 'Ergative Construction'. *Studies in Language*, 16: 1, 91–138.

Mel'čuk, I. 1993–2000. *Cours de morphologie générale. Vol. 1–5*. Montréal/Paris: Presses de l'Université de Montréal/Éditions du C.N.R.S.

Mel'čuk, I. 1996. Lexical Functions: A Tool for the Description of Lexical Relations in the Lexicon. In: Wanner (ed.) 1996: 37–102.

Mel'čuk, I. 1997. Grammatical Cases, Basic Verbal Construction, and Voice in Maasai: Towards a Better Analysis of the Concepts. In: W. Dressler *et al.* (eds.), *Towards Progress in Morphology*, Amsterdam/Philadelphia: John Benjamins, 131–170.

Mel'čuk, I. 2001. *Communicative Organization of Sentences in Natural Language*. Amsterdam/Philadelphia: John Benjamins.

Mel'čuk, I. 2004. Actants in Semantics and Syntax I/II: Actants in Semantics/Actants in Syntax. *Linguistics*, 42: 1, 1–66; 42: 2, 247–291.

Mel'čuk, I. 2006a. *Aspects of the Theory of Morphology*. Berlin: Mouton de Gruyter.

Mel'čuk, I. 2006b. Calculus of Possibilities as a Technique in Linguistic Typology. In: F. Ameka, A. Dench & N. Evans (eds.), *Catching Language. The Standing Challenge of Grammar Writing*, Berlin/New York: Mouton de Gruyter, 171–205.

Mel'čuk, I. 2009. Dependency in Natural Language. In: A. Polguère & I. Mel'čuk (eds.), *Dependency in Linguistic Description*, Amsterdam/Philadelphia: John Benjamins, 1–110.

Mel'čuk, I. 2011. Word Order in Russian. In: I. Boguslavskij, L. Iomdin & L. Krysin (eds.), *Slovo i jazyk (Sbornik statej k vos′midesjatiletiju akademika Ju.D. Apresjana)*, Moskva: Jazyki slavjanskix kul′tur, 499–525.

Mel'čuk, I. 2012. *Semantics: From Meaning to Text.* [Vol. 1.] Amsterdam/Philadelphia: John Benjamins.

Mel'čuk, I. 2013. *Semantics: From Meaning to Text*. Vol. 2. Amsterdam/Philadelphia: John Benjamins.

Mel'čuk, I. 2015. *Semantics: From Meaning to Text*. Vol. 3. Amsterdam/Philadelphia: John Benjamins.

Mel'čuk, I. et al. 1984–1999. *Dictionnaire explicatif et combinatoire du français contemporain : Recherches lexico-sémantiques*. I–IV. Montréal : Les Presses de l'Université de Montréal.

Mel'čuk, I., Clas, A. & Polguère, A. 1995. *Introduction à la lexicologie explicative et combinatoire*. Louvain-la-Neuve: Duculot.

Mel'čuk, I. & Pertsov, N. 1987. *Surface Syntax of English. A Formal Model Within the Meaning-Text Framework*. Amsterdam/Philadelphia: John Benjamins.

Mel'čuk, I. & Polguère, A. 2007. *Lexique actif du français. L'apprentissage du vocabulaire fondé sur 20 000 dérivations sémantiques et collocations du français*. Bruxelles : De Boeck.

Mel'čuk, I. & Wanner, L. 2001. Towards a Lexicographic Approach to Lexical Transfer in Machine Translation (Illustrated by the German-Russian Pair). Machine Translation, 16, 21–87.

Mel'čuk, I. & Wanner, L. 2006. Syntactic Mismatches in Machine Translation. *Machine Translation*, 20, 81–138.

Mel'čuk, I. & Wanner, L. 2008. Morphological Mismatches in Machine Translation. Machine Translation, 22: 3, 101–152.

Mel'čuk, I. & Zholkovsky, A. 1984. *Explanatory Combinatorial Dictionary of Modern Russian*. Wiener Slawistischer Almanach: Wien.
[See also http://olst.ling.umontreal.ca/pdf/Melcuk_Zholkovsky_1984.pdf]

Milićević, J. 2007. *La paraphrase. Modélisation de la paraphrase langagière*. Bern: Peter Lang.

Molino, J. 1985. Où en est la morphologie? *Langages*, 78, 5–40.

MPiPL 8. 1964. *Mašinnyj perevod i prikladnaja lingvistika [Machine Translation and Applied Linguistics]*, 8. Moslva: 1-yj Moskovskij gosudarstvennyj institut inostrannyx jazykov imeni M. Toreza.

Nagel, E., Suppes, P. & Tarski, A. (eds.). 1962. *Logic, Methodology and Philosophy of Science*. Stanford, CA: Stanford University Press.

Padučeva, E. V. 1985. *Vyskazyvanie u ego sootnesënnost′ s dejstvitel′nost′ju [The Proposition and Its Relation to Reality]*. Moskva: Nauka.

Padučeva, E. V. & Uspenskij, V. A. 1979. Podležaščee ili skazuemoe? [A Subject or a Copula's Attribute?] *Izvestija AN SSSR, serija lit-ry i jazyka*, 38: 4, 349–360. [Reprinted in: Padučeva, E. V., 2009, *Stat′i raznyx let*. Moskva: Jazyki slavjanskix kul′tur, 119–133.]

Polguère, A. 1990. *Structuration et mise en jeu procédurale d'un modèle linguistique déclaratif dans un cadre de génération de texte*. Montréal : Université de Montréal, Dép. de linguistique et de traduction [thèse de doctorat].

Polguère, A. 1992. Remarques sur les réseaux sémantiques Sens ⇔ Texte. In: A. Clas (réd.), *Le mot, les mots, les bons mots*, Montréal : Les Presses de l'Université de Montréal, 109–148.

Polguère, A. 2009. Lexical Systems: Graph Models of Natural Language Lexicons, *Language Resources and Evaluation*, 43: 1, 41–55.

Queneau, R. 1963. *Bords : mathématiciens, précurseurs, encyclopédistes*. Paris : Hermann.

Rosenblueth, A. & Wiener, N. 1945. The Role of Models in Science. *Philosophy of Science*, 12: 4, 316–321.

Saussure, de, Ferdinand. 1916[1962]. *Cours de linguistique générale*. Paris : Payot.

Tesnière, L. 1959. *Éléments de syntaxe structurale*. Paris : Klincksieck.

Thompson, S., Park, J. & Li, Ch. 2006. *A Reference Frammar of Wappo*. Berkeley/Los Angeles/London: University of California Press; see also: http://escholarship.org/uc/item/0dv86220.

Tucker, A. & Tompo ole Mpaayei, J. 1955. *A Maasai Grammar with Vocabulary*. London: Longmans, Green and Cº.

Vincze, O., Mosqueira, E. & Alonso Ramos, M. 2011. An Online Collocation Dictionary of Spanish. In: I. Boguslavsky & L. Wanner (eds.), *Proceedings of the 5th International Conference on the Meaning-Text Theory*, Barcelona, Sept. 8-9 2011, 275–286.

Wanner, L. (ed.). 1996. *Lexical Functions in Lexicography and Natural Language Processing*. Amsterdam/Philadelphia: John Benjamins.

Wierzbicka, A. 1969. *Dociekania semantyczne [Semantic Explorations]*. Wrocław/Warszawa/ Kraków: Wydawnictwo PAN.

Wierzbicka, A. 1972. *Semantic Primitives*. Frankfurt am Main: Athenäum.

Wierzbicka, A. 1980. *Lingua Mentalis. The Semantics of Natural Language*. Sydney etc.: Academic Press.

Wierzbicka, A. 1987. *English Speech Verbs: A Semantic Dictionary*. Sydney etc.: Academic Press.

Wierzbicka, A. 1991. *Cross-Cultural Pragmatics. The Semantics of Human Interaction*. Berlin/New York: Mouton de Gruyter.

Wierzbicka, A. 1996. *Semantics. Primes and Universals*. Oxford/New York: Oxford University Press.

Wierzbicka, A. 1999. *Emotions across Languages and Cultures. Diversity and Universals*. Cambridge—Paris: Cambridge University Press—Éditions de la Maison des Sciences de l'Homme.

Wierzbicka, A. 2006. *English: Meaning and Culture.* New York: Oxford University Press.

Žolkovskij, A. K. 1964a. Predislovie [Foreword]. *MPiPL*, 8, 3–16.

Žolkovskij, A. K. 1964b. O pravilax semantičeskogo analiza [Rules for Semantic Analysis]. *MPiPL*, 8, 17–32.

Žolkovskij, A. K. 1964c. Leksika celesoobraznoj dejatel´nosti [Vocabulary of Teleological Activity]. *MPiPL*, 8, 67–103.

Žolkovskij, A. K., Leont´eva, N. N. & Martem´janov, Ju. N. 1961. O principial´nom ispol´zovanii smysla pri mašinnom perevode [On an Essential Use of Meaning in Machine Translation]. In: *Mašinnyj perevod*, vol. 2, Moskva: Institut točnoj mexaniki i vyčislitel´noj texniki AN SSSR, 17–46.

Žolkovskij, A. K. & Mel´čuk, I. A. 1965. O vozmožnom metode i instrumentax semantičeskogo sinteza [On a Possible Method and Some Tools of Semantic Synthesis]. *Naučno-texničeskaja informacija*, No. 5, 23–28.

Žolkovskij, A. K. & Mel´čuk, I. A. 1966. O sisteme semantičeskogo sinteza. I. Stroenie slovarja [A System for Semantic Synthesis. I. The Structure of the Dictionary]. *Naučno-texničeskaja informacija*, No. 11, 48–55.

Žolkovskij, A. K. & Mel´čuk, I. A. 1967. O semantičeskom sinteze [On Semantic Synthesis]. *Problemy kibernetiki*, 19, 177–238.

Abbreviations and Notations

-A	: actant
ACC	: accusative
ACT	: active
Adj	: adjective
/C/	: consonant
Comm-	: communicative
D-	: deep
DAT	: dative
ECD	: *Explanatory-Combinatorial Dictionary*
FEM	: feminine (grammeme)
(fem)	: feminine (syntactic feature)
GEN	: genitive
iff	: if and only if
L	: given lexical unit
L('σ')	: lexical unit with the meaning 'σ'
L	: given language
LDOCE	: *Longman's Dictionary of Contemporary English*
LF	: lexical function
LMT	: *Language: From Meaning to Text* (the present book)
lit.	: literal translation (gloss)
LU	: lexical unit
⌜$L_1 + L_2 + \ldots + L_n$⌝	: idiom
MASC	: masculine (grammeme)

ABBREVIATIONS AND NOTATIONS

(masc)	: masculine (syntactic feature)
Morph-	: morphological
MTM	: Meaning-Text model
MTT	: Meaning-Text theory
N	: noun
NOM	: nominative
NUM	: numeral
PART	: participle
PASS	: passive
Phon-	: phonic
Phonem-	: phonemic
Phonet-	: phonetic
PL	: plural
-R	: representation
-Rel	: relation
s	: given sign
S	: given sentence
S-	: surface-
Sem-	: semantic
SG	: singular
Synt-	: syntactic
'σ'	: given meaning
T	: given text
V	: verb
/V/	: vowel
Λ	: empty set
Ø	: zero linguistic sign

ABBREVIATIONS AND NOTATIONS

*X	: incorrect expression X
#X	: pragmatically unacceptable expression X
$\mathbf{m_1 + m_2}$	: "+" separates morphs in a wordform and specifies their mutual order
$x \in X$	: element x belongs to set X
$X \subset Y$	: set X is included in set Y
$X \equiv Y$	: X and Y are equivalent
$X \cong Y$	: X and Y are nearly-equivalent
$X \not\equiv Y$	: X and Y are not equivalent
$X \Leftrightarrow Y$	: X and Y of two adjacent levels of representation correspond to each other
xyz	: the context of a rule
/xyz/	: phonemic transcription
[xyz]	: phonetic transcription
{X}	: set X
X ⟨Y⟩	: Y is a variant of X
$\oplus$	operation of linguistic union

Subject and Name Index with a Glossary

The terms without corresponding page numbers are not mentioned in the text; they are introduced for a better coherence of the Index.

ablative construction	see construction, ablative
actant, semantic (of a semanteme 'σ'/ of a lexeme L('σ')) 10, 47, 158	a semantic dependent of a semanteme 'σ' / of a lexeme L('σ')—that is, an argument of the predicate 'σ'; e.g., in *John is reading a book*, the meanings 'John' and 'book' are the arguments of the predicate 'read': 'read(John, book)' ≡ 'John←1–read–2→book'
actant, syntactic (of lexeme L) 8, 11, 56, 159	a syntactic dependent of lexeme L that either corresponds to one of its Sem-actants, or manifests syntactic behavior identical or similar to that of such a dependent; e.g., in *John is reading a book*, the lexemes JOHN and BOOK are syntactic actants of READ: JOHN←**subject**–READ–**direct-object**→BOOK Syntactic actants of a lexeme can be deep-syntactic or surface-syntactic.
affix 125, 129, 211	a morph that is not a radical; e.g., **-ed** in *answer+**ed*** and **re-** in ***re**+write*.
agreement 61, 112, 124, 128, 137, 173	one of the two types of morphological dependency (the other one is **government**): a noun imposes on an adjective or a verb some grammemes that correspond to its own grammemes or its agreement class; e.g., *I* requires the form *am* of the verb BE; *Sp. calles* 'streets' requires the form *anchas* of the adjective ANCHO 'wide'.

agreement class	a set of nouns that impose the same grammemes on adjectives and verbs; there are two types of agreement classes—namely, noun class *vs.* gender.
alternation 31, 33, 85, 123	a morphonological operation that modifies the segmental signifier of a linguistic sign in order either to express something—e.g., a grammeme, as in *sing ~ sang*, or to adapt this sign to the context of its use—e.g., as in *wife*+∅ ~ *wive*+*s*. Alternations of the first type are meaningful, and those of the second type, meaningless.
analysis, linguistic 3–4, 25–26, 43, 70	the operation by which a speaker or a linguistic model passes from text to meaning; it is performed on sentence *S* (more precisely, on its phonetic or graphic representation): $S \Rightarrow \text{Synt/SemR}(S)$. The inverse operation is linguistic synthesis.
analytical form (of an LU L) 129, 135, 192	a phrase consisting of two or more wordforms that is an inflectional form of an LU L and expresses a value of an inflectional category; e.g., *have been singing* is an analytical form of SING, expressing PERFECT and PROGRESSIVE.
antecedent (of a substitute pronoun PRON) 60	a lexeme in utterance **U** to which the substitute pronoun PRON refers; e.g., *Girls like it when you think of them*, where GIRLS is the antecedent of the pronoun **them**.
apophony [= **A**] 123	a non-segmental linguistic sign whose signifier is an alternation either of phonemes or of prosodemes; e.g., a phonemic apophony: *sang* is formed from *sing* by the apophony A_{PAST}; an accentual apophony: *cónflict*$_{(N)}$ is formed from *conflíct*$_{(V)}$ by the apophony A_{NOUN}.
Apresjan, Jurij 23, 88, 142, 152, 163	Russian linguist (b. 1930), one of the founders of the Meaning-Text approach; known for his work in Russianistics, general linguistics, semantics, lexicology, lexicography, and computational linguistics.

argument (of a predicate) 6–7, 47–48, 92, 171	a meaning filling the open slot (= argument position) of a predicate; e.g., the predicate 'ask(X, Y, Z)'—as in *John asked Mary to dance*—has three argument positions and, accordingly, three arguments: X, who is asking; Y, who is being asked; and Z, what is to be done by Y.
argument position (of a predicate) 6–7	an open slot (= place) of a predicate 'σ' that receives a meaning (= an argument of 'σ'); e.g., the predicate 'ask' has three argument positions: '_ ask _ to _'.
autonomy (of a linguistic expression)	see Definition 4, p. 130.
base (of a collocation) 76, 78, 92–93, 99, 179, 205	the element of a collocation that is freely chosen by the Speaker for its meaning (the other element is the collocate).
black box 21	an imaginary device that has observable inputs and outputs, but whose internal structure is not accessible: it has to be deduced from the observation of the black box's reactions to different manipulations of its inputs.
Cantor, Georg	German mathematician (1845–1918), creator of the set theory.
case 7–8, 82, 112, 136–141, 209	an inflectional category of the noun whose grammemes mark the noun's different syntactic roles; e.g., English has two cases in personal pronouns: the nominative *I, he, ...* ~ the oblique *me, him, ...*
case, ergative 139	a case whose main function is to mark a noun used as the syntactic subject of a transitive verb.
case, accusative 136–138	a case whose main function is to mark a noun used as a direct object of a transitive verb; e.g., in Latin: *Occidit host+em*$_{ACC}$ '[He] kills the enemy' or *Captat musc+as*$_{ACC}$ '[He] catches flies'.
case, nominative 8, 113, 136–140, 158, 175, 213	a case whose main function is to mark a noun used for naming an entity or a fact.

case, subjective 8, 140	a case whose main function to mark a noun used as the syntactic subject of any verb; it cannot be used for naming.
'cause1' 106, 145	an English semanteme: non-agentive (≈ involuntary) causation; 'X causes1 Y' = 'X is the cause of Y' (e.g., in *Poverty **causes** hunger*).
'cause2' 106, 145	an English semanteme: agentive (≈ voluntary) causation: 'X causes2 Y' = 'X is the causer of Y' (e.g., in *You **caused** it all by telling lies*).
Chomsky, Noam 19	American linguist (b. 1927), creator of Generative Grammar (= Generativism) and the theory of Universal Grammar.
cliché	a semantically compositional phraseme stored and used as a whole; e.g., *Speedy recovery!*, *You must be joking*, *Wet paint*, *killer whale*.
clitic 132, 212, 216	a stressless or toneless wordform, which cannot stand alone and necessarily leans prosodically on a particular stressed wordform (called its host); e.g., *Fr.* **je**, **te** and **la** в *Je te la donne* 'I you$_{SG}$ it give'= 'I give it to you$_{SG}$'.
collocate (in a collocation) 76, 92–93, 205	the element of a collocation that is chosen by the Speaker for a given meaning as a function of the collocation's base. Collocates are described by syntagmatic lexical functions.
collocation 54, 76, 78, 91–94, 99, 104–105, 167, 178, 205, 210	a compositional phraseme one element of which (= the base) is chosen freely by the Speaker for its meaning independently of the other element (= the collocate), while the latter is chosen as a function of the base.
communicate, to	one of the two major modes of producing speech (the other being [*to*] signal): transmit to somebody information about a state of affairs in a form that allows for negation and interrogation; e.g., the communicated *I admire this!* vs. the signaled *Wow!*

communicatively dominant node (of a SemS 'S') 11, 48, 71–75	a meaning to which the whole semantic structure 'S' can be reduced without deformation of the information (but of course with a loss). Thus:
	
	   'Sun←1–shine' ⇔ *The Sun is shining.*
	                                     the shining of the Sun
	vs.
	   'Sun←1–shine' ⇔ *the shining Sun.*
	
	The Comm-dominant node is indicated by underlining.

compositional (a complex sign $s_1 s_2$) 54, 120, 130, 205	a complex linguistic sign $s_1 s_2$ that can be constructed out of simpler signs s_1 and s_2 according to general rules of **L**; formally, $s_1 s_2 = s_1 \oplus s_2$. See Definition 3, p. 120.
compounding	one of the two mechanisms of word formation (the other being derivation): word formation carried out by putting together two (or more) radicals: e.g., **road**+**test** or *Ger.* **München**+ **reise** lit. 'Munich trip' = 'trip to Munich'.
congruence 173	a subtype of agreement (= agreement *in absentia*): the agreement of a substitute pronoun with its source, which is not present in the clause; e.g., *Sp.* *Toma las revistas y pon***las** *aquí* 'Take the revues and put them here', where *las* is the plural feminine form of the pronoun ÉL 'he' in the accusative, resulting from the agreement with the wordform REVISTAS$_{(fem)PL}$, which this pronoun replaces.
conjunction 86, 147	a logical operation corresponding to 'and' and denoted by ∧; **A** ∧ **B** is true iff both **A** and **B** are true.
connotation, lexical (of an LU L) 157	a meaning that is associated with the referent of L by language **L**, but is not part of L's definition; e.g., TIGRESS 'female tiger' has a lexical connotation of «violent reaction to an offense» (*Jean is a real tigress!*).
construction, ablative absolute (in Latin) 87	a construction "$N_{ABL} + V_{PARTICIPLE}$" that means ≈ 'with N that (was) V-ed'; e.g., *Lat. testamento facto* lit. 'with.testament made' = 'when the testament was made' or *mortuo Alexandro* lit. 'with.dead Alexander' = 'when Alexander died'.

construction, ergative 139–141, 213	a predicative (Subject←Main_Verb) construction whose Subject is marked by a case different from the nominative.
construction, nominative 213	a predicative (Subject←Main_Verb) construction whose Subject is marked by the nominative.
context (of a rule) 11, 70	that part of a rule that controls its applicability without being affected by it; the context is shown by shading.
conversion[1] (morphological) 121–123	a morphological operation that changes elements in the syntactics of the sign it applies to, usually to express a meaning; e.g., the modification $BOMB_{(N)} \Rightarrow BOMB_{(V)}$—that is, converting a noun into a verb—carries the meaning 'apply to Y'.
conversion[2] (syntactic) 96	a syntactic operation that changes the correspondence between semantic and deep-syntactic actants of the lexical unit L it applies to, usually to adapt the government pattern of L to communicative and/or pragmatic conditions of its use. For instance, $KILL_{ACT} \Rightarrow KILL_{PASS}$ ($John_{X \Leftrightarrow I}$ killed the wolf$_{Y \Leftrightarrow II}$ ~ The wolf$_{Y \Leftrightarrow I}$ was killed by John$_{X \Leftrightarrow II}$); the passive voice is one of grammatical means used to perform syntactic conversion.
cumulative expression 29, 84, 206–207, 209	the expression of several grammemes by one single morpheme; e.g., *Lat. puell+as* 'girls', where **-as** expresses the grammemes PL and ACC.
decomposition of meaning 71, 88–90, 103, 142–151, 156	the representation of a given meaning in terms of several simpler meanings; e.g., 'X assassinates Y' = 'X murders Y for political reasons'.
definiendum 156	that part of a definition that is defined.
definiens	that part of a definition that defines the definiendum.
denotation (of sign **s**) 27, 47, 128–129, 175	the infinite set of entities or facts of the real world to which the signified of **s** can refer.

SUBJECT AND NAME INDEX

dependency
13–14, 40, 48, 53, 61, 63, 72, 123, 196
an antireflexive and antisymmetrical binary relation in terms of which is described the semantic, syntactic and morphological organization of natural language. See *5.5*, p. 170*ff.*

dependency, deep-syntactic
16
a linguistically universal syntactic relation that links lexical units in a DSyntS; a particular DSynt-relation is a generalization over a set of specific syntactic constructions of all languages.

dependency, morphological
a morphological relation that links lexemes in an utterance; a particular Morph-relation indicates the impact of a lexeme on the grammemes of another lexeme

dependency, semantic
61, 172–173
a semantic relation that links semantemes in a SemS. Sem-relations are purely distinctive: they serve to distinguish the arguments of a given predicate, but do not carry meaning themselves.

dependency, surface-syntactic
60, 176–179
a language-specific syntactic relation that links lexemes in a SSyntS; a SSynt-relation represents a family of syntactic constructions of **L**.

dependency tree, syntactic
53, 63, 78, 177
a formalism used to represent the syntactic structure of a sentence: a graph such that 1) each of its nodes—except one node **n**—receives only one entering arc and 2) one, and only one, node **n** does not receive entering arcs; **n** is called the top node of the tree.

dependent, prototypical (of a SSyntRel)
177–178
the dependent member of a SSyntRel **r** that is acceptable with any governor of **r**.

derivation
one of the two mechanisms of word formation (the other being compounding): word formation carried out by morphological operations (affixation, apophony, reduplication, conversion) applied to a radical; e.g., *work*+*er*, *read*+*er*, *march*+*er*, etc.; ***mini***+*bar*, ***mini***+*skirt*, ***mini***+ *war*, etc.; *oil* ~ [to] *oil*, *salt* ~ [to] *salt*, [a] *saw* ~ [to] *saw*, etc.

derivative, semantic
see semantic derivative.

diathesis (of an LU L) 140, 213	the correspondence between semantic and deep-syntactic actants of L; e.g., GIVE, *X gives Y to Z*, has the following diathesis: $X \Leftrightarrow \text{I}, Y \Leftrightarrow \text{II}, Z \Leftrightarrow \text{III}$; the diathesis of BE GIVEN, *Z is given Y by X*, is $X \Leftrightarrow \text{III}, Y \Leftrightarrow \text{II}, Z \Leftrightarrow \text{I}$. L's diathesis is described by the government pattern of L.
diathesis, basic 140	the diathesis of the lexical unit L specified for L in L's dictionary entry.
dictionary, active 153–154	a dictionary designed to assist in the production of texts.
dictionary, passive 153	a dictionary designed to assist in the understanding of texts.
disjunction, exclusive (= strict) 86	a logical operation corresponding to 'either … or' and denoted by $\overline{\vee}$; $A \overline{\vee} B$ is true iff **A** is false and **B** is true, or vice versa.
disjunction, inclusive 147, 169	a logical operation corresponding to 'or' and denoted by $\vee$; $A \vee B$ is true iff at least one of **A** and **B** is true.
distribution, complementary (of elements A and B) 65, 110	Elements **A** and **B** are said to be in complementary distribution iff each of them is found exclusively in the contexts different from the possible contexts of the other; e.g., **A** appears only in contexts $X_1 A X_2$, while **B** only in contexts $Y_1 B Y_2$, $X \neq Y$.
DSyntA, DSynt-actant	see actant, deep-syntactic
egocentricity (of natural language) 28	a property of natural language consisting of the fact that the Speaker (= 'I') plays a central role in the lexical and grammatical organization of any language; e.g., the meanings of many words, grammemes and syntactic constructions include direct reference to 'I' (= the Speaker): 'here' = 'place where **I** utter *here*' or '$L_{(V)\text{PRES(ent)}}$' = 'fact denoted by $L_{(V)}$ takes place when **I** utter the verb form $L_{(V)\text{PRES}}$' (such elements are shifters).

SUBJECT AND NAME INDEX 237

enantiosemy 201	the semantic relation between two senses of one polysemous word (= between two lexemes of the same vocable) or between two etymologically identical words—in one language or in different languages—such that they are semantically opposite; e.g., HOST 'who receives guests' *vs.* GUEST (both nouns stem from the same Indo-European root) or HOST *vs.* HOST(ILE).
ergative case	see case, ergative
ergative construction	see construction, ergative
expletive pronoun	see pronoun, expletive
factive verb	see verb, factive
feature, syntactic (of a lexical unit L) 124, 172, 211, 215	a property of an LU L (specified in its syntactics), characterizing L's capacity/incapacity to be used in a particular construction; e.g., «(postpos)» encodes the capacity of an adjective to be postposed—without any dependent—to the noun modified: *alone*, *available*, *imaginable*, *possible*, etc. (as in *all means available*).
formal grammar 19, 24, 200	a logical device (= system of rules of a particular type) that specifies a set—as a rule, infinite.
Frege, Gotlob 68, 129	German mathematician and logician (1848–1925), creator of predicate logic; he established the crucial distinction between the meaning [= the signified] of a sign and its denotation/referent.
fusion 170	a phenomenon that consists of having a single lexical expression as an element of the value of an LF **f** applied to a keyword L such that it combines the meaning of L and that of **f**; e.g., Magn(*fog*) = //***pea-soup*** 'very dense fog' or Labreal$_{12}$(*bomb*$_{(N)}$) = //***bomb***$_{(V)}$ 'attack with bombs' (where *pea-soup* and *bomb*$_{(V)}$ are fused elements of the value of the corresponding LFs).

238   SUBJECT AND NAME INDEX

gender 123, 125	one of the two types of agreement class (the other one is noun class): it is the agreement class characterized by a low number of different classes (2 or 3), a direct link to sexual gender, the absence of a non-cumulative marker, etc.; e.g., the two genders of French or Spanish, the three genders of Latin and Russian.
generic component (of a meaning 'σ') 103	the component '$σ_1$' of the meaning 'σ' such that its denotation $D('σ_1')$ is the closest kind (= *genus proximum*) of the denotation D('σ'); the remainder of 'σ'—that is, '$σ_2$' = 'σ' – '$σ_1$' —represents the specific component(s); e.g., the generic component of 'murder' is 'kill', while the generic component of 'assassinate' is 'murder'.
glide 112	a phone that is neither vowel nor consonant; e.g., [w] in *Sp. rueda* [r̄wéða] 'wheel'.
government 61, 80	one of the two types of morphological dependency (the other one is agreement): lexeme L imposes on its syntactic dependent a grammeme as a function of L's propertiers; e.g., the verb SEE requires the oblique case from its object: *John sees **me/him/us***.
government pattern [= GP] (of an LU L) 80, 93, 125, 158, 159, 164, 168	a formalism used to specify L's basic diathesis: a matrix whose columns correspond to Sem- and DSynt-actants of L, and lines, to different surface means that implement these actants.
grammar 5, 10, 12, 28, 151	one of the two major components of language **L** (the other one is the lexicon) that contains all the rules specifying the behavior of **L**'s lexical units in terms of classes of these units.
grammar, formal	see formal grammar.
grammeme 12, 53, 55, 61, 64–65, 74-75, 79–80, 84, 120, 128, 135, 172, 175–176, 206–208	an element of an inflectional category (= an inflectional vaule); e.g., grammemes of tense: PRES, PAST and FUT (*I write ~ I wrote ~ I will write*); grammemes of person: 1, 2, 3 (*I am ~ you are ~ he is*); grammemes of number: SG and PL (*step ~ steps*).

SUBJECT AND NAME INDEX 239

iconicity 212	a property of a linguistic sign consisting of the fact that its signified and signifier are logically linked in such a way that the signifier reflects by its form—to some extent—the signified; e.g., the sign MEOW! is iconic, since its signifier /mɪáᵒ/ is acoustically similar to a cat's cry.
idiom 5, 54, 61, 78, 155, 200	a non-compositional phraseme; e.g., ⌐KICK THE BUCKET⌐ ≈ 'die'.
inflection 80, 135	one of the two mechanisms of morphology that produces individual wordforms (the other one is word formation).
inflectional category 12, 53, 61, 129, 135	a set of mutually opposed significations that distinguish the forms of the same lexeme (they are called grammemes); e.g., NUMBER = {SG, PL} or TENSE = {PRES, PAST, FUT}.
interface 10, 33	the shared boundary between two components of a system; e.g., the semantics-syntax interface in an MTM is the deep-syntactic structure: a DSyntS is produced by semantic rules and is processed by syntactic rules—in order to be turned into an actual sentence.
isolating language 131, 135	a language that does not have inflection and very little derivation, which means that its lexemes (= words) are invariant; e.g., Mandarin Chinese and Vietnamese.
isomorphic 36	Sets **A** and **B** are isomorphic iff 1) all their elements stand in one-to-one correspondence and 2) for any two elements of one set which are linked by a relation **r**, their corresponding elements in the other set are also linked by **r** (oriented the same way).
izafet 173, 198	a nominal suffix (in Iranian languages) attached to a noun to show that this noun is postpositionally modified—by an adjective, a noun, a prepositional phrase or a relative clause; e.g., *Pers.* ketab 'book' ~ ketab+e män lit. 'book-IZAFET I' = 'my book'.

Jakobson, Roman 27, 86	Russian philologist and linguist (1896–1982), who lived in Czechoslovakia and in the USA; known for his studies in semiotics and Slavistics, especially for his theoretical work on phonology and morphology.
keyword (of a lexical function **f**) 61, 78, 92, 94–96, 98, 102, 170	**f**'s argument L—that is, the base of the collocation (described by **f**) that consists of L and an element of the value **f**(L); e.g., in Magn($rain_{(N)}$), RAIN$_{(N)}$ is the keyword of the LF Magn.
laryngeal (phone; same as glottal phone) 183	(a phone) pronounced in the larynx—that is, deep in the throat.
lexeme 5, 54, 64, 73, 89, 102, 103*ff*, 129, 130, 135, 158	a word taken in one well-defined sense—more precisely, a set of all wordforms and analytical form phrases that differ only by inflectional significations; see Definition 10, p. 135. A lexeme can, of course, contain just one wordform: JUST, ABROAD, WHERE.
lexeme, fictitious 54–55, 61, 79, 206	symbol representing in the DSyntS a syntactic construction that carries a meaning of lexical type
lexical	related to a lexical unit.
lexical cooccurrence, restricted 39, 90*ff*, 105, 107, 160	the possibility/impossibility of combining LUs L_1 and L_2—in order to express a given meaning—that depends on individual properties of L_1 and/or L_2.
lexical unit [= LU] 5, 53, 54, 156, 200	a lexeme or an idiom.
lexical unit, full (= semantically loaded) 47, 53–54, 77	an LU that carries meaning in a given utterance—that is, that corresponds to a fragment of the SemR of the utterance.
lexical unit, empty 97, 160	an LU that does not carry meaning in a given utterance—that is, that does not correspond to a fragment of the SemR of the utterance.

SUBJECT AND NAME INDEX

lexical function [= LF] 8, 39, 53–54, 78, 91–94, 160, 210	a function **f** that associates with an LU L (L being **f**'s keyword) a set **f**(L) of LUs (**f**'s value) that express, as a function of L, a given meaning 'σ'(**f**).
lexical function, paradigmatic 94, 96–97, 160, 205	a lexical function **f** that associates with its keyword L a set **f**(L) of LUs that are L's semantic derivatives; a semantic derivative of L is used in text instead of L. For instance, the LF S_1 describes agent nouns: S_1(*speak*) = *speaker*, S_1(*stunt*) = *stuntman*, S_1(*steal*) = *thief*.
lexical function, syntagmatic 94, 97–102, 160–161, 206	a lexical function **f** that associates with its keyword L a set **f**(L) of LUs that are L's collocates; a collocate of L is used in text together with L. For instance, the LF Magn describes intensifiers: Magn(*appetite*)=*ravenous*, Magn(*sleep*) = *like a log*, Magn(*clear*) = *crystal-*.
lexicographic number 5, 148	code (most often numerical or alphanumerical) that identifies the sense of a polysemous word; e.g., BOXI.a 'container', BOXI.b 'contents of a boxI.a', BOXII 'square on paper…', BOXIII (in a theater), etc.
lexicon 5, 10, 27, 134, 151*ff*, 163	one of the two major components of language **L** (the other one is the grammar) that contains **L**'s LUs supplied with all the information necessary for their use according to the grammar of **L**.
linguistic union	see union, linguistic
linguistics x–xi, 18, 37, 39, 42	the science of natural language
linguistics, diachronic xi	that branch of linguistics that deals with the historic development of languages.
linguistics, neuro- xi	that branch of linguistics that deals with the processing of language in the human brain.
linguistics, psycho- xi	that branch of linguistics that deals with the processing of language in the human psyche.

linguistics, socio- xi	that branch of linguistics that deals with the functioning of a language in the society that speaks it.
linguistics, synchronic 14, 18	that branch of linguistics that deals with a language considered strictly in the given period of time.
logical (= vicious) circle 144–145, 156	the appearance of a definiendum in its definiens; e.g., X in the right-hand part of the expression X = Y + Z+ **X** + W. The presence of a logical circle in a system of definitions leads to absurdity.
meaning, linguistic 2, 3-4, 6, 24–25, 32, 34–36, 41, 46, 50, 67, 142*ff*	the invariant of a set of synonymous paraphrases.
meaning, (linguistic) communicative 44	information about communicative organization of a propositional meaning; e.g., Rheme ~Theme, Given ~ New, Focalized ~ Non-focalized, etc.
meaning, (linguistic) propositional 44	the most important part of the meaning of a sentence—that which can be expressed in terms of logical propositions. Cf. meaning, communicative and meaning, rhetorical.
meaning, (linguistic) rhetorical 44	information about rhetorical (≈ artistic) effects intended by the Speaker; e.g., **formal, colloquial, poetic**, etc.
Meaning-Text approach xii, 34*ff*, 109, 117, 120, 151, 170	an approach to the study of natural languages based on the idea that a language is a device that associates a given meaning with all the texts that carry it (and vice versa).
Meaning-Text linguistic model 23*ff*, 41*ff*	a model of language that appears as a set of formal rules ensuring the transition from any meaning to all the texts that carry it (and vice versa).
megamorph 85, 207	a segmental sign expressing simultaneously several morphemes
metalanguage	a language used to describe another language.
metalanguage, linguistic 37, 117, 119, 147	a formal system of concepts constructed by linguists for describing (= modeling) natural languages.

SUBJECT AND NAME INDEX

minimal X 30, 132–133	X that does not include other Xs of the same nature. See Definition 6, p. 132.
model, functional	see Definition 1, p. 3.
module (of a Meaning-Text model) 2, 3-4, 6, 24–25, 32, 34–36, 41, 46, 50, 67, 142*ff*	one of the six major components of a Meaning-Text model; see Section *3.1*, p. 42.
mood 28, 55, 207	an inflectional category of the verb whose grammemes mark the relation between the utterance and the real world as established by the Speaker; e.g., *He reads.* ~ *Read!* ~ *that he read* ~ *If he were reading* ~ *He would read*.
morph 7, 84, 85, 120–121, 124, 129, 209, 211	an elementary segmental sign; e.g., **head-, -s, anti-, for, where, Wow!**
morpheme 65, 84–85, 206–207	a set of morphs that 1) have identical signifieds and 2) are distributed as a function of immediate context within a wordform; e.g., **leaf-** and **leav-** (in *leaves*) belong to the morpheme {LEAF}; /s/, /z/ and /ɪz/ belong to the morpheme {PL}. A morpheme can, of course, contain just one morph: e.g., {FOR} or {WOW!}.
morphology 5, 31, 42, 117	that component of language that deals with constructing 1) new lexemes (word formation) and 2) individual word-forms of given lexemes (inflection); the corresponding branch of linguistics.
nominative case	see case, nominative.
nominative construction	see construction, nominative.
noun class 29, 125, 127, 208	one of the two types of agreement class (the other one is the gender): agreement class characterized by a high number of different classes (from 4 to ≈ 100), no direct link to sexual gender, the presence of a non-cumulative marker, etc. (e.g., ≈ 20 noun classes of Bantu languages).

244　　　SUBJECT AND NAME INDEX

paradigmatic axis
38, 87
: one of two imaginary axes (the other one is the syntagmatic axis)—that along which mutually exclusive linguistic units are opposed. This axis corresponds to the operation of selection carried out by the Speaker on linguistic units stored in his memory.

paraphrase
(of sentence S)
25, 33–36, 204–205
: a sentence S' synonymous with sentence S.

paraphrasing
(of sentence S)
33, 50, 71, 76–77, 93, 180
: the producing of sentences $\{S'_i\}$ synonymous with sentence S.

passive
75, 97, 137, 140, 213
: a voice grammeme marking a modification of the verb's basic diathesis under which the DSyntA **I** changes its correspondence to a SemA.

passive, demotional
140–141
: a passive marking the simple demotion of one DSynt-actant of the verb, without promoting another DSynt-actant (usually, the demotion of **I** to **III**).

passive, partial
140–141
: a passive marking the operation that affects only one of several DSynt-actants of the verb.

performative verb
: see verb, performative

pharyngeal (phone)
183
: a phone articulated in the pharynx—that is, very deep in the throat.

phone (of **L**)
42, 110–111, 203
: a linguistic sound of language **L**, which is naturally distinguished and reproduced by **L**'s speakers. Phones are shown in print by square brackets; e.g., [æ], [l], [ɫ], [k], [kʰ] are English phones.

phoneme (of **L**)
110–112, 203
: a set of phones of **L** such that they never distinguish two signs of **L**. Phonemes are shown in print by slashes; e.g., /æ/, /l/, /k/ are English phonemes. A phoneme can, of course, contain just one phone: *Eng.* /b/, /z/, /r/.

phraseme (lexical) 54, 91, 117–118, 207	a non-free phrase—that is, a phrase that cannot be regularly constructed by the Speaker in a predictable way from its components, but must be stored in his memory and reproduced as a whole. Phrasemes are subdivided into non-compositional phrasemes—idioms (*kick the bucket*)—and compositional phrasemes—collocations (*pay attention*, *dense traffic*) and clichés (*What time is it?*; the latter include pragmatemes such as *No parking* or *Wet paint*).
phraseologized expression	see phraseme.
plurale tantum (*Lat.* 'plural only') 79	a noun having only the plural form; e.g., OATS, GLASSES 'corrective lenses' and PANTS.
pragmateme	a cliché restricted by the situation of its use; e.g., *Wrong way* [on a road sign] or *Hold the line* [on the phone].
predicate, semantic	see semantic predicate.
prefix 28–29, 127, 134, 208	an affix that precedes the radical; e.g., ***re***+*write* or ***mini***+*bar*.
presupposition 71, 89, 90, 106–107, 168, 209	that part of a complex meaning 'σ' that continues to be affirmed even when the whole meaning 'σ' is negated. Thus, the meaning 'X helps Y to do Z' contains the presupposition '|[Y does Z]|' and the statement 'X adds his efforts to those of Y's'; when one says *John did not help Mary prepare the dinner*, he denies only the statement 'John added his efforts to those of Mary's', while still affirming 'Mary was preparing the dinner'.
«PRIMERNO» 'maybe' 206	a fictitious lexeme that represents the Russian approximative-quantificative construction of the type *knig desjat´* lit. 'books ten' = 'maybe ten books'.
primitive, semantic 51, 144, 146–147, 156, 214	a chunk of linguistic meaning indecomposable in terms of other meanings of the same language.

prolepsis 114, 136, 202	an element of a clause that expresses its Theme, is positioned at its absolute beginning and syntactically is only loosely linked to the rest of it; e.g., ***This movie***, *it is simply gorgeous*.
pronominalization 52, 54, 61	the introduction, into the SSyntS of the sentence, of substitute pronouns (such as HE, IT or WHICH) which replace some of coreferential nouns.
pronoun, meteorological 128	the pronoun IT2 (*Fr.* IL2, *Ger.* ES2, etc.) used as a dummy subject with meteorological verbs and verbal expressions: *It rains, It hails, It dawns*.
pronoun, expletive 128	the pronoun IT3 (*Fr.* IL3, *Ger.* ES3, etc.) used as a dummy subject with verbs and verbal expressions that govern an infinitive or a THAT-clause; e.g., *It is useful to sleep, It seems that John has left*.
pronoun, substitute 52, 54, 60–64	a 3rd person pronoun that replaces, in an utterance, a specific noun (= its source): HE, SHE, IT, THEY, WHO$_{(rel)}$, WHICH$_{(rel)}$, ...
propaganda word 27, 202	a word whose meaning includes a component of the form 'I hating and/or despising the whole class of Xs'; e.g., all ethnic slurs, such as KRAUT or RUSSKY.
proposition, logical	an expression that is either true or false. Thus, the sentence *Two plus three is five* expresses a true proposition, while *Man is immortal* is a false proposition, and *Come to me and be my love!* does not express a proposition at all.
propositional meaning	see meaning, propositional.
prosodeme (of **L**) 52, 121	a set of prosodies of **L** such that they never distinguish two signs of **L**. Prosodemes are shown by slashes.
prosody 81, 174	Prosodies represent one of the four expressive means of natural language: they are pauses, stresses, intonation contours, and rhythm. (The other expressive means of natural language include structural words, word order, and syntactic morphology—markers of agreement and government.)

prosody, semantic 52	a prosody that carries meaning: interrogative or exclamatory intonation, expression of irony or imploration, etc.
prosody, syntactic 59, 176	a prosody that is used to express the syntactic structure: first of all, phrasing—that is, forming phonological phrases separated by pauses and carrying particular intonational contours.
prototypical	see dependent, prototypical
quasi-predicate 47–48	a meaning that designates an entity (like a semantic name), but has actant slots (like a semantic predicate); e.g., 'letter from X to Y about Z' or 'minister of Y of country Z'.
radical 112, 124–127, 129, 211	a morph that contributes the lion's share of the information to the syntactics of the wordform **w** to which this morph belongs—in the first place, the information concerning the interlexemic cooccurrence of **w**; e.g., **belong-, phenomen-, foot-, through**. See affix.
referent (of the sign **s**) 44-46, 113, 129, 157	an entity or fact in the real world to which the signified of the sign **s**, used in a particular utterance, refers; e.g., the referent of the noun BOOK in the sentence *Give me this book!* is the particular book the Speaker wants. A specific referent of **s** is an element of **s**'s denotation.
referential status (of a semanteme) 45, 129	a property of a semanteme 'σ' used in a particular utterance that is determined by the type of the referent that 'σ' has. For instance, this referent can be individual ('σ' refers to one particular entity/fact) or generic ('σ' refers to a class of entities/fact); the Speaker and/or the Addressee can/cannot fully identify the referent of 'σ' based only on the utterance; etc.
representation, conceptual 36, 45, 50, 66–69	a symbolic representation of a psychic reflection of a "chunk" of reality.
representation, linguistic (of utterance **U**) 14, 30–32, 38, 41*ff*, 68	a symbolic representation of essential aspects of an utterance **U**.

representation linguistic, phonetic (of utterance **U**) 24	a representation of utterance **U** as a string of phones supplied with the necessary prosodies [= a phonetic transcription of **U**].
representation (linguistic), semantic (of utterance **U**) 6, 24, 38, 46	a representation of the meaning of a family of more or less synonymous utterances (including also **U**) in terms of semantemes and links between them.
resumptive clitic 179	a clitic that repeats a surface-syntactic actant.
Rheme, semantic 44	the part of the meaning of the sentence that the Speaker wants to communicate; e.g., 'Mary [**left for Jamaica**]$_{Rheme}$'. Cf. Theme, semantic.
rhetorical meaning	see meaning, rhetorical
rhetorical relation	a relation between two fragments of a text that reflects the Speaker's attitude or intentions rather than an "objective" fact; e.g., the adverb FOR EXAMPLE expresses the rhetorical relation of exemplification.
Saussure, de, Ferdinand 86, 118–119	Swiss linguist (1857–1913), who laid the foundation of modern linguistics; he introduced the notion of linguistic sign.
segment (of **L**) 121	a string of phonemes of **L** that can be a signifier.
segmental (sign of **L**) 7, 84–85, 120–121, 133	a sign of **L** whose signifier is a segment.
semanteme (of **L**) 47, 72, 129, 143, 146*ff*	a semantic unit (of **L**)—the meaning of a full lexical unit (of **L**).
SemA, Sem-actant	see actant, semantic
semantic decomposition	see decomposition of meaning

semantic derivative (of an LU L) 54, 205	LU L' whose meaning includes that of LU L such that the semantic difference between them is regular in language **L** and can be expressed by a morphological means—as a rule, by an affix; e.g., THIEF is a semantic derivative of STEAL, along with such cases as WORK ~ WORKER, STUNT ~ STUNTMAN, etc. Semantic derivatives are described by paradigmatic lexical functions.
semantic name 47	a meaning denoting an entity that is not essentially involved in a situation: a being, an object, a substance, etc.; e.g., 'boy', 'tiger', '[a] rock', 'tree', 'Sun', 'sand', 'air'.
semantic network	see structure, semantic.
semantic predicate 7, 47, 209	a meaning 'σ' that denotes a fact and is incomplete without some other meanings 'σ_i' for which 'σ' has open positions (= slots, places); 'σ_i' are arguments of 'σ'; e.g., the predicate 'convinced' has two argument positions (two arguments), X and Y: $$X\ is.convinced.that\ Y.$$
semantic structure	see structure, semantic.
semantics 31, 42	that component of language that deals with constructing deep-syntactic structures of sentences from their semantic structure; the corresponding branch of linguistics.
sentence 30–31	a maximal fragment of text within which the rules of a language **L** apply; it can appear between two full pauses and carries prosodies characteristic of **L**'s sentences.
shifter 237	a linguistic sign whose signified includes the reference to 'I' = 'Speaker'; e.g., 'now' = 'moment in which the Speaker utters *now*'. See egocentricity of natural language.
sign, linguistic 118*ff*	an ordered triplet ⟨signified, signifier, syntactics⟩; see Definition 3, p. 120.

sign, linguistic, empty 126–129, 141, 207	a linguistic sign whose signified is empty: e.g., the expletive IT in English, as in *It is true that John is in London*.
sign, linguistic, zero [= Ø] 7, 127–128	a linguistic sign whose signifier is empty: e.g., -$Ø_{SG}$, which marks the singular in English nouns as opposed to -s: **boy+Ø** *vs.* **boy+s**.
signal, to 170	one of the two major ways of producing speech (the other one is [*to*] communicate): expressing speech acts or the Speaker's inner states in a form that does not allow for negation or interrogation; e.g., the signaled *Ouch!* vs. the communicated *It hurt!*
signalative, a 28, 30	a linguistic expression that signals rather than communicates; for more, see Mel'čuk 2012: 134*ff.*
source of a pronoun 54, 60	the noun replaced by a substitute pronoun; e.g., in the phrase *the novel₁ the author of which* [WHICH ⇐ NOVEL₂], the noun NOVEL₁ is the antecedent of the pronoun WHICH, and NOVEL₂, which is present in the syntactic structure, but not in the phrase itself, where it is replaced by WHICH, is its source.
Speaker [with a capital "S"] 2	the author of the utterance in question—that is, the first participant in a given speech act.
specific components (of a meaning 'σ')	any component (of a meaning 'σ') different from the generic component
Sprachbund (German, lit. 'language union') 216	a group of languages that develop common features because of their protracted contacts.
SSyntA, SSynt-actant	see actant, surface-syntactic
structure, deep-syntactic 9, 33, 52*ff*	a formal representation of the syntactic organization of the sentence at the deep sublevel—a dependency tree whose nodes are labeled with semantically full lexical units of **L** present in the sentence and branches, with universal deep-syntactic relations.

SUBJECT AND NAME INDEX 251

structure, semantic 6, 33, 44, 46*ff*	a formal representation of the propositional meaning of a family of synonymous sentences—a network whose nodes are labeled with semantemes of **L** and the arcs, with the numbers of predicate-argument relations.
structure, surface-syntactic 59*ff*	a formal representation of the syntactic organization of the sentence at the surface sublevel—a dependency tree whose nodes are labeled with all lexemes of **L** present in the sentence and branches, with language-specific surface-syntactic relations of **L**.
subject, syntactic 8, 59, 62, 112*ff*, 128, 137*ff*, 185, 212	that SSynt-actant of the Main Verb that is syntactically most privileged in **L**.
subjective case	see case, subjective.
suffix 7–8, 28, 120, 123, 126–132, 173, 178, 213	an affix that follows the radical; e.g., *John's* or *suppli+er+s*.
suprafix 121–122	an elementary sign whose signifier is a prosodeme (a tone or a stress) on a given syllable.
suppressive 213	a voice grammeme marking the blocking of one of the verb's DSynt-actants.
syntactic group, simple [= SSG] 82–83	the type of maximal phrase according to its part of speech which does not contain inside any other phrase and is represented by a linear pattern with numbered positions foreseen for the elements of the phrase; there are varieties of SSG for nouns, verbs, adjectives, and adverbs.
syntactics 72, 80, 85, 119, 120, 124–126, 128–129, 211	one of the three components of a linguistic sign **s**—a set of data that specify the cooccurrence of **s** with other signs and cannot be deduced from **s**'s signified or signifier.
syntagmatic axis 39, 87	one of two imaginary axes (the other one is the paradigmatic axis)—that along which the linguistic units are combined. This axis corresponds to the operation of **combination** carried out by the Speaker on the linguistic units selected by him along the paradigmatic axis.

syntax 31, 42, 43, 129, 184	that component of language that deals with constructing sentences from their syntactic structures; the corresponding branch of linguistics.
synthesis, linguistic 2–4, 25–26, 39, 70, 76	the operation by which a speaker or a linguistic model passes from meaning to text; it is performed on the syntactic or the semantic representation of sentence S: $$\text{Synt/SemR}(S) \Rightarrow S.$$ The inverse operation is linguistic analysis.
thematic element 126, 207	a semantically empty morph required after a stem in some forms. Four verbal thematic elements in Latin determine the distribution of verbs into four conjugation groups: -ā- (*compar*+*ā*+*re* 'compare') -ē- (*noc* +*ē*+*re* 'harm') -ĕ- (*bib* +*ĕ*+*re* 'drink') -ī- (*dorm* +*ī*+*re* 'sleep')
Theme, semantic 44, 75, 95, 114, 195, 202	that part of the meaning of a sentence about which the Speaker wants to communicate something, this something being the Rheme; e.g., '[**Mary**]$_{\text{Theme}}$ [left for Jamaica]$_{\text{Rheme}}$'. Cf. Rheme, semantic.
'«they»' 140–141, 179	the meaning of an indefinite personal pronoun corresponding to the meaning of *Fr.* ON or *Ger.* MAN; in English, the pronoun THEY can be used in this sense: *As **they** say in Maine, we have nine months of winter and three months of poor sledding.*
transcription, phonemic 203	the notation of texts in terms of phonemic symbols (in slashes): /kóld/ *cold*, /kóral/ *coral*, /kɔrǽl/ *corral*.
transcription, phonetic 24, 203	the notation of texts in terms of phonetic symbols (in square brackets): e.g., [kʰóɫd] *cold*. Phonetic transcription shows the different phones appearing in different contexts; e.g., in English, phonetic transcription shows the aspiration of voiceless stops in an appropriate position: e.g., [kʰóɫd] vs. [skóɫd], [kʰórəɫ] vs. [kɔrǽɫ].

SUBJECT AND NAME INDEX

"transcription, semantic" 24, 51
: a metaphorical designation for representing linguistic meaning in a formal way; e.g., in terms of Meaning-Text semantic networks.

union, linguistic (⊕) 65, 129, 142
: the operation that combines language **L**'s units according to rules (= grammar) of **L** and particular properties of these units specified in their syntactics.

valence, syntactic active (of a lexical unit L) 184
: the set of the types of syntactic units which can be joined to L as expressions implementing L's actants; e.g., the English noun OBEDIENCE has the following active Synt-valence:

$$X \Leftrightarrow \text{I} \Leftrightarrow \text{N's/A}_{(poss)}(\text{N}) \ [\textit{John's/his obedience}]$$
$$Y \Leftrightarrow \text{II} \Leftrightarrow \textit{to } \text{N} \ [\textit{obedience to Mary}]$$

The active Synt-valence of L is specified by the government pattern of L.

valence, syntactic passive (of a lexical expression L) 171, 174–175
: the set of the types of syntactic units to which L can be joined in a particular syntactic role within a well-formed expression without affecting their status and well-formedness; e.g., the passive Synt-valency of the English noun includes 1) the subject of a finite verb, 2) the DirO of a transitive verb, 3) the complement of a preposition, 4) the attribute with a copula, etc. The passive Synt-valence of L is specified by L's part of speech and syntactic features.

verb, factive 87
: a verb that implies the truth of its clausal complement; e.g., in *John knows that Mary is at home*, 'Mary is at home' must be true (you cannot continue this sentence with ... *but this is not true*).

verb, performative 28
: a verb whose use in the 1st person singular in the present indicative constitutes the action denoted by the verb; e.g., in order to take an oath, the Speaker has to utter *I swear*, and in order to thank, he has to say *Thank you*.

verb, qualificative 140
: a verb that expresses a quality—that is, has an adjectival meaning; e.g., Chinese *pàng* 'be.fat', *kōng* 'be.empty', etc., which can be used both attributively (as modifiers to a noun) and predicatively (as Main Verbs).

voice 137, 140–141	a verbal inflectional category whose grammemes mark a modification of the basic diathesis of the verb, under which either its Sem-actants remain intact while DSynt-actants are permutated or suppressed, or the Sem-actants are referentially identified and some DSynt-actants are suppressed.
Wierzbicka, Anna /v'ežb'ícka/ 51, 88, 142, 146–147	Polish linguist, based in Australia (b. 1938); one of the creators of modern linguistic semantics, the author of the methodology of semantic decomposition and the semantic primitive theory.
word formation	one of the two mechanisms of morphology that produces new lexemes (the other one is inflection). Word formation is divided into compounding and derivation.
word, structural 61, 79	a lexeme that is used either to mark syntactic structure (e.g., the conjunction THAT, the prepositions AGAINST and ON in *fight **against*** N and *insist **on*** N) or to express a grammeme (e.g., the auxiliary verbs BE and HAVE, the articles).
wordform 30, 64, 130, 133–135, 212–213	a word taken in one well-defined sense and in a particular grammatical form; e.g., **pencils**, **sprang**, **my**, **went**, **given**, **with**, **to**, etc. See Definitions 7–9, p. 133.
zero, linguistic	see sign linguistic, zero
Zholkovsky, Alexander 88, 142, 152	Russian linguist and literary study specialist (b. 1937), based in the USA; one of the founders of the Meaning-Text linguistic approach. He is known for his work on semantics and on the Somali language, as well as on the structural poetics and literary theory and history.

Index of Languages

Albanian 179	Indo-European family, Albanian branch; Albania.
Alutor 28, 121, 180	Chukchi-Kamchatka family; Kamchatka peninsula, Russia.
Arabic 100	Afro-Asiatic family, Semitic branch.
Bantu 29, 208	A group of 522 languages in Africa: a sub-branch of the Volta-Congo branch of the Congo-Kordofanian family. The word *bantu* includes the radical **-ntu** 'man, human being' and the prefix of noun class II, **ba**-; in this case, **ba**- marks the plural (the singular being *muntu*). Thus, the self-denomination *Bantu* means simply 'people'.
Chinantec 121	Oto-Manguean; Mexico.
Chinese [Mandarin] 100	Sino-Tibetan family (840 million native speakers).
Dutch 99	Indo-European family, Germanic branch.
Dyirbal 122, 212	Australian family (264 related languages); Australia.
English 7–13, 34, 54–55, 67, 83, 99, 147, 184*ff*, 200, 202, 203, 205, 208, 212, 213	Indo-European family, Germanic branch.
Eskimo 126	at least three closely related languages: Yupik (Siberian Eskimo), Inuktitut (Canadian Eskimo), and Greenlandic (Kalaallisut); Eskimo-Aleut family.

French 9, 26, 99, 134, 211	Indo-European family, Italic branch, Romance sub-branch.
Georgian 209	Kartvelian (= South-Caucasian) family; Georgia.
German 9, 99, 100, 121, 134, 200, 203–204, 211	Indo-European family, Germanic branch.
Hebrew 207	Afro-Asiatic family, Semitic branch.
Hungarian 101	Uralic family, Ugric branch. (This branch also includes, along with Hungarian, two minor languages spoken in Northern Siberia, on the lower Ob river: Khanty and Mansi.)
Japanese 29, 202	Japonic family.
Kirundi 127	Congo-Kordofanian family, Volta-Congo branch, Bantu sub-branch (see *Bantu languages*); Burundi. The radical **-rundi** denotes a specific ethnic group, and **ki-**, the noun class VII prefix, means 'language' (cf. **Ki**+*kongo*, **Ki**+*nyarwanda*, **Ki**+*swahili*, etc.).
Korean 7–14, 99, 203	Language isolate; many consider it a member of the Altaic family.
Latin 84, 173, 199, 208	Indo-European family, Italic branch; dead, Ancient Rome.
Maasai 136–141, 213	Nilo-Saharan family, Nilotic branch; Kenya.
Megrelian 139	Kartvelian (= South-Caucasian) family; Georgia.
Penan, Eastern 163	Austronesian family, Bornean branch; Malaysia, Sarawak, Borneo.
Persian 178, 198	Indo-European family, Iranian branch.

INDEX OF LANGUAGES

Polish   Indo-European family, Slavic branch.
135, 212, 213

Russian   Indo-European family, Slavic branch.
7–14, 45–46, 84, 101, 103–108, 112*ff*, 124, 131, 132, 138, 145, 157–158, 164, 175, 206–207, 208, 209, 212, 215

Spanish   Indo-European family, Italic branch, Romance sub-branch.
123, 128, 132, 179, 200, 207, 213

Swahili   Congo-Kordofanian family, Volta-Congo branch, Bantu sub-
29, 208   branch (see *Bantu languages*); Tanzania and several other East-African countries.

Tabassaran   Nakh-Daghestanian (= North-Caucasian) family, Lezgian branch;
195   North Caucasus, Russia.

Turkish   Altaic family, Turkic branch; Turkey.
206

Wappo   dead (the last speaker died in 1990); one of two languages of the
139–140   Yuki family, California, USA.

Yiddish   Indo-European family, German branch (the language of Ash-
123   kenazi Jews).

www.ingramcontent.com/pod-product-compliance
Lightning Source LLC
Chambersburg PA
CBHW051113230426
43667CB00014B/2560